LIFE IN THE RURAL WORKHOUSE

WINCANTON WORKHOUSE, SOMERSET, 1834-1900

P.W. Randell

Pen Press

© Peter Randell 2010

All rights reserved

No part of this publication may be reproduced, stored in a retrieval system, or transmitted in any form or by any means, without the prior permission in writing of the publisher, nor be otherwise circulated in any form of binding or cover other than that in which it is published and without a similar condition including this condition being imposed on the subsequent purchaser.

First published in Great Britain by Pen Press

All paper used in the printing of this book has been made from wood grown in managed, sustainable forests.

ISBN13: 978-1-907499-75-3

Printed and bound in the UK
Pen Press is an imprint of Indepenpress Publishing Limited
25 Eastern Place
Brighton
BN2 1GJ

A catalogue record of this book is available from
the British Library

Cover design by Jacqueline Abromeit

Contents

Acknowledgements	i
Tables	ii
Explanation of terms	iv
Introduction	**vi**
1. Setting the Scene	1
2. Creation of the Wincanton Union and Workhouse	7
3. Admission to the Workhouse	16
4. Work	31
5. Food and Drink	40
6. Shelter for the Vulnerable.	51
a) The Aged and Infirm	51
b) The Sick	57
c) Lunatics	68
7. Children and their Education	76
a) Treatment	76
b) Education	86
8. Life for the Unwanted	101
a) Bastardy	101
b) Vagrants	104
9. Offences, Crimes and Punishment	113
a) Offences	113
b) Punishments	121
10. Sex and Cruelty	126
a) Sex	126
b) Cruelty	130

11. Religion and Death 133
    a) Religion 133
    b) Death 138

12. Special Days 144

13. Inmates thoughts on their lives 150

14. Life for some Workhouse Officers 156
    a) Master and Matron. 156
    b) The Schoolteachers. 161
    c) The Porter 167

15. Odds and Ends 171
    a) Classification 171
    b) Segregation 174
    c) Rules, Regulations and Routine. 175
    d) Safety and Comfort (?) 177
    e) The Visiting Committee. 182

Conclusion 184

APPENDICES 191
Appendix 1a – Dietary for the Able-bodied 192
Appendix 1b – Dietary for Children 194

Appendix 2 196
    a) Letter from Jane Sergeant to the Local Government Board. 196
    b) Letter from G. Gould to the Local Government Board. 196
    c) Letter from Solomon Dewfall to the Local Government Board, March 1884 197
    d) Letters from Richard Lewis to the Local Government Board. 197

Appendix 3 – Poem by Richard Lewis 201

Appendix 4 – Letter from James Walter 203

Notes and References 205

For the long-forgotten inmates and staff of the Wincanton Union Workhouse.

Acknowledgements

I wish to record my thanks to the staff at both the Public Record Office in London and Somerset Record Office for their assistance and help in my research. I am grateful to the University of Lancaster for permitting me to undertake part-time research into the Wincanton Poor Law Union, some of which forms the basis of this book and to Professor Eric Evans who was my supervisor during that period and who gave freely of his time and knowledge to provide a broader background to my study.

Tables

Table 1.	Relief to the Poor based on the Price of Bread and Number of Dependents	2
Table 2a.	Numbers receiving Relief 1838-1863	16
Table 2b.	Numbers receiving Relief 1873-1898 (excluding vagrants)	17
Table 3.	Authority for Admission to the Workhouse	18
Table 4.	Reasons for Admission to Wincanton Workhouse	23
Table 5.	Age on Admission to Wincanton Workhouse	24
Table 6a.	Occupation before Admission	25
Table 6b.	Age of Inmates of Wincanton Workhouse on Census days 1841, 1881 and 1891.	26
Table 6c.	Occupation of Inmates of Wincanton Workhouse on Census days in 1881 and 1891	26
Table 7.	Multiple Admissions, 1837-8, 1870-1	28
Table 8.	Length of stay in the Wincanton Workhouse	29
Table 9.	Sale of Produce	37
Table 10.	'Substances used per week in Dietary, 1851'	40
Table 11.	Alcohol Consumption and Cost in Wincanton Workhouse 1871-1893	49
Table 12a.	Admissions of Paupers over 60 years of age to the Workhouse	54
Table 12b.	Reasons for the Admission of those over 60	54
Table 13.	Number and Location of Lunatics in the Wincanton Union	69
Table 14.	Ages of Lunatics in Wincanton Union and Workhouse	70
Table 15.	Average Number of Children attending Wincanton Workhouse Schools	90
Table 16.	Experience and Qualifications of Teachers	94
Table 17.	Vagrant Admissions 1889-1893	109

Table 18a.	Inmates committed to Prison, 1835-1842	124
Table 18b.	Periods of Detention 1835-1842	124
Table 19.	Religious Beliefs of those admitted to the Workhouse	135
Table 20.	Ages on death in Wincanton Workhouse 1866-1900	139
Table 21.	Age of Schoolteachers on appointment	162
Table 22.	Duration of tenure of Schoolteachers	162
Table 23.	Teachers moving to other Appointments	165
Table 24.	Reasons for resignation of teachers 1837-1891	166
Table 25.	Children admitted to the Workhouse with parent(s)	174

Explanation of terms

Old Poor Law	The system under which the poor were helped between 1601 and 1834
New Poor Law	The system under which the poor were helped after 1834
Independent poor	Those poor people who managed without help from the poor rates.
Pauper	A poor person who received help from the poor rates.
Able-bodied	Paupers who were judged fit to work.
Non able-bodied	Paupers who were not fit to work such as the sick and infirm
Poor Rates	A tax levied at local level on all property.
Poorhouse	A building used to accommodate paupers before 1834.
Workhouse	A building used to accommodate paupers after 1834.
House	Word commonly used instead of 'Workhouse'.
House of Correction	A prison.
Oakum	Loose fibre obtained by unpicking old rope.
¼d	a farthing
2 farthings =	½d, a halfpenny
4 farthings =	1d, a penny
12 pennies =	1s, one shilling (equivalent to 5p)
20 shillings =	£1
21 shillings =	1 Guinea.

Quarter	28 pounds weight
Cwt.	one hundredweight, 112 pounds weight
20 cwt.	one ton
Lady Day	25th March
Michaelmas Day	25th September.

Introduction

The year 1834 was a turning point in the treatment of the poor. In that year the Old Poor Law with its poorhouses was swept away and replaced by the New Poor Law with its workhouses. These workhouses soon became places of dread for the poor and the system itself engendered criticism from a broader section of the community. In 1836 one M.P., Thomas Wakeley, condemned the way in which the poor were treated in no uncertain terms, "The object of the poor law undoubtedly was to turn the workhouses into prisons.........and to subject paupers to every species of hardship and degradation." Another M.P., Richard Oastler, went even further when he referred to it as "a most horrible system of dastardly murder.......damnable, infernal, detestable, despotic, unchristian, unconstitutional, and unnatural." While these Radical Tories may have been more influenced by their hatred of industrialization, urbanization, centralization and had a romanticized view of the countryside, than by having actual first-hand knowledge of the new workhouses, their words helped to create an image of them which lasted throughout the nineteenth century and long after they ceased to exist.

My own interest in the Wincanton Workhouse developed from two family episodes which occurred while I was growing up in Bruton in the 1950s and early 1960s. Having relatives in Wincanton it was common for my mother and I to cycle there during the summer months to visit them. We often returned along Shadwell Lane and, on one occasion, as we turned the corner to go under the railway arch, I asked what was the large building which seemed to tower above us on our left. My mother replied that it was 'Town View' which was an Old People's Home and then, in almost a whisper, added that formerly it had been the Workhouse. She would explain no more even though born in 1908 she would have witnessed its last days and transformation. I also had two elderly maiden aunts, sisters of my grandfather, who lived together in retirement in the same small cottage that their father had rented in Pitcombe from the Hobhouse family. On more than one occasion I remember that they made my mother promise that if ever they became unable to remain independent she should make arrangements for them to go into any nursing home or old peoples' home except Town View in Wincanton. To them, born in 1879 and 1881, it was, and always would be, the Workhouse.

Many years later when I had the opportunity to undertake some research on the Wincanton Poor Law Union a somewhat different picture began to emerge. It became clear that it was essential to place the conditions in the Workhouse in the context of the living and working conditions of the independent poor outside of the Workhouse. For many of these life was extremely hard and unpleasant. Wages in East Somerset remained low for most of the nineteenth century. In 1834 wages in the Bruton area were reported to be about 8s a week and by 1867 for the Wincanton Union as a whole they had risen to 9s a week. The rent of a cottage could account for a quarter of this sum. The family budget could be supplemented by the labour of wives who could earn about 8d a day and children, especially boys who were often sent out at the age of six or seven to scare birds, lead the plough or pick apples, to earn about 1s 6d a week. Such labour would of course be for a twelve-hour day.

William Bird, who was the Relieving Officer for the Wincanton District in 1867, commented that he "Cannot make out how they live at all. They have nothing to eat and drink but bread and cheese and cider, and sometimes a bit of pork." This reference to diet is very similar to the evidence provided by the Overseers of Bruton for the parish of Bruton, Henry Hobhouse for the Hundred of Bruton and the Rector of North Cadbury for his parish in 1834 when they stated that, "Bread and potatoes, with a rasher of bacon occasionally is the usual food."

The cottages in which the poor were forced to live were often damp, dilapidated, and without water or sanitary facilities. In 1901 George Sweetman recalled the cottage on the north side of the High Street in Wincanton where he grew up in the 1840s:

"The house had a small lobby, turning to the left was a living room, stone floor, with large fire place…The front window was of small leaded panes of glass. There was a back house reached by 3 or 4 steps. It was very damp being several feet under the garden level. The stairs began in the back house. In the outer room upstairs, my brother and I slept. In the front room my father and mother, and curtained off my sister then about 18….. There was a garden at the back, uncultivated, with a common privy, open to the world at the top of the garden, in a most dilapidated condition. There were four families who had access to these back premises, not much under 20 persons."

Thirty years later a local newspaper described four cottages in Wincanton and clearly there had been few improvements:

"The living rooms are generally without plastering……… the ceilings look as if they have never been plastered. The living rooms in No. 1 and 2 are about six feet in height; the others are about 7 feet. The floors were once paved with rough stone in irregular pieces, but at present the stones are split into bits…..The state of dilapidation of the whole is beyond description……..there are many holes through the rotten thatch…..The condition of some of the rooms is that they cannot be occupied, so that the crowding in others must be pretty considerable. The fearful state of ruin, dirt and squalor cannot easily be described."

Cottages throughout the Union were very poor. In 1852 it was reported that in Kington Magna they "are small, very crowded and badly ventilated." In 1867 cottages in Corten Denham had two rooms ten feet by twelve feet with little drainage; in North Cadbury,

"The cottages are generally bad, some overcrowded", and the same in Shepton Montague. There was little evidence of any improvement by the 1890s as in Charlton Horethorne in 1891 a man, his wife and nine children slept in two rooms and in Buckhorn Weston an Inquest Jury found that a child had died from "exposure to cold in a dilapidated bedroom." Two years later it was alleged that "landowners allow the cottages to tumble down, or they are not fit for pigs to live in."

Most cottages had no water supply at all or one that was totally inadequate. In 1884 in Milborne Port it was found that, "In one (*Water*) Closet inspected water was flowing through it and leading direct to a spring from which drinking water was drawn." An inspection in 1872 in Bruton found that most of the house wells were "unmistakeably polluted" and that Patwell, which many of the poor used, was frequently flooded by the river Brue into which "house drains conveying excremental matter open" a few yards above the well. A subsequent Report in 1885 found no improvement and pointed out that, "At the top of the town, on a height called Tolbury Hill, there are 36 houses containing 145 persons, destitute of any water supply."

In a Report in 1872 Dr. Heginbothom, a local doctor and Medical Officer of Health, found sanitation in Bruton dreadful as privies "were without exception foul and unwholesome." He saw that many were "a perforated board suspended over a shallow ditch open to public view." This was a finding which was not unlike Sweetman's description in Wincanton thirty years before. Heginbothom also reported, "some cottages have none, the inmates being thrown on the hospitality of their neighbours or of the public street."

With wages so low, their diet so basic and cottages so deplorable in the countryside in 1834 and the years which followed, those who were charged with administering the Poor Law were faced with an almost insurmountable problem. If they provided the pauper with better food and conditions they would encourage the independent labouring poor to give up and seek help but if they imposed worse conditions, if that was actually possible, they would face a humanitarian outcry. This is the context against which the operation of the Wincanton Workhouse has to be seen and judged and not from present day standards. It is far too easy to view the past from the comforts of the present when the Welfare State ensures that the vast majority have shelter, food and medical treatment from 'the cradle to the grave'. The poor in the nineteenth century could take none of these for granted.

For the historian studying the nineteenth century there is an abundance of written material, produced by an army of clerks. The Wincanton Poor Law Union is no exception, for example in the National Archives at Kew in London, amongst other documents, are some seventeen very large correspondence files up to 1900 which contain copies of thousands and thousands of letters, all of them carefully arranged in date-order and numbered, sent from and to the Wincanton Board of Guardians; the decisions reached at every weekly Board Meeting from 1835 to 1900 were recorded in detail in nineteen volumes of Minutes preserved in Somerset Record Office. Together they provide a wealth of information.

On the other hand, a huge amount of written material has been destroyed, some of it by the Guardians themselves. On 5th August 1891 for an unspecified reason, probably associated with the lack of storage space, they resolved to dispose of a considerable quantity of material and accepted a tender of 4s per cwt. for waste paper from George Sweetman. As well as paper they sold some 319 of their old record books, including 11 Vagrant Books, 14 Porter's Books, 2 Chaplain's Report Books, 17 Necessaries Books, 54 Provisions Books, 5 Visitors' Books, 10 Day Books, and 4 Pauper Class Books. (1)

Such books would have provided so many details of daily life in the Workhouse. Nevertheless the surviving material does give a comprehensive insight into conditions within the House and the attitudes of those who received and administered the necessary help.

The following is an account of some aspects of a single workhouse in a rural area of England. It is but one example from more than 640 that existed and served their local communities throughout the Victorian age and early twentieth century. In the late 1920s the Wincanton Workhouse became an Old People's Home and was finally demolished in the early 1970s: a housing estate being built on the site so that all that remains is the southern boundary wall. The Workhouse and its inmates may be long gone but the memory lingers.

1. Setting the Scene

Two Statutes passed in 1597 and 1601 created the Elizabethan Poor Law which was the first attempt to establish a uniform system of relief for the poor. The Acts made each parish responsible for its own poor so from 1601 until the major change caused by the Poor Law Amendment Act of 1834 it was left to parish officers and ratepayers to deal with and solve all the problems which related to the poor. The key officer in the system was the Overseer of the Poor whose role was defined in the 1601 Act:

- to collect a compulsory tax or poor rate from all householders and occupiers of land
- to distribute relief to the sick, the old, orphans and the destitute
- to set unemployed adults to work
- to punish the undeserving poor, namely "sturdy rogues and vagabonds", by sending them to Houses of Correction after a whipping.

The Overseers, who were unpaid, were elected annually by the ratepayers assembled together as the Parish Vestry and had no choice but to serve as it was seen as part of the responsibility of the wealthier members towards their community. Failure to do so resulted in a fine and possible imprisonment by a local Justice of the Peace, although in some circumstances it was possible for them to employ a deputy in their place.

In the following two hundred years there were a number of developments designed to allow the system to function more effectively. It soon became clear that some parishes were more generous than others in the relief which was granted and so attracted the poor from neighbouring areas. This placed an increased financial burden upon the ratepayers and created a surplus of labour in some parishes and a shortage in others. The result was that in 1662 an Act of Settlement was passed by Parliament which, along with subsequent Acts, stated that a poor person or pauper could only receive help in his or her parish of Settlement or origin. This was usually the parish in which a person was born, but Settlement could also be gained through serving an apprenticeship or a period of residence. On marriage a woman took the place of origin of her husband.

In the 1790s there was a significant increase in poverty which resulted from the long term effects of the Industrial and Agricultural Revolutions and more immediately from shortages and high prices during the war against the French. From 1795 to try and help the poor the unofficial Speenhamland System spread across some of the counties of Southern England, although it was not extensively used in Somerset. Under the System relief was granted to the poor based upon the price of bread and the number of dependents in the family. In the 1830s a version of this system was in operation in the Magistrates' Division of Wincanton, from which the examples in Table 1 are taken.

Table 1. Relief to the Poor based on the Price of Bread and Number of Dependents

Price of a 4 lb loaf of Bread	7d	14d	21d
Required for a Labouring Man	1s 10d	3s 7d	5s 1d
Required for a Woman, a Boy or Girl above 14 years	1s 6d	2s 8d	3s 8d
Required for a Boy or Girl aged 14, 13, 12	1s 1d	2s 3d	3s 3d
Required for a Boy or Girl aged 11 and under	1s 0d	1s 9d	2s 5d
Total required to be earned by the family	5s 5d	10s 3d	14s 5d

If the income from all members of a family was below the required total then the difference was made up out of the poor rates.

The majority of the poor received relief in their own homes, sometimes in cash and sometimes in kind, such as bread, coal or wood. This was known as Outdoor Relief. In addition most parishes owned one or more cottages in which the poor could live if they were homeless or destitute. Parishes acquired these cottages through time: some were received as the result of a bequest in a Will, some through purchase and others when the existing owner or tenant could no longer manage unaided and so in return for relief handed the cottage over to the Parish. While most Parishes owned one or two such cottages, larger places such as Bruton, Henstridge or Wincanton could possess a dozen or more.

In some towns in the eighteenth century there was a move towards housing the poor together, often on the grounds of cost, in one building which was usually known as the Poorhouse or occasionally the Workhouse. In the Wincanton area there were three of these Poorhouses, one each in Bruton, Henstridge and Wincanton which together could accommodate about one hundred and seventy paupers. These were the poor who could not manage on their own, such as the old, sick, infirm, lunatics and orphans until they could be apprenticed. This was known as Indoor Relief. While the paupers who were still able-bodied were encouraged to work, often in the form of spinning, it was not seen as a punishment, or deterrence or designed to make a financial profit. It was to allow the poor to maintain some self-respect by continuing to make a contribution to their community.

There were criticisms of the Poorhouses such as the way in which different groups were mixed together and found expression in the poetry of men like George Crabbe:

>There children dwell who know no parents' care……..
>Heartbroken matrons on their joyless bed,
>Forsaken wives, and mothers never wed;
>Dejected widows with unheeded tears,
>And crippled age with more than childhood fears;
>The lame, the blind, and, far the happiest they!

> The moping idiot and the madman gay.
> Here too the sick their final doom receive.

On the other hand the Overseers' Account Books for Bruton Poorhouse, established in 1734, indicate that the paupers were certainly well fed with weekly purchases of such items as potatoes, vegetables, milk, cheese, butter and tobacco. It would appear that about one pound of beef was bought for each inmate each week. Little wonder that there were many complaints when the new system was introduced after 1834.

For the poor the Elizabethan Poor Law was a form of local insurance or welfare system long before the Welfare State was introduced. They knew what kind and level of assistance they could expect in various clearly defined circumstances. There were, nevertheless, implications for their behaviour as unacceptable conduct could threaten their existing relief or that which they might apply for in the future. In this sense it was a form of social control which encouraged deference. From the point of view of the ratepayers, the wealthier classes, it reinforced their social superiority and kept the countryside peaceful.

In the late eighteenth and early nineteenth centuries, however, concern mounted about the operation and effectiveness of the Poor Law. The huge increase in the population along with the disruption and squalor created by the Industrial Revolution and the changes in rural areas during the Agricultural Revolution, placed the system under great strain. Numbers seeking relief rose dramatically and hence so did the cost to ratepayers. At national level between 1783 and 1785 the average expenditure on poor relief was £2,000,000 but by 1812-1813 it was £6,560,000, peaking at £6,790,000 between 1819 and 1823. At a local level the parishes which were to form the Wincanton Union spent £3,856 in 1775-1776 and £20,274 in 1812-1813, an increase of over 425%.

Many ratepayers began to demand that some form of action be taken.

In addition the Poor Law was being criticized on a number of grounds such as creating over-dependence by the poor, encouraging large families to obtain more relief and preventing labour moving freely around the country as a result of the Settlement Laws. The latter also led to dubious practices by some Overseers such as dumping unmarried pregnant women over parish boundaries so that the illegitimate child would not gain a settlement in their parish by being born there and thus become a burden on the poor rates. Many ratepayers had supported the Poor Law as they considered that it helped to maintain social stability. That belief, however, was severely shaken in the late 1820s and early 1830s when, as a result of economic depression and severe weather, unrest became widespread.

In 1830-1831 the South of England was swept by a series of disturbances, called "The Swing Riots", after a mythical Captain Swing, their supposed leader. Considerable alarm was caused amongst local farmers and landowners by the fear of arson attacks and the destruction of threshing machines. Sir Richard Colt Hoare of Stourhead noted that "the fires are coming near us" and as a result advised all his tenant farmers to stop using their machines "if they wish to save their ricks." The Steward of the Earl of Ilchester at Redlynch reported, "large bodies of idle labourers armed with Bludgeons", but he added that he felt both the Earl's and Sir Richard's property was safe as they had protected their labourers in the past. In fact when at Stourhead "a mob of insurgents passed his house, they did not do the least mischief." Others in the area were less fortunate as in December 1830 'The Times' reported that, "a mob of several hundred persons assembled at Henstridge, where they destroyed threshing machines belonging to Mr Gray and Sir William Medlycott." The Wincanton Magistrates took immediate action when they "entered into spirited resolutions to enforce the law with the utmost vigour against all offenders. They also appointed and swore several hundreds of special constables." Few of those involved in these disturbances were ever caught although three teenage labourers, aged sixteen, eighteen and nineteen, were tried at Dorchester for riot at Henstridge but their involvement cannot have been significant as each was sentenced to enter into a recognisance for £50 to keep the peace for two years. (2)

At national level the Government's response was swift and decisive with thousands of arrests and hundreds of imprisonments and transportations to Australia, along with a small number of executions. Such was the alarm the Swing Riots engendered amongst the landowning classes that the Government established a Royal Commission to investigate the way in which some 15,000 parishes administered the existing Poor Law. The Commissioners amassed a huge amount of evidence but in reality ignored much of it as before they started they had already decided that the principal cause of the problems was that many able-bodied labourers, both male and female, were not working but seeking relief. Their Report therefore cited the evidence which supported this view and ignored the rest. The outcome of their Report was the Poor Law Amendment Act of 1834.

2. Creation of the Wincanton Union and Workhouse

The Poor Law Amendment Act or the New Poor Law changed the philosophy on which the poor law system was based. In future it was to be one of 'less eligibility' which was to be achieved through the deterrent workhouse: that is to say, conditions within the workhouses were to be worse than those of the poorest independent labourer outside of the workhouse. In this way it would encourage all able-bodied labourers to seek work and turn to the poor law only when facing destitution.

In addition the 1834 Act altered significantly the administrative system as the Overseers and the 15,000 parishes ceased to control poor relief and in their place was a more centralized system, based in London. At the centre was the Poor Law Commission, re-named the Poor Law Board in 1847 and the Local Government Board in 1871, which decided national policy. England and Wales were divided into nine Districts each under the control of an Inspector, initially called Assistant Poor Law Commissioners, appointed by the Central Board and whose function was to implement its decisions in their Districts. Their first task was to amalgamate groups of parishes into Unions, usually centred on a local market town. The ratepayers in each parish elected one Guardian, or in the case of the larger ones of Bruton, Castle Cary, Henstridge, Milborne Port and Wincanton, two, who formed the Board of Guardians which was responsible for the administration of poor relief at local level. To do this they employed paid officials such as a Clerk, Relieving Officers, Master and Matron of the Workhouse, and Schoolteachers.

The administrative system created in 1834 was so successful at local level that its functions were extended during the course of the nineteenth century to include the Registration of Births, Marriages and Deaths, Vaccination, School Attendance and Public Health throughout the Union. In this way it appeared that local people remained in control of their own affairs, a sensitive issue at times during that century, and so helped to prevent conflict with central authorities

Robert Weale was the Assistant Poor Law Commissioner who was responsible for creating the new Unions in the West Country, which he accomplished by September 1837. He explained that, "My object was to take a Market town for a centre, and to unite such Parishes to it as were connected to it." Wincanton was the flourishing market town he selected in East Somerset as it served a wide rural area, was the base of the local Magistrates' Division created in 1831 and was a crossroads on coach and mail routes between London, Bristol and the South West. It was also the largest centre of population in that area. He joined together thirty-nine parishes to form the Wincanton Poor Law Union and in so doing he ignored estate boundaries, the old Hundred administrative boundaries as the thirty-nine parishes were drawn from six different hundreds, and even County boundaries as two parishes, Buckhorn Weston and Kington Magna, were in Dorset. The total population included within the Union as recorded in the 1831 Census was 21,096 and it covered an area of 65,019 acres.

The Board of Guardians of the Wincanton Union held its first meeting on 31st December 1835, with a potential attendance of forty-four elected Guardians and any local Magistrates who wished to attend as ex-officio Guardians. Such numbers would have made their weekly meetings very cumbersome and it soon became clear that a core of up to ten Guardians formed the basic group, joined by others on the occasions when they attended the weekly Wednesday Market in Wincanton or when there were key decisions and appointments to be made. The weekly meetings started promptly at 10 am, moved to 11 am in May 1850 as business became more routine, lasted for about three hours and were not open to the public until 1892 when determined criticism from the local press and the leakage of information forced a change. To that point the Guardians had retained the traditional view that once elected they were not directly responsible to the ratepayers who had elected them.

The Wincanton Board appears to have been competent and conscientious throughout the century as on only five occasions during the period 1836 to 1900 did they fail to form a quorum, and then usually as a result of bad weather. During the same period some seventy-six meetings attracted thirty or more of the Guardians and forty-four of these were concerned with the appointment of their Chairman or officials. There was a pronounced increase in attendance in the late 1890s, with at least eight meetings having more than thirty Guardians in attendance for no specific reason. In this respect the Local Government Act of 1894 was a success as it made the Guardians more inclined to respect the wishes of the electorate and attend to their duties. One local newspaper was favourably impressed with the Guardians at this period, "The attendance of members was never so good as now, and perhaps the business was never characterized by so much common sense."

To facilitate their business and to undertake the detailed specialist work required they immediately adopted a bureaucratic committee system. It was the recommendations of these various committees, amongst other matters, which the full Board considered each Wednesday. It was many of the same men who appeared on each committee, for example in 1838 five of the seven members of the Building Committee were also on the Visiting Committee and in 1880 eight of the twelve Visiting Committee members were on the Assessment Committee and six on the School Attendance Committee. There was also a close correlation between the membership of committees and general attendance so that of the thirteen members appointed to the Visiting Committee in 1840-1, eight attended more than half of the regular weekly meetings. In 1880 five of the Visiting Committee of twelve attended more than thirty-five of the weekly meetings. As well as the regular committees there were 'ad hoc' ones which investigated and reported on a wide range of topics including vagrancy, overcrowding, the consumption of spirits, the baking of bread, fire escapes, water pipes, building alterations and complaints against officials. There may be little doubt that these regular attenders worked extremely hard on behalf of both the ratepayers and the poor of the district.

The Guardians met each week in the Board Room which was located at the front of the Workhouse, to the right of the Entrance Hall and which was some twenty-two feet long and fifteen feet wide. It had three large windows which looked out over the Terrace and Drive. Its wooden floor was made from 1¼ inch thick deal planks with a moulded skirting eleven inches high and it had a Bell pull system connecting it to other rooms in the House. It was heated with a fire in a Best Registers Sheffield Grate "with best bright steel polished fire irons and neat very strong pattern cast iron Fender." To conduct business there was an oak-framed table which had a top 1½ inches thick made of "Honduras best Mahogony", ten feet long and tapered from four feet wide at one end to three feet at the other, eighteen oak chairs with turned legs and three Bench seats each seven feet six inches long. For the Chairman there was "one large Elbow Chair with dark leather stuffed with horsehair" and a similar one for the Vice Chairman "but less important in appearance." It was without any doubt the best room in appearance and with the best furnishings in the whole building and it was here that the Board met for the rest of the century, except between January and April 1871 when the increased numbers of inmates forced it to be turned into a temporary sleeping room. It was also used from August 1877 to October 1878 by the local Magistrates to hold their Monthly Meeting when the Town Hall was destroyed by fire.

Not unsurprisingly as the 1831 Census had shown that 46.6% of families in the area were employed in agriculture, small tenant farmers, often referred to as yeomen, dominated the Board of Guardians. At no stage in the nineteenth century did their representation fall below 60% of the total Board and peaked at 93% in 1860. Periods of service of twenty or thirty years were not uncommon: of the forty-nine Guardians present at the first meeting fourteen were still attending in the mid- 1850s, three a decade later and Thomas Gifford of North Cadbury until 1875. Of the forty-four elected in 1860 seven were still present in 1880 and three in 1890. A few ex-officio Guardians also played a prominent part with the longest serving member of all being Charles Barton who attended for over fifty years, forty-one of them as Chairman. Between 1854 and 1897 he was supported by another ex-officio Guardian, T.E. Rogers of Yarlington, as Vice-Chairman. This duration of tenure and regular attendance by some members meant that there was considerable continuity in the approach to poor relief and a wealth of experience. On the other hand, it led to a lack of innovation and change with the continuation for decades of some policies, which were severely criticized at the end of the century.

The Guardians inherited the three Poorhouses at Bruton, Henstridge and Wincanton which were inspected by one of their Committees and based upon its recommendations their initial inclination on 27th January 1836 was to continue to house the aged and infirm at Bruton and Henstridge but agreed "that it is absolutely necessary to erect a new Workhouse for the general purposes of the Union." The following month they amended their decision so that on a temporary basis the aged would be housed at Bruton, single women and children at Henstridge and the able-bodied at Wincanton. A further investigation revealed that the Poorhouses at Bruton and Henstridge were not ideal for the intended purposes, that the numbers to be accommodated were small and that costs would be significantly reduced by the use of just one centralized house. In April therefore the Guardians decided to close the Poorhouses in these two towns and transfer the inmates to the one in Wincanton in May until a new Workhouse was constructed on a site to the west of the town off Wright's Lane, (now known as Shadwell Lane) called Yarn's Barton, an area of ten acres which they purchased on 9th April 1836 for £350. (3)

As experience of building the proposed workhouses was very limited the Poor Law Commissioners published specimen plans in their early Reports. The Wincanton Board decided to adopt one which was not included but was very similar, was designed by George Wilkinson of London and had been adopted by many Unions in the adjoining counties. This decision too was influenced by cost. Unfortunately the choice of site and plan were to haunt the Guardians for the rest of the century as the design did not allow for the total separation of the different classes of paupers, such as the able-bodied and the aged and the site was so small that once the Workhouse building was erected there was little space for additional buildings to make improvements or even for sufficient cultivation, especially as the remaining land sloped away to the east and west and on the southern side some 10,000 square feet had a slope of forty-five degrees.

The Contract for building was awarded to Maurice Davis of Langport with a tender of £3,550, which included making an estimated 300,000 bricks on the site. With the foundation stone laid on 29th March 1837, he was given a completion date of 29th September in that year, extended to 1st February 1838 after the Guardians decided to amend their original plan to allow them to accommodate 200 instead of 140 paupers. The total cost of the building, which was completed on schedule, along with fixtures, fittings and all the contents was £6,775 15s 0d, a sum which was borrowed by means of an Exchequer Loan and repaid in annual instalments until 1856, with each parish making a proportional contribution.

From the very beginning the function of the Workhouse was clear: it was to act as a deterrent, especially to the able-bodied. Time and again this was re-iterated by the Central Board,

> "The sole object of the workhouse is to give relief to the destitute poor in such a manner as shall satisfy the necessary wants, without making pauperism attractive, or otherwise injuring the industrious classes."

It was a sentiment with which the Wincanton Board of Guardians agreed, even at the end of the century, "It was wrong to go on a basis which would place any pauper in receipt of relief in a better position than a low-paid labourer in the same class of life."

The design of the Workhouse fostered this end by giving distinct accommodation to each category of inmate. There were separate yards, flanked by dayrooms with sleeping accommodation above, creating a geometric design. Along the outside walls of the buildings and against the boundary walls were a number of outbuildings which were added at various times, such as vagrant wards, stone breaking cell, carpenter's shop, fumigating room, mortuary and wash house. In the centre was the Dining Hall, which also served as a Chapel, because all paupers required access to it from their separate wings, and immediately above was the accommodation for the Master and Matron, placing them in a strategic position with windows which gave them a view over each yard and with quick access to all parts of the building. To the left of the Entrance Hall was the Porter's Room and Receiving Wards.

The very accommodation available in the Wincanton Workhouse also conformed to the guiding principle of deterrence. The three Poorhouses pre-1834 could house in total of about 170 paupers, or some 0.81% of the 1831 population of the area: the new Workhouse contained 200 places, suitable for 0.96% of the population. After 1834 there was no intention to build more accommodation but rather some with a different purpose. For more than thirty years its primary function was to deter the able-bodied and their dependents from entering. As their numbers decreased more attention was paid to the treatment of other categories, notably the aged, sick, infirm and children. This change in emphasis led to a major building programme in 1870 to construct, amongst other things, Infectious Wards and a separate Schoolroom for children. The result of this activity was that the accommodation increased nominally to 307.

The completed Workhouse revealed the ambivalent attitude that nineteenth century society possessed towards workhouses as it was isolated on the western edge of Wincanton, because no one wanted the inmates as close neighbours. As late as 1898 the owner of the field next door complained that he had picked up a three-peck basket full of waste bread in that field. Early Ordnance Survey Maps show that there were virtually no other buildings to the west of the River Cale. On the other hand the Workhouse was a substantial brick building, certainly not hidden away, as it stood two storeys high on a rise in the land. It would have been a prominent feature for any traveller coming from the direction of Castle Cary, Yeovil, Shepton Montague or Bruton and visible from many parts of Wincanton itself. (4)

The Wincanton Workhouse represented a regime committed to deterrence, uniformity and rigid discipline for all and it was to this building that the former inmates of the Poorhouses transferred in 1838.

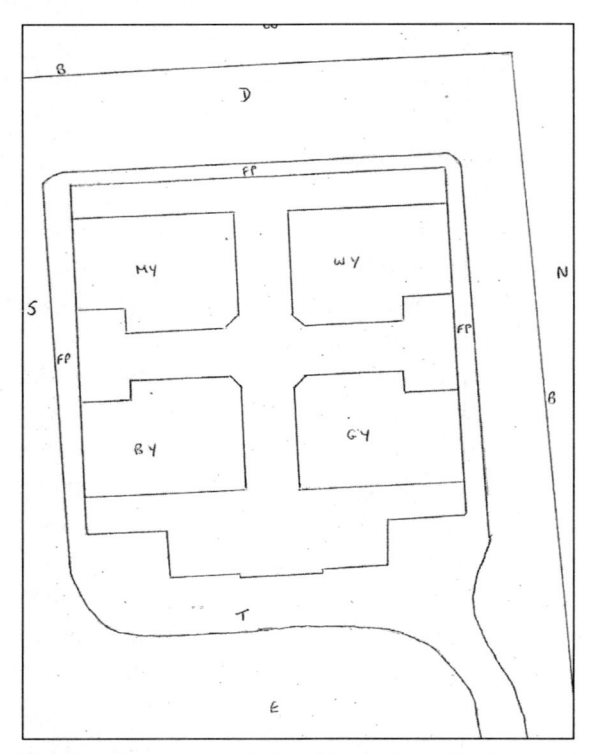

Original Plan of the Wincanton Workhouse

N. S. E. W.	North, South, East and West.
B	Boundary Wall
D	Drying Ground
FP	Footpath
T	Terrace
MY	Men's Yard
WY	Women's Yard
BY	Boys' Yard
GY	Girls' Yard

Extensions to the Wincanton Workhouse by 1900

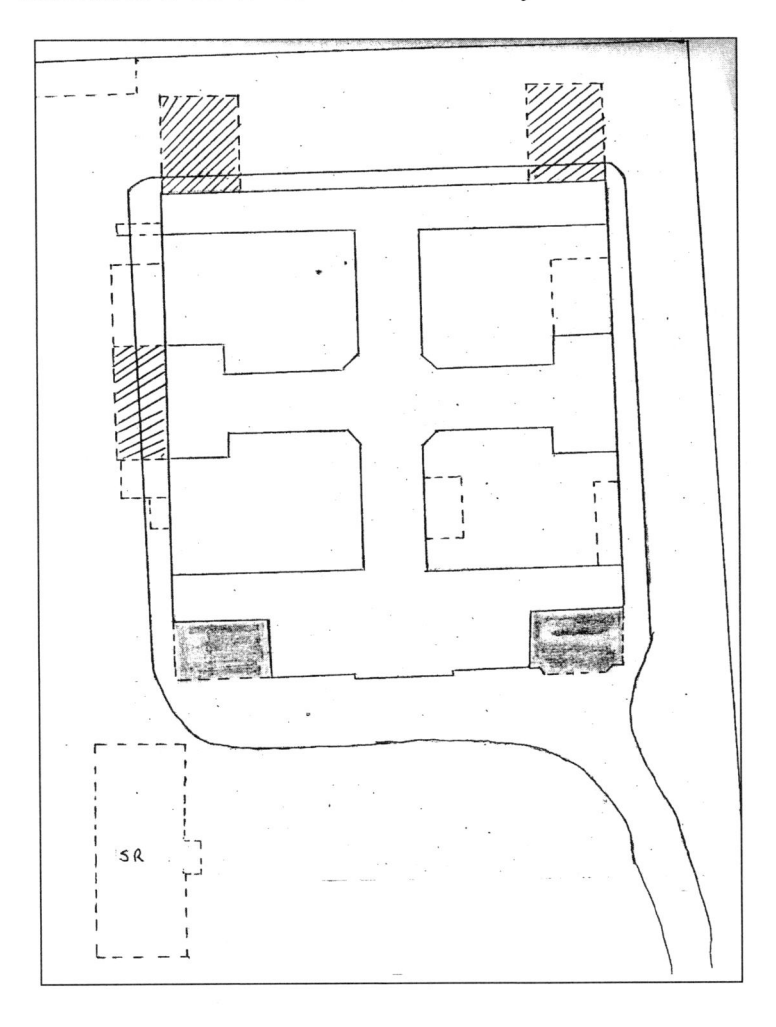

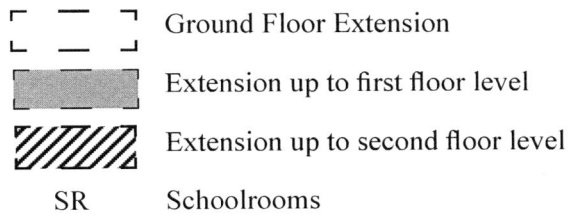

Ground Floor Extension

Extension up to first floor level

Extension up to second floor level

SR   Schoolrooms

3. Admission to the Workhouse

Workhouses have achieved a prominent position in the popular imagination yet in reality the vast majority of paupers received Outdoor Relief in their own homes and only a minority Indoor Relief in the Workhouse. In the first thirty years after the formation of the Wincanton Union in only two years of particular hardship, 1848 and 1850, did Indoor Relief numbers reach 10% of the total number relieved and in other years such as 1858 and 1859 was just over 6%. The more rigorous enforcement of the Workhouse Test after 1870 led to an increase in those receiving Indoor Relief, both nationally and in Wincanton where it peaked at 18% in the 1880s, declining to between 12% and 15% in the 1890s. These percentages represented between 0.6% and 1.5% of the total population of the area. In numerical terms, therefore, the number of inmates was small as may be seen from Tables 2a and 2b covering the period 1838 to 1898, during which time statistical reporting methods to the Central Boards changed.

Table 2a.   Numbers receiving Relief 1838-1863

Year ending Lady Day	Indoor Relief	Outdoor Relief
1838	147	2799
1843	286	3202
1848	548	3496
1853	254	3293
1858	186	2696
1863	189	2218

Table 2b. Numbers receiving Relief 1873-1898 (excluding vagrants)

Year	Indoor Relief		Outdoor Relief	
	1 January	1 July	1 January	1 July
1873	214	199	1322	1267
1878	191	192	1075	1028
1883	226	184	1153	1060
1888	189	152	967	991
1893	126	116	939	935
1898	147	131	941	905

For many of those who were forced to enter the confines of the Workhouse for whatever reason, it could have been a traumatic experience, one which some paupers tried desperately to avoid, appealing for Outdoor Relief to the Relieving Officer, the Board of Guardians and, in a small number of cases, to the Central Board itself. Once a decision had been taken it was seldom changed and examples throughout the Minute Books show that transference from Outdoor Relief to Indoor Relief was the more common route, as John and Rebecca Shears found in June 1858 when their Outdoor Relief of two loaves a week was stopped and they were ordered to the House on account of "habitual intoxication."

To gain admission to the Workhouse a pauper required a signed Order and as Table 3 shows this could be obtained from different sources. It is clear that the Relieving Officer was the key figure, with the Board of Guardians or individual Guardians in their own parishes making a significant contribution. In the early years the Overseers continued to issue such Orders but these markedly decreased after 1842, except in specific unusual years and had ceased altogether by the 1890s. The Master had the authority to allow admissions in emergency situations, "sudden and urgent necessity" was the phrase used, subject to the subsequent approval of the Board of Guardians. By 1870 the local Police could require the admission of categories such as tramps and anyone they discovered homeless and destitute, although usually the actual admission Order was signed by the Master.

Table 3. Authority for Admission to the Workhouse

Admitting Officer	1836	1837	1838	1870	1871	1872	1873	1890	1891	1892
Overseers	25	17	10	4	18	1				
Relieving Officers	43	132	287	355	226	288	284	159	134	125
Master	8	5	18	48	15	8	15	9	21	12
Medical Officer	1									
Board of Guardians	98	87	66	3	1		1	8	2	4
Born in House		7	8							
Police				5						
From other Unions				5	5	6	17	1	4	2
From Lunatic Asylum					3					

(The totals for 1871 will probably be greater as no figures were given for May and June.)

Once the Order had been signed the pauper had to travel to the Workhouse and this was usually on foot, although horses and carts were hired for the aged, infirm and those too weak to walk through malnutrition and general destitution, the cost being borne by the parish of Settlement. For some it would have been a long walk as the furthest parish in the Union was nine and a half miles from Wincanton and at least eighteen parishes were five miles or more from the Workhouse. The last stage of the walk must have been soul destroying, especially for the elderly as for many of them this would be their last place of residence. Going along Wright's Lane the perimeter wall of the Workhouse grounds would be above their heads and was surmounted near the gates with wrought iron railings two and a half feet high with spear-shaped ends. The two wrought iron gates, each five feet wide and six feet high, hung from square Doulting stone pillars. Once through the gates the pauper was on an eighteen foot wide gravel drive which followed an almost semi-circular uphill route to the Terrace which ran along the front of the Workhouse and was twenty-nine feet wide: ample space for any carts carrying paupers or carriages with their wealthier visitors to turn. To save money the Board of Guardians purchased five hundred loads of Cheriton Hill stone which was broken up into gravel by the able-bodied male paupers in the Workhouse and then used on the drive and Terrace where it was eight inches deep.

All the time looming above the paupers, rising from the Terrace, was the two-storey brick Workhouse with its rows of sash windows. The approach and the building itself were at once both impressive and intimidating. Eventually they came to the large central front door made from yellow Christiana deal, complete with its knocker which they would have to use as the door was kept locked. It had a twelve-inch draw-back lock and two twelve inch bolts as well as a strong barrel chain. From 1863 it also had a bell attached to it, "large enough to be heard all over the premises". The door was unlocked by the Master or Porter who would examine the Order for Admission. Before crossing the threshold shoes and boots had to be cleaned on a cast iron scraper let into stone and then on a doormat inside, which cost 5s 6d to replace in July 1857.

The Entrance Hall originally had a brick floor but this was replaced with Keinton stone slabs in August 1850. Against the walls were deal seats eleven inches wide and one and a half inches thick with two rails fixed to the wall to act as a back rest. From here the paupers were ushered to the left into the Male and Female Receiving Wards, both of which were sparsely furnished with the same deal seats around the wall but with a single four inch wide back rail fixed to the wall fifteen inches above the seat. The walls in these rooms, as in all the rooms used by the paupers, were plastered and coated with white lime. Here they waited for the daily visit of the Medical Officer as one of his tasks was to pronounce on the condition of the pauper and he or she was allocated to the appropriate category based upon the Medical Officer's decision. The Wincanton Board was also very clear that only their Medical Officer could admit or discharge paupers from the Sick Wards.

The system after 1834 allowed for seven categories of inmates:

Class 1	Men infirm through age or any other cause
Class 2	Able bodied men, and youths above the age of fifteen years
Class 3	Boys above the age of seven years, and under that of fifteen
Class 4	Women infirm through age or any other cause
Class 5	Able bodied women, and girls above the age of fifteen years
Class 6	Girls above the age of seven years, and under that of fifteen
Class 7	Children under seven years of age.

The allocation of the class was crucial as it had implications for other areas such as the nature of the work set and the diet.

Once the class was allocated the pauper was ready to move on and face what for some was another ordeal, "the pauper shall be thoroughly cleansed, and shall be clothed in a workhouse dress, and the clothes which he wore at the time of his admission shall be purified." In the days before a regular water supply many of the paupers who entered a workhouse were not only diseased but also filthy and their clothes often in a terrible condition, sometimes described as little more than rags. It was said of John Harding aged 50, that he "Came in in a diseased state", and that Ann Parsons was a "Dirty idle woman." Near the Receiving Rooms and adjoining the Porter's Bedroom was the necessary Bathroom which contained two deal baths, six feet long and three feet six inches deep, let nine inches into the ground and placed across the room under the window. All hot water was brought in buckets from the kitchen and emptied in the same way.

Once clean and deprived of their own clothes each of the paupers was given a complete set of linen. Men received a shirt, waistcoat, trousers, jacket with one pocket, stockings and boots and women a dress made of linsey woolsey, which was a coarse woollen cloth, shoes, stockings and a shawl. In 1862 the shawls for the girls were replaced with a cloak made of a pattern cloth which cost 5s 6d a yard. Initially all clothing was in the same dull grey which may be seen as part of the de-humanizing process but also made the paupers clearly identifiable when outside of the Workhouse. Expenditure on clothing was to be a constant feature in the Ledgers for the rest of the century. In 1838 the original purchase of three hundred yards of linsey woolsey cost £18; by 1850 some £149 was being spent on clothing for the inmates and over £223 in 1875. In addition in June 1836 Mr Read received £19 1s 8d for shoes and George Bond £10 2s 0d in January 1837. He also received £1 17s 11d for shoe mending in November of the same year. The Guardians appear to have been strict in their requirements as in April 1836 they had no hesitation in sending back to one of their suppliers thirteen "Suits of Men's Clothing" as they were not of the colour and quality ordered.

Clothing provided a fruitful source of complaints, usually centred on allegations that clean linen was not provided weekly, for example in July 1864 William Parsons complained that he had not received a clean shirt for a fortnight and stockings for three weeks. A few months later he and two other men alleged that their shirts, stockings and handkerchiefs had not been changed for three weeks. In the first instance the Matron, who was responsible for the supply of linen, was warned to be more careful and in the second asked to resign as this was the culmination of a number of other matters. One unsatisfactory practice was eradicated early as in 1841 some of the male paupers complained that when they received their fresh linen on Fridays they were often compelled to change in the yards. The Board ordered the Master to discontinue this practice and to place the change of linen in the respective bedrooms every Saturday evening "that all the paupers might appear in clean linen Sunday morning" when they attended Church. Public appearances obviously mattered and the system remained in place for the rest of the century.

As some of the pauper inmates soon discovered that the Workhouse clothes were superior to their own, the Discharge Books and Minute Books indicate that absconding with Union clothes was not uncommon:

> "22 November 1837 William Ashford. Absconded. Taking with him belonging to the Union 1 New Pair Shoes 1 Stockings, Trousers, 1 Shirt & Waistcoat. 9 June 1838 Jane Hopkins. Absconded. Taking 1 pr Shoes 1 Frock & 1 Pinafore belonging to the Union."

The local Magistrates' Records reveal that when caught the offenders faced hard labour in Shepton Mallet Gaol for periods of seven to twenty-one days, for example on 29th August 1859 George Wall received twenty-one days with hard labour for his fourth such offence. By 1850 the Guardians had become aware that a gang of boys aged about sixteen were being repeatedly admitted to the Workhouse as they had no work, absconding with the Union clothing, selling it, returning and giving themselves up and serving their sentences before re-offending. In August 1850 therefore the Board decided to provide distinctive clothes for those who had absconded before and sold Union clothes although they were advised by the Poor Law Board that the clothes should be "marked with the name of the Union, but not that so the Mark or Stamp shall be publicly visible." (5)

Clean and clothed the new inmates were taken to their respective section of the Workhouse: an experience which, especially for families and married couples, was the next traumatic part of the process as it involved separation. Every room was identified with its name by lettering which had cost 10s 6d in June 1836 when done by Kimber.

The few surviving Admission and Discharge Books give some indication of the reasons why paupers were admitted to the Wincanton Workhouse and may be seen in Table 4.

Table 4. Reasons for Admission to Wincanton Workhouse

	1837	1838	1870	1871	1872	1873	1890	1891	1892
No home	32	6		1					
Unemployed	43	27							
Ill health	37	19	67	38	49	27	17	25	17
Pregnant	7	15	8	7	11	6	10	6	7
Deserted by husband or parents	25	13	3	19	11	26		5	3
Husband in Army	1	2							
Age	1								
Destitution		121	193	129	139	150	105	69	97
Idiot/Insane		3		4	3		2	5	2
Infirm			29	30	21	32	8	5	3
Drink			2		1	3		3	
Returned from Service			6	3	6	10		8	3
Removed from another Union				4	5		1		3
Brought by Police				1		3	1	1	
Deaf and Dumb						1		1	
Returned from Gaol						1	3		1
With parents							20	19	4

23

Destitution, the reason specified by the Central Board, was by far the largest factor but a significant number were also admitted as a result of illness or infirmity, the latter covering a range of conditions, from those which were long term, sometimes associated with age, to those of a more temporary nature such as a broken or fractured limb. Those deserted by a husband, father, mother or both continued to be an important group throughout the period whereas age was rarely specified as a factor in its own right. In 1870-1871 some ninety-five or 13.2% of the 722 paupers admitted were over sixty years of age and of the eighty-six for whom a reason was specified thirty-four were infirm, twenty-five ill, another twenty-five destitute and two were removed from other Unions.

The poor of any age were vulnerable as the statistics in the sample years in Table 5 indicate.

Table 5.   Age on Admission to Wincanton Workhouse

	1837-1838	1870-1871	1890-1891
10 and under	226	214	58
11-19	84	96	11
20-29	122	118	35
30-39	56	73	29
40-49	71	68	42
50-59	30	58	58
60-69	24	54	82
70-79	9	26	21
80 and over	2	15	3
Total	624	722	339

Throughout the period children under ten years of age constituted an important group and significant attention was paid to them. The figures also show a major change in the function of the Workhouse as the percentage of admissions for those over sixty years of age increased dramatically, from 5.6% of all admissions in 1837-1838 to 30.7% in 1890-1891. The Guardians had to amend their policies and the very layout of their Workhouse to cater for this change.

In most of the cases of those above fifteen years of age the Admissions Registers specified an occupation and Table 6a indicates that in the sample years 62.3% to 80.1% were from unskilled labouring occupations. Men were usually referred to a 'Labourers' and women as 'Servants'. In addition, however, there was a vast range of other occupations represented, many of which reflected the predominantly rural nature of the area, but also one which did have small industries based in the larger towns. Wool comber, silk worker, glover, cooper, tailor, butcher, rag woman, weaver, carpenter, blacksmith, lime burner, shepherd, quarrier and washerwoman were just a few and while some of these were more skilled and required an apprenticeship, others were not and could so easily have been placed in the more general category of 'labourer'.

Table 6a.   Occupation before Admission

	1837-1838	1870-1871	1890-1891
Labourer	189	157	122
Servant	81	102	34
Others	67	115	60
Total	337	374	216

A single event such as a Census provided a snap-shot of the inmates of workhouses on just one day. Tables 6b and 6c are based upon the 1841, 1881 and 1891 Census Returns for the Wincanton Workhouse and show similar patterns to those in Tables 5 and 6a. An increasing percentage were aged sixty and over, from 10.9% in 1841 to 32.6% in 1891 and a declining percentage were aged ten and under, 35.6% in 1841, 28.3% in 1881 and 24.1% in 1891. Once again the unskilled formed a significant group of at least 64% to 66%. On Census day in 1881 thirteen paupers were classed as Imbeciles, of whom four were male and nine female. There were also five blind inmates, four males and one female, along with one Deaf and Dumb female and one dumb male. The inability of older men to cope on their own may be suggested by the presence of twenty-four widowers compared with thirteen widows.

Table 6b. Age of Inmates of Wincanton Workhouse on Census days 1841, 1881 and 1891.

Age	1841	1881	1891
10 and under	36	64	34
11-19	23	34	14
20-29	7	21	9
30-39	16	13	14
40-49	5	17	7
50-59	3	12	17
60-69	7	20	19
70-79	4	36	22
80 and over	0	9	5
Total	101	226	141

Table 6c. Occupation of Inmates of Wincanton Workhouse on Census days in 1881 and 1891

	1881	1891
Labourer	49	37
Servant	27	24
Others	42	31
Total	118	92

As so many of the occupations in the area were connected with agriculture it is not surprising that there were some fluctuations in the timing of admissions to the Workhouse. The nine full years covered by the Admission Registers indicate that January and February were together the peak period for entry with 501 or 19.5% of the total. Lack of employment on the farms, the often bitter weather and increase in illness forced some who could otherwise manage to seek assistance. With the coming of Spring and the warmer weather the lowest pair of months for admission were March and April with 365 or 14.2%. The largest single monthly admission was fifty-eight in July 1870, which may have been the result of the more rigorous enforcement of the Workhouse Test rather than any other factor. The second largest monthly admission came in October 1838 and was probably related to adverse weather.

In addition admission from the different parishes in the Union varied significantly and was often connected with population totals. Parishes with larger populations tended to send more paupers to Wincanton: Bruton provided 10.8% of all admissions, Castle Cary 9% and Henstridge 5.4%. Parishes with small populations sent far fewer which may suggest either a more close-knit social structure within them or that there had been, or still was, a policy by the landowners to prevent anyone who might become a pauper from gaining Settlement, usually by failing to provide cottage accommodation, the so-called 'close' parishes. In reality this meant that labourers lived in one parish and worked in another, often with a long walk in the morning and evening. Of the 2,563 admissions in the years covered just two came from Sutton Montis, three from Maperton and four from Lovington. The parishes of Alford and Wheathill sent none at all. Other parishes with a relatively small population such as Stoke Trister sent ninety and Buckhorn Weston seventy-two which may suggest the presence of individuals or families who created specific problems or a policy by local landowners to tie a cottage to employment and if the work ceased or was seasonal the family became homeless and frequently destitute.

The admission of families increased numbers rapidly. In 1837-1838 the entry into the Wincanton Workhouse of sixty-four married couples led to the admission of ninety-one children with them, and fifty-three mothers and five fathers added a further one hundred and four children. In 1870-1871 eighteen couples brought thirty-three children and thirty-three single parents sixty-nine children. These figures were distorted by some families remaining in the Workhouse for just a short time, leaving and then seeking re-admission, for example, Silas Deacon, a cooper from Bruton, was admitted and discharged with his wife and four children on four separate occasions between August 1836 and the end of June 1838.

It was not only families who were admitted and discharged more than once as may be seen in Table 7.

Table 7.   Multiple Admission, 1837-8, 1870-1

No. of occasions	No. of individuals 1837-1838	No. of individuals 1870-1871
Twice	31	26
Three times	8	17
Four times	4	10
Five times	2	7
More than five times	1	7

These paupers were frequently referred to as the "Ins and Outs", and would enter the Workhouse often with a specific problem such as illness or in periods of cold weather, then go out to try to find work and return after a few days or a week if they failed.

During the first twenty years of the operation of the Wincanton Union the Guardians occasionally attempted to keep some families out of the Workhouse by accepting one child into it. The youngest child of seven of widower William Gant of South Brewham was admitted in December 1837; one of the six children of George Trim and his wife in January 1846; the five-month old child of widower William Pitman of Horsington as he could not nurse the baby in November 1850; and widowers Henry Abbot and Charles Wills both had one child admitted in November 1855 from their families of four and five children respectively. After the death of the wife of John

Cooper of Castle Cary in November 1853 the Guardians agreed to admit his two stepchildren into the Workhouse as he had three more children of his own under sixteen years of age. In most cases the men involved were able-bodied but widowers, which in itself is an indication of the dangers of childbirth for women at this period, and the offer of the House for a child prevented the admission of a whole family, especially in cases where the father was employed, and it was by far the cheapest option for the ratepayers. (6)

Multiple admissions meant that the length of stay in the Workhouse of some paupers was quite short, while for the aged it could be more long term. The trend towards a longer period of residence in 1870-1871 may well be an indication of the changing nature of the Workhouse. For those who had experienced the old system pre-1834 the new Union Workhouse must have been quite a shock so, for example, Honor and George Fleetwood were admitted and discharged on the same day, 30th October 1838.

Table 8.   Length of stay in the Wincanton Workhouse

No. of days	No. of paupers 25 March 1836 to 31 December 1838	No. of paupers 1870-1871
1 day or less	2	4
2-7	164	39
8-14	117	23
15-30	107	45
31-60	129	47
61-120	76	55
121-365	70	92
Over 365	7	91

Soon after the workhouses were constructed they became known as the "Poor Man's Bastille", but they were not prisons as most inmates could leave when they wished, although there were obvious exceptions such as orphans. The usual procedure was to make a verbal request to the Master and then the able-bodied would be detained for a further set period of two or three hours to perform a task after their last meal, which was usually breakfast, and then permitted to leave. The non-able bodied on the other hand could leave immediately. In 1871 of the 313 discharges some 179 were at the paupers' own request and they took with them ninety-three children. Twenty years later in 1891 of 187 discharges 115 were at their own request, taking twenty-eight children. The remainder of the discharges were for a variety of other reasons: a small number absconded; some, especially older children, went out to service; a few to asylums, hospitals or gaol; and each year some died, twenty-one in 1871 and thirteen in 1891.

The multiple admissions and the high turnover rate indicates that many poor people were living a very precarious economic existence so that a small unexpected event such as bad weather or illness could be a disaster which forced them to turn to the Poor Law. The Workhouse with all its rules, regulations and family separation was less of a threat than total destitution outside. Some appear to have been unconcerned about the consequences of social rejection or disgrace especially if many of their neighbours were in a similar position. In this sense the deterrent effect of the Workhouse was not as great as it supporters had hoped.

4. Work

Compulsory labour for all the able-bodied, both male and female, was the order of the day, especially as from 25th March 1837 the Guardians implemented the Order from the Poor Law Commissioners which required all relief to the able-bodied to be in the workhouse, except in cases "of sudden or urgent necessity or of sickness." The partially able-bodied, the aged, lunatics and children when not in School, were required to undertake tasks within their capability or as directed by the Medical Officer. At their meeting on 4th July 1838 the Wincanton Board resolved,
> "That all the Paupers in the house shall be employed in any work of which they may be capable."

This was virtually the same as a resolution which they had agreed two years earlier before their new Workhouse was constructed and was to remain in place for the rest of the century. The Guardians were also quite clear that refusal to perform the task set would lead to a punishment. Initially this might entail stopping the normal diet and placing the offender in the Refractory Ward with just bread and water and could lead eventually to an appearance before a Magistrate which would probably mean imprisonment with hard labour for up to one month.

Work started immediately after breakfast, continued until dinner-time, resumed after that meal and lasted until late afternoon or such time as the allotted task was completed. It was designed to be hard physical labour occupying a long period of the day. As a result it was anticipated that this aspect of life in the workhouse would be a major factor in discouraging the able-bodied from seeking poor relief and encourage them to find paid employment. The 1834 Report itself had urged that they should all be subjected to such work as "all labour is irksome to those who are unaccustomed to labour."

The Wincanton Board implemented a range of tasks during the nineteenth century, with varying results. In September 1838 they considered the purchase of one of Herbert's small Corn Mills but after a year's investigation decided that it was impractical and did not go ahead with that scheme. Their initial preferred labour therefore for able-bodied males, and one used in many other workhouses, was bone crushing. The bones, which were obtained from local sources, were crushed into bone dust and then sold mainly for fertilizer at a significant profit, so, for example, in February 1845 the Guardians sold eighty quarters of bone dust to a Mr Lush at 22s a quarter while purchasing five tons of bones from William Fry at 5s per ton. It was seen as an appropriate form of labour as it did not interfere with or threaten the work of labourers outside of the Workhouse. The able-bodied males were given a pestle and mortar and in dry weather sat in the open air in one of the yards to crush their allotted twenty pounds and in wet weather in open fronted sheds constructed along the boundary wall.

As the Guardians insisted that only dry bones should be supplied, which may not have been entirely possible, they were confident that no putrid matter would be present which might create a health hazard. In February 1845 they also constructed a shed thirty feet long by twelve feet wide attached to a boundary wall in which to store the bones and the bone dust. In December 1845 their Medical Officer, William Brunton, was prepared to certify that, "crushing bones has no injurious effects either on the health of those employed in it, nor on the inmates of the house generally." There were odd problems such as in the winter of 1841-2 when the Clerk was unable to purchase any bones in the town and was directed to try to obtain a ton of them from Horsington. In addition in March 1843 John and Charles Willis, who had been paupers in the House, were charged with robbery when they stole a quantity of green bones buried in the Workhouse garden. This episode does suggest that attempts were made to ensure that bones were only crushed when they were suitably clean and until such a stage had been reached were buried out of the way.

While the system of bone crushing might have been operating effectively in the Wincanton Workhouse that was not the case elsewhere. A scandal was created in Andover when it was discovered that some of the inmates who claimed to be starving were eating bits of putrid meat still on the bones. After a series of investigations the Poor Law Commissioners banned bone crushing in all Unions from 1st January 1846. The Wincanton Board was horrified and started a detailed correspondence with the Central Board designed to change its mind. They claimed no ill-effects in their Workhouse, that they had invested a considerable sum of money, that there was a ready market for the bone dust, that there was no other permanent labour available which would not affect labourers outside of the House and that they needed more time to establish another system in its place. In a separate letter the Medical Officer went so far as to claim that the able-bodied men preferred crushing bones to any other labour "as the strong and industrious men, by crushing the given weight of bones in a less time, have then an hour or two at their own disposal." The most the Guardians achieved was a three-month suspension of the Order until 1 April 1846. Four years later in February 1850 faced with an increase in the number of male able-bodied inmates they attempted again to persuade the Poor Law Board to suspend the Order for three months but this time they failed. The result was that they had to place more emphasis upon their other form of labour - cracking stone. (7)

Cracking stone into gravel for roads and paths had operated from the formation of the Union and had included the gravel for the Terrace and drive of the Workhouse itself but it had been of secondary importance for the employment of male paupers. Each was required to crack twenty-eight pounds of stone a day and, as with the bones, the labour was performed in the yards on dry days and in an open shed on wet ones. It was alleged that in some respects it was not an occupation which would act as a deterrent as

> "all the stone to be procured here being of a very soft and porous nature cannot afford nothing like labour for a really able-bodied man."

The Guardians purchased large quantities such as one hundred yards of stone from James Sweetman at 2s per yard in November 1861. There was some variation in the sale price of the resulting gravel, for example when it failed to sell at 5s per ton in January 1848 it was reduced to 4s and the following month to 3s when the Rev. J. Phabayn purchased fifteen tons. In the year ending Lady Day 1871 the Guardians made a profit from stone breaking of £17 5s 6d.

As the number of able-bodied men entering the Workhouse decreased later in the century cracking stone ceased. In December 1893, however, the Visiting Committee recommended that it should be resumed as there were two able-bodied men in the House. The Guardians agreed but the Master protested that it had been so long since it was last undertaken that there was no longer any suitable accommodation. A compromise was reached so that stone breaking should occur in a yard "weather permitting." (8)

A small number of able-bodied males had the opportunity to be involved in the cultivation of vegetables in the gardens which were in front of the Workhouse, on its eastern side and sloped down to Wrights Lane. In general, however, the gardens were the preserve of the elderly men, assisted at various times by some of the boys as this was perceived as good training for the latter and also occupied them out of school hours. For the elderly men it provided some relief from the hours of tedium they experienced in the dayrooms and possibly gave them a sense of still fulfilling a useful function. In March 1838 the Guardians had spent £2 16s 0d on purchasing wheelbarrows to be used in the gardens and most years a small sum was spent on seeds, such as £1 0d 8d to Thomas White in March 1847. While most of the produce grown was for internal consumption a small amount was sold. In relation to the numbers in the House the actual quantity produced was limited as the space available for growing was not extensive.

The major employment of the able-bodied females was clear, "all the household work to be performed and executed by the able-bodied women, and Girls above the age of seven years."

The Guardians were careful to instruct the Matron, who was responsible for this aspect of workhouse life, that she must ensure that the able-bodied women and girls when performing this work did not have contact with able-bodied men or boys above the age of seven years. Initially this labour was also for "women pregnant with and the mothers of Bastard Children" but under pressure from the Poor Law Inspectors this practice was discontinued in August 1853.

As the Workhouse had many large rooms, originally housed 200 inmates, and later nominally 307, some of whom were far from clean in their habits, this work, which was well underway by 9 am was both essential and time-consuming. Everyday all the rooms and passages were swept and in most cases the floors scrubbed on hands and knees. In 1893 the whole House was referred to as "scrupulously clean" and five years later one Visitor noted, "the perfect cleanliness of the house", although he did acknowledge that that had not always been the case under the previous Matron. The able-bodied women also undertook all the washing for the House and for this purpose a Washhouse had been built which opened into the Women's Yard. It contained two boiling coppers, one holding sixty gallons of water and the other fifty gallons and both were filled manually. Underneath each was the fire to heat the water. In addition there were smaller washing tubs, one of which for example cost £2 1s 0d in November 1836. For all this washing and cleaning huge amounts of soap were required and the Guardians purchased this in large quantities, for example in 1855-6 best yellow soap was costing them £2 6s 0d per hundredweight.

This type of labour entailed considerable physical effort, especially for the women working in the hot, damp atmosphere in the Washhouse but it was not until 1864 that they were allowed an extra drink of one pint of tea. Some of the elderly or infirm females may have been encouraged to knit as 8s 8d was paid to George Crocker in December 1837 for knitting needles. Such domestic labour was not well received by all paupers. When Rebecca Gerrad was discharged the Master noted, "Very Idle woman. Said she would rather starve than work for nothing."

Oakum picking had been investigated as a possible occupation for able-bodied women when the Union was formed but its inland position and the expense of the material led to the view that it would not be economical. Faced with an inadequate amount of labour in 1850 the idea was again explored but the Poor Law Board Inspector noted, "no oakum can be taken from any sea port to Wincanton and back without a loss equal to its worth." The idea was abandoned although periodically small quantities were purchased for punishment labour for able-bodied paupers reported disorderly or refractory.

A range of other activities were manifest from time to time. Able-bodied women were required to make and mend the clothes of the inmates if the occasion arose. If additional labour was needed, as for example occurred in the early 1850s when larger numbers entered the House, straw was purchased to make straw mats. The mothers of bastard children had to undertake wool picking in a separate room for the glove industry. For a small number of able-bodied women there were occasionally opportunities for other work in the House. From the formation of the Union the Guardians had used an appropriate female pauper as the Cook, such as Frances Dyke who was paid 3s a week in 1836, but with a shortage of suitable females from the 1850s it was more common for an outside person to be appointed. How successful the pauper Cooks were at large scale catering following a rigid set menu, is impossible to determine. Few complaints reached the Guardians at their weekly meetings and those which did concentrated on the externally produced food such as the bread, milk and butter rather than the internally cooked meals. The Cook operated in a kitchen to the east of the Dining Hall, some twenty feet long by sixteen feet wide, which contained a deal table four feet wide and eight feet long for the preparation of food and a large fireplace with iron range. Alongside the kitchen was a scullery which extended into the Girls' Yard but from which there was no access. It contained a deal sink that was two feet six inches wide and six inches deep and lined with seven pounds of lead.

Another female pauper was employed as the Nurse and if necessary an additional inmate to assist. It was a far from satisfactory arrangement, for example in April 1853 Mary Moorse was given one month's notice for disobedience to the Master and allowing the room assistant Mary Ann Cross to ill treat some of the patients. The problem was that the salary was so low, being at that stage just £10 a year, that it failed to attract a person with any real experience or qualifications. When Moorse left the only candidate was Elizabeth Parker, another pauper in the House. Raising the salary did little to improve the quality.

There was the expectation that labour in the House, as well as occupying the inmates, would produce tangible financial results for the benefit of the ratepayers and help to offset the running costs of the Union. The sums involved, however, were not considerable, depending so much on the number and condition of the inmates. Statistics published in the 1850s give an indication of the annual sums involved.

Table 9.   Sale of Produce

	Garden Produce			Produce of Labour		
	£	s	d	£	s	d
To Lady Day 1850	7	1	8	20	11	3¼
To Lady Day 1851	6	12	0	19	5	3
To Lady Day 1852	5	4	7	27	15	6
To Lady Day 1856	9	9	10	9	18	8

In addition in the year ending Michaelmas 1857 the sale of produce from labour realised £10 17s 6d.

Two contradictory problems developed at various times during the nineteenth century in the Wincanton Workhouse in relation to the work of the able-bodied paupers. The first problem was that at times there was a shortage of labour to perform the necessary functions of the House. On four occasions between 1853 and 1864 the Guardians were forced to advertise for a 'Maid of all Work' to assist with the household work or in the kitchen as there were no able-bodied women or older girls capable of doing it. In April 1895 to his consternation Inspector Preston-Thomas found a tramp washing the floors of the Men's bedrooms "on account of the scarcity of able-bodied labour in the house." In the following year it was reported that there were no able-bodied males to assist at pauper funerals.

The second problem was that other times there was a surplus of able-bodied paupers, especially males, and insufficient labour available. The cessation of bone crushing, as the Guardians predicted, removed much suitable labour and in February 1850 one Poor Law Inspector noted, "There are <u>38</u> able-bodied, single men in the WH, & <u>no work</u>, which can properly be so called." The following year another Inspector commented that in Wincanton, "there are many young and able men in the WH…..and little labour for them to perform." As a temporary measure the Guardians appointed a former sergeant in the 17th Lancers, Robert Hale of Wincanton, as Superintendent of Labour to ensure that what labour existed was rigorously performed. The Central Board also suggested that "spade labour in the workhouse garden has been found an efficient mode of employing the able-bodied", but their own Inspector pointed out that the garden space at Wincanton was very limited. The Guardians remained reluctant to purchase additional land because of the cost to the ratepayers, even though there were fields on two sides of the existing Workhouse property. The result was that at the end of the century the then Inspector, Preston-Thomas, could complain, "The want of land for the employment of the men who now sit idle is very unfortunate." (9)

There remained throughout the Victorian period a fundamental ambivalence towards institutional work: on the one hand it was seen as a duty, with the Workhouse intended to rehabilitate the able-bodied labourer and to improve his or her chances of independence; on the other hand, it was regarded by inmates as a punishment. This important principle relating to labour contained within the 1834 Act was implemented at local level in the Wincanton Workhouse with some degree of laxity, mainly because the numbers of indoor able-bodied paupers at any one time was not considerable and they were not perceived for most of the period as a major problem.

5. Food and Drink

The Poor Law Commissioners were absolutely clear about the principle which should be adopted when framing the dietary. The inmates of the workhouse were to have

> "an adequate supply of wholesome food, not superior in quantity or quality to that which the labouring classes in the respective neighbourhoods provide for themselves."

Once again the idea was to deter the poor from entering the workhouse by not providing anything like the diet which had been available in some poorhouses pre-1834. It soon became apparent however that while this might be a sound principle in theory it was unrealistic in practice as it was impossible to adopt in a workhouse a dietary which could give the inmates food which was inferior in quantity or quality to that of some of the independent labourers outside of the workhouse. Throughout the nineteenth century observers of the agricultural labourers agreed that in the West County that diet was already extremely poor.

The diet adopted in the Wincanton Workhouse placed great emphasis upon bread and gruel, made from oatmeal, as Table 10 shows.

Table 10.   'Substances used per week in Dietary, 1851'

	Men	Women
	oz	oz
Bread	111	96
Cheese	50	12
Bacon	6	5
Vegetables (including potatoes)	44	40
Peas	24	24
Suet Pudding	20	16
Gruel	10½ pints	10½ pints

A man could expect seven ounces of bread every morning for breakfast and six or seven ounces for ten other meals during the week and a woman one ounce less for each of these meals. Both men and women started the day with one and a half pints of gruel. Meat was very scarce and vegetables appeared for at least five meals during the week. For a complete dietary sheet see Appendix 1a. The aged and infirm received minor concessions such as tea and sugar at breakfast and some butter. Children above nine years of age were allowed the same quantities as women and children under nine received quantities at the discretion of the Board. (See Appendix 1b) The Medical Officer directed the diet of the sick. The diet was one area where the class to which a pauper was allocated on admission was crucial.

Items of food such as the bread were carefully weighed and the gruel measured out so that each pauper received exactly the amount allotted and so that disputes could not develop. Such a procedure did not, however, succeed in eradicating complaints completely, for example, in 1872 Jane Sergeant wrote to the Local Government Board to allege that,

> "there is a great deal of difficulty made hear between some of the inmates the mistress and the Master give them the best of everything to live with and some of us sometimes have not our laurince." (*allowance*)

An interesting comparison may be found in 1838 in relation to male prisoners sentenced to hard labour at Shepton Mallet House of Correction. Here a man could expect per week 112 oz of bread, 140 oz of potatoes, 8oz meat and 17½ pints of oatmeal gruel.

The Officers in the Workhouse experienced a somewhat enhanced diet as part of their terms of employment. In 1865 for example it was stated to be five and a quarter pounds of meat, one pound of bacon, seven pounds of bread, two pounds of flour, seven pounds of potatoes, four ounces of tea, one pound of sugar, one third of a pound of butter and three-quarters of a pound of cheese for each officer per week. In January 1838 some £9 2s 8¾d was paid for the

Master's Rations and in September 1857 the quarter's rations for all the Officers and servants amounted to £81 19s 2½d.

Supplying the Union and Workhouse with provisions was a significant source of income for some traders. In the early years of the existence of the Workhouse the General Ledgers show that the quarterly bread contract was worth an average of £14, that for meat £10, for groceries £8, for oatmeal £3 and for milk £2. Advertizements appeared on a regular basis in local newspapers requesting tenders:

> "Bakers, Butchers and Grocers, desirous of CONTRACTING with the Board of Guardians for the Supply of the Union and Workhouse at Wincanton with PROVISIONS and STORES, from the 25th Instant to the 24th June next, are requested to apply at the Poor Law Union Office in Wincanton aforesaid, for the form of Tender and all other particulars. Each tender, *accompanied by a letter from some individual of known responsibility undertaking to become bound in the sum required by the Board, for the due performance of the Contract* must be delivered, free of expense, at the office aforesaid, by or before nine o'clock in the morning of the 22nd of March inst. Wincanton 1 March 1837."

The Annual Accounts show that the cost of provisions for the inmates and officers in the Workhouse rose dramatically through the decades: in the first year of operation of the new Workhouse in 1838 some £614 5s 6¾d was spent whereas in 1875 it was £1,684 18s 10d, which represented about 3s per pauper per week. Increasing numbers using the House and rises in prices indicated that the system established by the 1834 Act did not eradicate poverty but rather committed the local ratepayers to an on-going expenditure.

The food supplied to the Workhouse provided a fertile source for complaints. As early as May 1838 there were complaints about the bread supplied and the following month the supplier's contract was terminated. In December 1846 the Medical Officer complained about the bread supplied and fifty years later complaints were still being made when the bread was found to be sour and the contractor ordered to take it back. Meat was alleged to be too fatty in 1888 and of an inferior quality in 1897. Milk was found to be less than ten percent cream in 1893 and at the same time it was ordered that in future it should not be skimmed by the deaf and dumb girl in the House. In the same year the old women complained about the butter but one of the Visiting Committee tasted it and found no serious cause for complaint although did acknowledge "it certainly is a little salty." Two years later butter was sent back, "it not being fit for the paupers." How far these were deliberate attempts to profit by supplying the Workhouse with inferior provisions or how far it reflected what was available at a time when so much of the food sold to the poor was adulterated in some way is impossible to determine from the surviving evidence.

At one extreme a pauper's complaint could be very dramatic, for example in July 1886 Richard Lewis did not like his dinner, shouted insults about the Master and Chairman of the Board of Guardians and then threw his soup on the floor. He earned six weeks with hard labour in Shepton Mallet Gaol. On the other hand, at times the food in the Workhouse was reported to be good, for example, in 1898 Mrs Emma Bracher, the one and only woman to be elected a Guardian in the Wincanton Union in the nineteenth century, noted in the Visitors' Book, "The dinner was good with plenty of Vegetables. I tasted & found very good."

Meals for all inmates, except the sick, were eaten in the Dining Hall, the main part of which was twenty-four feet square and which had two recesses on the north and south sides sixteen feet long and six feet deep. The walls above the point where the recesses joined the Dining Hall were supported by six cast iron pillars each five inches in diameter at their base, tapered slightly to four and a half inches in diameter at the top and were nine feet six inches high. All the inmates' seats in the main part of the Dining Hall faced east towards the Officers' Table and the seats in both recesses also faced this table. The deal seats of the inmates were similar to pews in a church: the part on which to sit was eighteen inches off the ground and ten inches wide with its back sixteen and a half inches high. In front of each seated pauper was a ledge eight inches wide and two feet six inches from the ground and which was attached to the back of the seat. It was on this ledge that their food was placed. On the end of each row was a round wooden knob on the top of the back of the seat. Each row was eighteen feet six inches long with a gangway at each end, designed to be wide enough for paupers to walk along in single file. In the recesses there were two pairs of rows each six feet six inches long and separated by a three feet wide gangway in the middle. The Master had a separate seat at the very front, to the south of an entrance door and raised two steps above floor level which gave him a clear view over all the seated paupers. It was under the watchful eye of the Master and other officers that the paupers ate their meals. The Chaplain conducted Services from the seat to the right of the entrance.

Ground Plan of Dining Hall/Chapel.

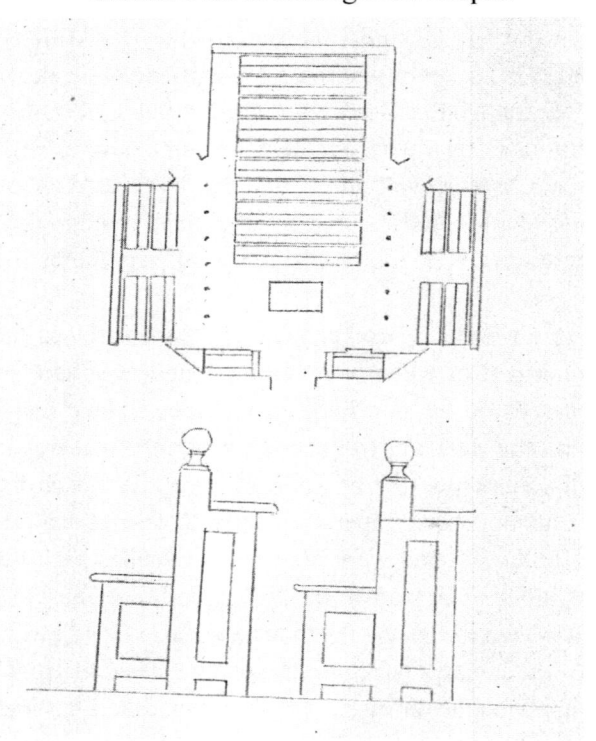

Cross section through seats in the Dining Hall/Chapel. (not to scale)

The inmates entered the Dining Hall in silence from their respective part of the House, great care being taken that the sexes did not touch or communicate in any way. All the meals were consumed in silence from tin ware plates, dishes and mugs, most of which were purchased in 1838 for £3 9s 5d but replacements and additions were made periodically such as 4s 8d for tin cups in August 1854. The Officers on the other hand were supplied with earthenware items. Despite the fact that the inmates were watched carefully during meals, they still managed to remove food from the Dining Hall. One reason was that they found the bread too much or too unpleasant and allegations were made that it was thrown over the boundary walls into neighbouring fields. Another reason emerged in 1846 when the Master discovered large quantities of bread, cheese, potatoes and pudding in the able-bodied women's bedroom. It appeared "that the women take the food from the Dining Hall to give to their infants between meals." Rather than demonstrate any concern or sympathy the Guardians ordered the practice to cease and passed the necessary byelaw. (10)

For the vast majority of the year the inmates faced the same monotonous diet but there were occasional variations which may be explained by five main reasons. First, in a few instances the Medical Officer made recommendations beyond the diet of the sick which were generally acted upon, for example in November 1853 he suggested parsnips and swede turnips as substitutes for potatoes and a ton of each was duly purchased. Two years later faced with an outbreak of scurvy as fresh vegetables were scarce he ordered that Lime Juice and Watercress be provided. Skin disease in 1864 led to the introduction of more rice but as it was largely ignored by the inmates beef and more potatoes were suggested. In 1892 he recommended that the children's diet be amended so that they could have treacle once a week and a stew or rice pudding instead of bacon.

Second, changes were forced upon the Guardians by external circumstances, usually shortages. In June 1840 six ounces of bread were substituted for potatoes for one month "in consequence of the difficulty of procuring good Potatoes." Early in November 1845 the Inspector for the West County, Tufnell, alerted the Poor Law Commissioners to likely potato crop failure,

> "the disease has spread so rapidly, affecting even potatoes that were dry and stored apparently sound.......I conclude that two thirds of the crop are lost."

He recommended that rice be substituted, although by May 1846 the Wincanton Board decided to provide bread and cheese for supper on Monday, Tuesday and Saturday: seven ounces of bread and two ounces of cheese for men and six ounces of bread and one and a half ounces of cheese for women. The failure of the crop as a result of potato blight was to affect the diet for nearly three months. When the Guardians faced difficulties in obtaining both potatoes and green vegetables in June 1853 rice and treacle were substituted for two months. The situation was slightly different in 1883 when the quantity of potatoes was halved and a portion of bread given instead because of "the dearness of potatoes." Cost as always played a part.

Third, special external events could lead to a change in the diet, for example in 1863 permission was given for a celebration meal on the day of the Wedding of the Prince of Wales. The inmates were provided with "100 lbs Beef, 80 Pints Cider, 20 Pints Beer, 12 lbs Currants, 6 lb Lard, 2 lbs Tea, 12 lbs Sugar, 1 lb Tobacco and ½ lb Snuff." A similar meal was provided for Queen Victoria's Jubilees in 1887 and 1897. In October 1890 the Workhouse received a large quantity of vegetables and fruit, the proceeds of the harvest festival at Galhampton. In the 1890s one Guardian, Bailward, sent the inmates forty to fifty rabbits annually during the winter months.

The fourth reason for a variation in the diet was for many of the inmates the most significant as it was a special meal to celebrate Christmas or the New Year. This time of year was one when the poor had traditionally been treated in many parishes and considerable harm was done to the image of the New Poor Law in some areas after 1834 when this tradition was discontinued. This does not seem to have been the case in the Wincanton Union which was more generous. In December 1836 the inhabitants of the town of Wincanton raised a subscription to provide the paupers in the Workhouse with a dinner of Beef and Plum Pudding on New Year's Day and this continued in subsequent years. By 1860 the meal had been transferred to Christmas Day and extended to include snuff, tobacco, along with tea and plum cake in the evening. New Year's Day became the occasion of another special treat when there was a tea with cake, often followed by some entertainment. Until 1863 such treats were as a result of public subscriptions but in that year a decision was taken to charge parishes based upon the number of paupers they had in the Workhouse. In the same year the one hundred and nine inmates were permitted one hundred and twelve pints of cider and thirty-six pints of beer. This tradition of an amended diet on Christmas Day remained for the rest of the century. In 1886 one local newspaper commented, "Once a year at any rate, these poor people have a day's enjoyment, and to them it is a red letter day."

The fifth reason for variation in the diet was caused by a change in attitude which developed late in the nineteenth century. It did not lead to significant alterations in what was provided but there was some liberalization. In April 1892 the inmates were permitted to have tea at breakfast and supper-time if they wished and two years later tea, sugar and milk was made available to female inmates at other times. There was less emphasis upon bacon as the meat and in 1892 the Guardians agreed to another meat meal to replace the bacon one. While these were not major changes they did offer some flexibility. Whatever the reasons the inmates would have been pleased to have some variation in the monotony of their usual diet. (11)

Alcohol had long been condemned for leading the labouring poor into poverty: money which could have been spent on food and supporting a family was squandered, it was claimed, on various forms of drink. Cider was very prevalent and was often given in part for wages but it was the largely unregulated beer-houses which were causing the most concern for the wealthier classes immediately pre –1834. Captain Chapman, who reported from the West Country for the Poor Law Commission in that year, found widespread condemnation.

"The baneful influence of the beer shops was universally complained of, they were represented as an encouragement to the abandoned and a source of irresistible temptation to the imprudent and thoughtless, and were considered as a most active means of demoralizing the labouring classes, and of increasing the poor rate."

The Wincanton Board of Guardians appeared to support this assertion for in the years which followed they had no hesitation in stopping Outdoor Relief and ordering into the Workhouse any pauper suspected of excessive indulgence. In November 1836 before the new Workhouse was erected they had to raise the wall in the Men's Yard of the Poorhouse "to prevent Cyder or any other articles from being handed over the same to the Paupers." They were likewise horrified when inmates such as Jonah Thompson were granted leave of absence for one day in 1842 and returned drunk: his punishment twelve hours in the Refractory Ward. Their own Officers received an allowance of beer each week, although as the century advanced some did opt to have one shilling a week instead, such as the Master and Matron in December 1892.

It is therefore somewhat surprising to discover that the inmates in the Wincanton Workhouse were abundantly supplied with alcohol, mainly through the exploitation of the medical loophole as alcohol could be prescribed by the Medical Officer if he believed it was necessary. It is impossible to determine if the Guardians supported this action for humanitarian reasons or whether at various times there was a lack of close scrutiny. It was a topic which caused some friction in the Workhouse between those who received alcohol and those who did not and increasingly irritated the temperance lobby which was strong in Wincanton itself and surrounding areas and in which the Non-Conformists played a prominent part. In the last twenty years of the nineteenth century under pressure from this temperance movement, the press, the Inspectors and the ratepayers, the Wincanton Guardians made a determined effort to reduce the quantities involved.

Table 11. Alcohol Consumption and Cost in Wincanton Workhouse 1871-1893

	Spirits pints	Wine pints	Malted Liquors gallons	Total Cost £	s	d
1871	84	281	449	58	17	10
1881	542	41	928	129	1	3
1885	296	3	1239	112	13	6
1891	122	29	1159	81	5	10
1892	85	1	1057	70	8	5
1893	65	0	415	30	7	6

The consumption of alcohol in this Workhouse in 1881 was prodigious compared with others in Somerset: 928 gallons of malted liquors in Wincanton but only one in Axbridge; 41 pints of wine in Wincanton and none in Taunton, Wells and Williton; 542 pints of spirits in Wincanton, which was the largest amount in Somerset, compared with just ten pints in Langport. No wonder alarm bells started to ring! In 1881 the Guardians asked their Medical Officer, Dr Wybrants, to review the supply of alcohol to his patients but he found it unnecessary to make any alterations. Nevertheless in the late 1880s and early 1890s reductions were made, although in 1893 as a letter to a local newspaper pointed out, expenditure on alcohol in the Wincanton Workhouse was 12s 3¾d per head compared with 3d per head in Axbridge and 4s 2d for Somerset. In general, however, further reviews by Committees in 1891 and 1892 had the desired effect as by 1904 it was claimed that the expenditure on alcohol for inmates had been reduced to 1s 7d. In June 1909 one Guardian, Mr Moore, referred to as "a strong temperance advocate", congratulated the Board on the fact that at that moment no alcohol was being used. He went on to allege, "that in times gone by, more intoxicants were used in this Union than in the whole of the Unions in Devon and Cornwall." Tea, coffee or cocoa, sugar and tobacco became the substitutes which may not have been the first choice of some of the inmates. As a letter to the press from 'A Poor Man's Friend' expressed it in 1883,

> "It would be a comfort to those who may ultimately fall on the parish funds to know that, whatever deprivations there may be in the Workhouse, they are not deprived of good wholesome drink."

The conclusion must be that overall the diet available in the Wincanton Workhouse was not a great deterrent to those who sought relief: they did after all prefer the Workhouse to starvation. No one ever starved to death in this Workhouse, although a few complained openly about what they considered an inadequate diet. In 1881 John Gould was set to crack stones "where I get scarcely anything to eat but dry bread and a few potatoes and nothing else to drink but a drop of cold water." The chief defect, however, was not the quantity or the calories provided but the lack of vitamins from fresh produce and, above all, the absolute monotony of constant repetition: the inmates knew exactly what to expect for each meal on each day. One newspaper summed up this monotony on the diet as it had been in the early years of Queen Victoria's reign, "The diet was peas and skilly, and for a change it was skilly and peas." In addition, another problem was the set meal times which proved unsatisfactory for the digestive systems of the elderly, infirm and young children and which led to some food being smuggled from the Dining Hall to be eaten between meals. For all its defects it remained for much of the century far superior to the diet of many of the labouring poor outside of the Workhouse. This fact, however, was little consolation to those who had experienced the poorhouses pre-1834. Immediately on being transferred to the Wincanton Poor House in May 1836 before the new Workhouse was erected, many of the paupers petitioned the Guardians for tea, sugar and butter but this request was firmly rejected. When Thomas Gulliver was discharged in September of the following year, the Master noted, "Wanted half a pint of Gin per day & a feather Bed to sleep on and Roast Beef for Dinner." (12)

6. Shelter for the Vulnerable

The aim behind the workhouses was to deter the poor from entering them except in cases of destitution and to achieve this end it was anticipated that the physical conditions within them would be spartan and unattractive to the poor. It soon became apparent, however, that the living conditions of many of the poor were so deplorable that it was impossible to create institutions in which they were worse or even similar. In the area covered by the Wincanton Union many cottages were very small, damp, lacked any sanitation or water supply and were far from weather proof. With wages so low there was little incentive for cottage owners to improve their properties as the tenants could not afford an increased rent. The emphasis in the Workhouses therefore shifted onto developing a rigorous regime rather than maintaining harsh physical conditions.

The Wincanton Workhouse gave basic shelter to those who needed it. Each class had their own Day Room on the ground floor with sleeping accommodation on the first floor. Each room was heated by a stove, open fire place or hot water pipes. For water a well was bored to a depth of sixty feet and for this Pratten the Well Sinker was paid £12 0s 0d but it proved to be inadequate and had to be bored down a further sixteen feet in 1842. In 1875 a constant supply of water was assured when the Workhouse was connected to the town water supply. Throughout the House the original specifications required a number of water closets which were connected to a large cesspool in front of the Workhouse. Such facilities could not be found in most labourers' cottages.

a) The Aged and Infirm

The Aged were usually defined as people above the age of sixty-five years, although many sets of statistics included those above sixty years and the Infirm consisted of those of any age who through some disability were incapable of earning an independent living. The 1834 Act envisaged that this class should in general continue to receive Outdoor Relief but it was recognised that there would be some who through age or the nature of their infirmity would require care in an institution. It soon became clear in rural areas that the proposed separate building for them would be far too expensive to maintain and so they were placed in the general workhouse. Once the new system was established opinion appeared to harden against any concessions to the aged and infirm as it was argued that this could encourage them to go into the workhouse and also discourage the young from saving for their old age.

The aged and infirm followed the same admissions procedure as all other inmates and received the same workhouse dress. Each went to their respective Day Rooms which for the elderly were far from comfortable. All around the walls of the Day Rooms were one and a half inch thick deal seats which were eleven inches wide and with a back rail four inches wide some fifteen inches above the seats. There were also four deal benches eight feet long "with strong backs for the old people (moveable at pleasure)." Here the aged and infirm would sit for the long monotonous hours of boring tedium with many of them having nothing to do, as in the earliest days there were no books or newspapers, even if they could read, although from 1843 a small number of books were kept under lock and key by the Master and their distribution superintended by the Chaplain. Work for this category was not an issue in the Wincanton Workhouse as the Guardians required the Master to allocate them light tasks if the Medical Officer concurred. This labour usually centred on some of the household chores for the women and activities in the garden for the men, although a small number with a required skill could work elsewhere, for example in 1845 John Foot looked after and repaired the shoes and boots in the small Shoe Room which was situated between the kitchen and the Dining Hall and for which he was allowed tea, butter and sugar.

There was originally one Day Room for the old men and one for the old women, each of which was heated by a stove and replaced by an open fire place in 1850. As the nature of the admissions and residence changed towards the end of the century re-arrangements were required and so by 1900 there were two Day Rooms for old men and so few able-bodied old women that they shared one Day Room with the infirm. The bedrooms for the aged and infirm on the first floor were the same as for the other classes and consisted of a large dormitory-style room with a row of beds on each of the longer sides. Once again the situation at the end of the century meant that the old men required an additional room. They slept in beds which were standard throughout the House: wrought iron bedsteads and mattresses stuffed with reed or straw, although difficulty in procuring the latter in 1860 led to the purchase of Cocoa Nut Fibre as an alternative. The beds were designed to be single for men and double for women and children.

It is difficult to produce an accurate estimate of the numbers of aged and infirm in the Wincanton Workhouse as for statistical purposes they were referred to as 'non able-bodied' and this category included all the sick as well. More evidence is available, especially later in the century, for the aged alone which in itself is indicative of the changed nature of the House. In 1854 there were thirty-eight aged and infirm paupers in the Workhouse out of a total of eighty-six, some 44.2%. Table 12a, based on the surviving Admission and Discharge Books, includes the numbers of those who were over sixty years of age on admission. There is some small degree of inaccuracy as a few paupers were admitted more than once, the most notorious being Alfred Clothier, a shoemaker, born in 1829 who was admitted and discharged eight times between March 1890 and October 1891.

Table 12a.   Admissions of Paupers over 60 years of age to the Workhouse

	Number over 60 admitted	Total Number admitted	Over 60 as a % of total admitted
1837	17	255	6.7
1838	23	393	5.9
1870	43	440	9.8
1871	52	319	16.3
1872	69	321	21.5
1873	73	323	22.6
1890	41	199	20.6
1891	58	164	35.4
1892	69	147	46.9

The Table shows clearly how the function of the Workhouse had changed and that the aged were not exempt from the campaign against Outdoor Relief in the early 1870s. Table 12b gives the reasons for their admission, although little indication was given for their destitution after 1870. One Report in 1899 suggested that most of the elderly who sought the shelter of a workhouse did so because of sickness or infirmity.

Table 12b.   Reasons for the Admission of those over 60

	1837	1838	1870	1871	1872	1873	1890	1891	1892
No work	9	2							
No home	4	4							
Illness	2	3	14	11	14	8	7	13	5
Infirm	1	3	13	19	8	14	3	3	1
Destitute		11	10	16	43	51	29	39	63
Imbecile					2		1		
Accident								1	
Not specified	1		7	6	2		1	2	

After 1880 the Local Government Inspectors recorded on their visits the numbers of old men and old women over sixty-five who were resident on the night preceding their visit. These statistics, which are not a complete picture as they excluded any elderly who were in the Infirmary, Infectious or Receiving Wards, suggest that for the last twenty years of the century between 11% and 27% of all inmates in the Wincanton Workhouse were there because of age alone. In fact about one third would probably be a more realistic estimate as in small rural workhouses the aged were often placed in Infirmary Wards as these were the only places where there was constant supervision. According to a Return by the Medical Officer of the Workhouse in 1903 of the sixty-six inmates over sixty years of age, forty were there as they could no longer take care of themselves as a result of mental or physical infirmity.

It was also clear that there was a significant sex difference: in eleven visits between 1880 and 1890 the Inspectors recorded 337 aged persons and of these 252 or 75% were old men and eighty-five or 25% were old women. The greatest variation was in March 1881 when there were thirty-eight old men and seven old women. Women were obviously able to maintain their independence longer than men, played a much greater role in helping and living with younger members of their family and possibly retained a level of affection which was greater than that of a male, especially if the latter had been a disciplinarian.

Not unsurprisingly as the composition and nature of the Workhouse changed there was more pressure for concessions for the aged and infirm. From the very beginning there had been small alterations centred around diet and hours but little else happened until the late 1880s despite the pleas of one local newspaper in 1834 which reminded its readers that there were "many old persons of most reputable character, and who have in their earlier days enjoyed the comforts of life", and who were now "the industrious and deserving portion of the poor." It was only in the late 1880s and 1890s as the scope of poverty was made apparent by the studies of men like Charles Booth that the Local Government Board bowed to political pressure and introduced changes for the aged and infirm: in 1892 both sexes were allowed tobacco in unspecified amounts; in 1894 old women were allowed 'dry tea' with sugar and milk; two Circulars in 1895 and 1896 abandoned the old concepts of fixed times for meals and bed, suggested that they have separate cubicles and that they should be allowed out for walks and to visit friends in their own clothes rather than in the distinctive workhouse dress; finally their diet was amended to permit a small allowance of milk pudding to break the interval between regular meals. The Wincanton Board did not comply with all concessions, for example they did not provide accommodation for married couples over sixty years of age on the grounds that they virtually never had any in their Workhouse, although they did point out that there was a room which "can be easily utilized for married couples if at any time required." There was some criticism of particular concessions, for example from Inspector Preston-Thomas who in 1898 complained that in the West Country leave of absence was being granted too freely "for it is not uncommon for them to come back the worse for liquor."

The degree of contentment amongst the aged and infirm is difficult to assess because of the wide range of abilities that were present in such a class: from those who were totally incapacitated to those who had a minor problem which necessitated short-term care. The few who wrote letters to the Central Boards all wanted Outdoor Relief and not to be sent to the Workhouse and this may reflect a much more general opinion amongst this category, assuming that they had their own shelter and were capable of looking after themselves. One problem for the elderly was that removal to the workhouse often deprived them of the community of a lifetime. The administrators of the system, however, were in no doubt that indoor relief was beneficial: in 1838 in reference to the aged and infirm the Wincanton Board reported, "They are better relieved and have more comforts." Inspector Tufnell also considered that on the whole the aged were satisfied with the workhouses as "congenial to their time of life." In the early twentieth century the presence of some of them was even felt to be beneficial as the Chaplain, Rev William Farrer, commented in 1909, "Some of them are excellent old folk whose influence is of very great value in softening their neighbours".

Not all the aged in the Workhouse were destined to be there permanently or until death as an unusual case revealed in October 1859,

> "On Tuesday last a wedding of an extraordinary nature took place at the Baptist Chapel of this town, the bride being at the advanced age of 75, the bridegroom 39. Such was the joy of the bride (who has been an inmate of the Union for a long time) in being united in holy wedlock, that she danced nearly the whole of the way up High-street. Both parties have been on their rounds through the town soliciting donations to get some household furniture." (13)

b. The Sick

The 1834 Act envisaged that the sick would continue to receive Outdoor Relief and so no attempt was made to establish the Workhouse as a hospital for the sick from the surrounding villages. The presence of the Medical Officer in the Workhouse did ensure that any paupers taken ill once in it would receive the appropriate medical treatment. It soon became apparent, however, that institutional provision was going to have to be made for the destitute sick who had no family or friends to look after them and for those whose insanitary and filthy cottages meant that any treatment by the District Medical Officer was unlikely to be successful.

By the time that the new Wincanton Workhouse was constructed the Poor Law Commissioners had directed the Guardians to have a room available for the sick, but it was not specifically designed as such. The Wincanton Board were concerned about the spread of infectious diseases within the House so their building plans envisaged an Infectious Ward on the ground floor but once again it was just another standard room which in one respect was inadequate as in 1841 it was discovered that paupers were getting out of the window at night. The solution, iron bars across it. As the Workhouse was not perceived as a hospital for such cases from the Union as a whole, it remained relatively under-used. If an infectious disease broke out in a parish it was left to the District Medical Officer to deal with it and on one occasion the Wincanton Board banned any sick paupers from being transferred to their Workhouse, "It was ordered that no Paupers labouring under sickness or disease of any kind be in future removed from his or her residence to this house."

As the decades passed the function of the Workhouse changed and so alterations became essential. As early as September 1847 the Poor Law Board advised the Guardians that additional hospital accommodation was necessary but they attempted to procrastinate, "as the season is so far advanced that the further consideration of the subject be deferred until the first Wednesday in February next." They were immediately informed that this was unacceptable and so on 22nd September formed a committee to study the issue. Not until April 1849 did they agree to build new accommodation when they added a Male and a Female Infirmary Ward on the western side of the House at a cost of £589 8s 0d, which they referred to as "commodious and comfortable Hospital accommodation."

At national level there was scathing criticism of workhouse infirmaries, highlighted by the Poor Law Board's own Medical Officer, Dr. Smith, who considered that many workhouses had become essentially asylums and infirmaries. In 1870 the Board itself acknowledged the change, "Workhouses, originally designed mainly as a test for the able-bodied, have been of necessity gradually transformed into infirmaries for the sick." Once again pressure was placed on the Wincanton Board but on this occasion plans that it had to transfer pauper children to a new separate schoolroom meant that additional space was generated in the Workhouse itself for the sick. They were not, however, purpose built rooms and so criticism continued from the Central Boards.

For the inmates of the Infirmary and Infectious Wards conditions could be far from satisfactory. In 1860 Inspector Gulson "found the Hospital wards less cleanly than elsewhere, and wet beds which could scarcely fail to produce cold and disease to the Patients." The beds were of course the same wrought iron ones with straw mattresses as were used elsewhere in the House but at least they were all single, even if they were closer together than the Inspectors would have wished. Poor classification in the House in general meant that the men in the Male Infirmary Ward shared a yard with the able-bodied men and the old men. In addition, the Infirmary Wards lacked a Day Room so the inmates had to stay in with the sick for much of the day and where, for example, when smoking was permitted in the 1890s they could cause annoyance to others. A common criticism was that the ventilation was inadequate which was a particular matter of concern in one of the Female Infirmary Wards as it was located on the first floor immediately over the Washhouse and so became very hot with the steam generated. The various wards were originally heated by open fires but by the 1890s it was felt that they should be replaced with stoves as little heat was given out, a none-too-pleasant experience for those who spent so much time in them. From June 1880 the floors were covered with cocoa matting. All inmates in the Infirmary and Infectious Wards received a weekly bath, although the baths themselves were not fixed and so were filled by means of buckets of hot water and emptied in the same way. One very unpleasant aspect for the inmates was that the Water Closets opened directly on to the Wards and with inadequate ventilation the resulting smell was frequently commented upon by Inspectors and visitors.

The Infectious Wards were also a cause for concern, leaving aside the lack of knowledge about disease and close proximity of inmates to each other which rendered cross-infection possible, as on the ground floor the floors themselves were made of cold Keinton stone and the wards originally shared a common entrance with other rooms. By the 1870s, however, alterations had been made and there was a separate entrance from the outside. It would have required a major building programme to create detached Infectious Wards and this did not occur until the twentieth century mainly on the grounds of cost. In 1898 Inspector Preston-Thomas was scathing in his criticism,

> "The accommodation for the sick is very ill-managed & unsatisfactory; the wards close & ill-ventilated with closets opening directly into them; there being no fixed baths nor day rooms."

On the other hand, the inmates could expect constant supervision for while the Master had overall responsibility for the accommodation of the sick and the male wards, the Matron supervised the women's wards as well as the cleanliness, food and supplies to all the sick. A great deal depended on the competence of the Medical Officer and any nurses (see below). From time to time items were added for the comfort and convenience of the sick, for example, from 1836 John Randall supplied Trusses: 4s single and 8s double, in 1862 some air cushions were purchased and in 1899 a wheelchair. Occasionally there were items for individual paupers such as a feather bed for one Parsons hired at the rate of 1s 6d a week for two months, this being a cheaper alternative than buying one for £3. Gifts that may have been designed to improve their spiritual comfort included texts and pictures from the Rev. J. Brown in July 1891.

After the alterations in the early 1870s there was an increase in the number of rooms referred to as 'Infirmary Wards' and by 1880 there were thirty-six beds in the Male Wards and forty-one in the Female ones, along with eight beds in each of the two Infectious Wards and a further two beds available for Lying-in. The annual visits of the Inspectors between 1880 and 1900 show that between 27.5% and 42.1% of all inmates in the Wincanton Workhouse were in the Infirmary Wards. The smallest number of beds occupied was thirty-nine in June 1892 and the largest seventy-six in March 1880 whereas the average number of males on each visit was twenty-nine and the average number of females twenty-six. On only five visits did the number of females exceed that of males. A Return to Parliament made for 1st July 1896 indicated that forty-three beds were occupied and of these thirteen were by the Sick and Bedridden and thirty by the Aged and Infirm. The nature of the Workhouse had certainly changed dramatically since 1834 as not only the aged, infirm and sick were present in increasingly large numbers but also it had become a refuge for others who could not cope on the outside or were unwanted elsewhere. By 1887 there were five blind inmates in the Wincanton Workhouse, three males and two females, along with three inmates who were deaf and dumb, one male and two females. For cases such as these the Workhouse performed a custodial function rather than one of treatment.

A Return in March 1870 showed that the Medical Officer in the Wincanton Workhouse had to deal with a wide range of illnesses as it included four inmates with fever, three with rheumatism, three with scrofula and seven with 'Nervous Debility'. Five inmates had epilepsy, three heart disease, one asthma, one had boils and there were two patients with fractures. From time to time venereal disease appeared, one female in July 1867 and two males in January 1868. In January 1877 a more detailed Return showed one case of gonorrhoea and one of secondary syphilis. The failure in many small workhouses to treat this disease had later consequences which led to increased poverty and had the potential to be passed on to children. The Medical Officer would also perform operations as necessary, for example in February 1858 William Brunton amputated all the toes of William White after his confinement in Bruton Lockup one weekend in frosty weather.

One great fear in an institution which housed so many destitute paupers was that infections would be introduced and spread. From the opening of the Workhouse the Board directed that the Medical Officer must report the appearance of any infectious or contagious disease to the Master and arrangements made to separate the affected inmate from the rest. Inevitably such diseases occurred with the most serious being an outbreak of smallpox with one death in January 1840. The Guardians ordered the vaccination of all young men, women and children in the House but it was still present four months later when paupers were banned from attending church, although no attempt was made to stop admissions and discharges from the House. The outbreak was over by the following month with no more deaths.

Children as always were particularly prone to illness and in 1875 there was a significant outbreak of scarlet fever that fortunately was "of a mild type no deaths having taken place." Although the original sufferer was quickly isolated, she was permitted an inadequate period of convalescence before returning to the school. The result was that by February 1875 there were ten children with the disease and a further eleven convalescing. The Local Government Board was highly critical of the speed with which the original girl was sent back to school and with the failure of the Guardians to trace the origin of the first case. In November 1894 there were several cases of whooping cough reported amongst the children and a year later eleven cases of measles amongst them. Greater contact with other children at the local Board School may well have played a part.

On the positive side the number of infectious cases remained small so that in their annual Reports for the last twenty years of the century the Inspectors noted just twenty-three cases. In addition residence in the Workhouse, especially for children, provided an ideal opportunity for compulsory vaccination against smallpox, for example between 1st October 1876 and 30th July 1882 some 222 inmates were vaccinated, of which nine were unsuccessful. In July 1894 the Visiting Committee reported that of the thirty-three children in the House they found that thirty-two had been vaccinated against smallpox, Christina Barber "at present unfit." Vaccination was an undertaking which the Guardians were to promote actively throughout the Union during the nineteenth century and as early as September 1840 were praised by one local newspaper for the "most prompt and energetic measures." (14)

For the sick paupers what really mattered was the calibre of, and care displayed by, the Medical staff. By the standards of the day the Medical Officers were well qualified: nine held the post in the Wincanton Workhouse between 1836 and 1900 and all were Members of the Royal College of Surgeons, with six being Licentiates of the Society of Apothecaries; three were also Licentiates of the Royal College of Physicians, one had an additional qualification in Midwifery and held the degree of M.D. In one respect these qualifications were a problem as, apart from the Clerk to the Board who had legal training, the Medical Officers were the only professionals in the system, yet they did not even have control over the Infirmaries which were supervised by the Master so they were unable to regulate conditions. On the other hand, the Minute Books from Wincanton indicate that it was rare for the Board of Guardians not to accept the recommendations of their Medical Officer.

The Medical Officer was non-resident but lived in the town as he was also the Medical Officer for one of the six Medical Districts, Wincanton East. He was required to attend the Workhouse daily to examine the new arrivals, allocate them to the appropriate class and to treat the sick in the House. For those who were sick and infirm he was expected to fill out a Bed Card which indicated the nature of the disease and the diet of each patient. These cards were then kept by the Nurse. He was given a room on the ground floor on the western side of the building as a Surgery, with windows which looked onto the Women's Yard on the eastern side and on the western side over the Drying Ground. The first Medical Officer, Dr. Brunton, requested that it be equipped with "a wash-hand Bason and Jug, a Bleeding bason, Towels, a Bed-pan, Night Convenience and a cupboard with drawers." The presence of a bleeding bason suggests that although the Medical Officers were well-qualified by the standards of the day, in many areas there was a lack of knowledge and the result was that the paupers were often treated with ancient practices.

Initially the salary paid was low having reached just £19 a year by 1850. This was increased to £40 in 1867 when it was found to be below that in other Unions in the County and the number of patients having increased, "averaging over 35 under his care." It was to remain at £40 for the rest of the century, although once compulsory vaccination was introduced into the Workhouse he received 1s 6d for each case. At first the Medical Officer was responsible for the cost of all the drugs which he supplied but one problem that arose from this system in some Unions was that Medical Officers prescribed very few drugs and then only the cheapest available which was not in the best interests of the patient. It was only in 1861 that the Guardians agreed to pay out of the poor rates for all Quinine and Cod Liver Oil prescribed. Quinine was used as a general tonic and as a medicine to reduce fever in such complaints as malaria, or the Ague as it was commonly called, which was still common in the area.

There were occasional complaints against the Medical Officer such as in March 1873 G. Gould claimed that he had a bad eye and neck but "The doctor if I ask him for any Medicine he only make Sport of me." Most proved to be unfounded, although in 1863 the Guardians criticized the then Medical Officer, John Parker, for not attending the Workhouse in person for several weeks but rather he "sent his unauthorized and not fully qualified assistant."

The overall impression created is that successive Medical Officers on the whole undertook their duties carefully and thoroughly within the constraints of the system in which they were required to operate. There is no evidence of innovation or experimentation but their care of the inmates did not lead to any widespread criticism and in most cases their recommendations in areas such as classification, diet and general care were implemented. It may be that at times they were more generous than others would have wished, most notably in their suggestions relating to alcohol. They were not immune from criticism, as may be seen from a comment by Inspector Tufnell in 1842, "like all men with a little smattering of learning, they are exceedingly fond of using the hardest names the dictionary can supply." He believed that through their excessive ordering of 'extras', they were "adding to the amount of pauperism and the poor rates."

The role of Nurses in the workhouses was another matter. For at least the first thirty years there was no national system to train nurses and even if there had been the parsimony of some of the Guardians would have prevented their employment for during the first decade of its existence the Wincanton Union paid their Workhouse nurse between £5 and £8 and year, rising to £10 in 1851. Many of the rural Guardians did not see any reason to employ a specialist as there was nearly always a pauper female in the House who had acted as a nurse at some time and as the number of sick was small the Matron was expected to supervise these Wards. In addition as many of those in the sick wards were aged and infirm they often required no specialist skill. In March 1837 B. Sweatman was paid £1 5s 10d for the quarter as the Nurse but once she was replaced by Ann Smith in November at a salary of £8 a year, she was paid 12s 6d as the laundress. In May 1840 Sarah Spratling was appointed as she was the only candidate but remained just until Michaelmas. In March 1844 Harriet Read, a pauper, was appointed as the acting Nurse at 3s per week until a permanent appointment was made. She proved to be of a sufficient standard so that she was still in post five years later.

The Wincanton Board initially tended to appoint mature women with no specialist experience, for example in 1851 Mary Moorse, a widow aged fifty-four, in 1853 Sophia Edwards, a widow aged fifty-eight and in 1861 Elizabeth Chown who was forty-eight, "a Farmer's daughter and Housekeeper to Mother." She had been attracted by a salary which had been increased to £20 to avoid appointing a pauper but she resigned a few months later as she "proved incompetent to discharge her duties." Their first appointment of a Nurse with previous workhouse experience came in 1864 with Caroline King who moved from the Bath Union Workhouse and when she left in 1871 for "a private appointment", they appointed Mary Stevenson from the Langport Union Workhouse, their longest serving nurse who remained until April 1884 when ill-health forced her resignation. These later appointments coincided with a change in attitude towards nursing in workhouses as their functions developed and was spearheaded by men like Dr. Smith. He stressed that in order to attend upon the sick, women in Lying-in Wards and to administer medicines under the direction of the Medical Officer, nurses had to display "great care and attention" and needed to be

> "a person of experience in the treatment of the sick, of great respectability of character, and of diligent and decorous habits."

The majority of those who were appointed to the Wincanton Workhouse after 1864 gave their occupation as 'Nurse', were all single and had an average age of approximately thirty-two.

For patients the conditions could be dreadful if the Nurse was incompetent or unsatisfactory. In March 1840 the Master complained that the pauper Nurse neglected her duty and the following month was dismissed when she absented herself from the House after attending a funeral. In 1853 Mary Moorse was dismissed for keeping the Infirmary Wards "in a dirty state", being intoxicated several times and above all allowing some of the patients to be ill-treated by Mary Ann Cross who was a pauper inmate who sometimes assisted in the Wards. In 1860 Inspector Gulson found the sick wards filthy and the beds wet. In 1897 when complaints of insolence and insubordination were made against the Nurse, it was also discovered that her supervision of one ward was so lax that a female patient had been placed on a bed-pan containing hot water by pauper assistants.

The nursing care in the Wincanton Workhouse did not provide an example of rapid change, innovation or progress in the last three decades of the nineteenth century, largely explained by the relatively small numbers and the lack of the need for specialized care. In 1866 publications such as 'The Lancet' had criticized the lack of a system of night-nursing in workhouses generally but it was to be more than a decade later that the Wincanton Board required the Nurse to sleep in the Infirmary and it was only in 1898 that a specific night nurse was obtained and then just on a temporary basis. The following year the Master was authorized to obtain a night nurse when necessary and recommended by the Medical Officer.

While the Guardians had been prepared to grant extra assistance on a temporary basis, such as Louisa Thomas as Assistant Nurse in June 1872, they were all drawn from the ranks of paupers. When Dr. MacDougall recommended that the Nurse be given more assistance in March 1894 this was granted as long as it was from a pauper and the Board stoutly resisted attempts to obtain another properly trained and qualified person. At long last in the 1890s, recognising the preponderance of aged and infirm men in the sick wards, the Guardians appointed the first Male Attendant in April 1895 at a salary of £20 "to attend to sick male inmates under the direction of the Nurse and Doctor and to make himself generally useful." When Henry Isgrove was appointed to the post the following year the Local Government

Board queried the appointment as he was a harness maker by trade, but were informed by the Guardians that they were satisfied "as he will be more an attendant than a nurse."

Wincanton Workhouse failed to attract suitable nurses for much of the period as the Guardians resolutely refused to pay an adequate remuneration, as the salary never rose above £28 a year, along with Board and Lodging, Coal, Candles and Washing and 1s a week instead of Beer if requested. The accommodation provided was often neglected so that the Visiting Committee reported in 1893 that the Nurses sitting room required papering and painting along with new floor covering,

> "the walls are very damp & wet…..the bedroom carpet is entirely worn out and a new set of ware seems to be required."

The result, largely to be expected, was a rapid turnover in staff, for example in the 1890s there were ten different female nurses whose dedication left much to be desired. The situation in this Workhouse was not unique for in 1902 Inspector Preston-Thomas reported that of one hundred and twelve nurses in his district less than twenty were trained. He attributed this position to the monotonous round of duties, the loneliness in small rural workhouses, low pay, subordination to the Matron, and the failure to recognise that nursing was a skilled occupation. (15)

The evidence shows that in the area of the facilities available for the sick poor, the Wincanton Board was not an innovator and generally lagged behind developments so that it usually required pressure from the Central Board or the Inspectorate to initiate change. The reluctance to provide increased facilities did not derive from a callous disregard for the interests of the paupers but rather partly from the failure to see the need for such improvements when frequently the opportunities available for the independent poor were so limited, partly because the number of sick paupers in the Workhouse at any one time in the first forty years at least of its existence was not great, and partly because they were so deeply imbued with the idea, if not of actually cutting costs, of ensuring that the poor rates did not increase. For so long they were content to drift along, untroubled by modern developments.

c) Lunatics

Before 1834 most lunatics remained with family or friends who received Outdoor Relief for them, while a small number who had no one to look after them or were difficult to manage were placed in the Poorhouses or in a local private asylum, such as the one operated by Charles Finch at Fisherton House near Salisbury. Lunacy was hardly mentioned in 1834 as the Report and subsequent Act were more concerned with those who would not work rather than those who could not. One clause, however, did ban the Guardians from detaining a "dangerous" lunatic in their workhouse for more than fourteen days, but so much depended on the definition of "dangerous". The Workhouse Medical Officer had to attend lunatics as necessary and regulate their diet but there was no mention of any treatment which aimed to cure or even alleviate their condition. That would have required more staff and so expenditure.

Although Somerset Lunatic Asylum was opened in 1848, for a number of years the Wincanton Board displayed a pronounced preference to retain lunatics in their Workhouse. Several reasons help to explain this tendency: the first centred on a difference in attitude as in the long term the function of the County Asylum was to operate as a curative institution but for most of the Guardians it was just another place of detention and they believed that they could do that as effectively and certainly more cheaply. This view was in fact one with which the Commissioners in Lunacy themselves concurred in the early days of its existence when they commented that the majority of the lunatics in workhouses

> "are congenitally imbecile or idiot and in all probability incapable of deriving much (if any) benefit from treatment in a lunatic asylum."

While they subsequently amended their views the Guardians did not. Second, and above all, it was a question of cost as a pauper lunatic in the Somerset County Asylum cost an average of 7s 7d a week to maintain, in the Wincanton Workhouse it was 2s 4d per head. Third, in many rural Workhouses, such as this one, the harmless lunatics performed useful household functions, a fact which the Commissioners in Lunacy acknowledged,

> "In many Workhouses, indeed, the services of these inmates are most valuable, and save the cost of much paid labour."

Table 13. Number and Location of Lunatics in the Wincanton Union

	County Asylum	Private Asylum	Workhouse	Relative	Total
1844 Month Total	0	5	6	25	36
1849 Year Ending Lady Day	9	0	11	13	33
1854 Day Count	14	0	11	16	41
1859 Day Count	9	0	13	12	34
1864 Day Count	20	0	8	14	42
1869 Day Count	19	0	12	15	46
1874 Year Ending Lady Day	24	1	10	10	45
1879 Year Ending Lady Day	33	1	16	7	57
1884 Year Ending Lady Day	42	3	13	11	69
1889 Year Ending Lady Day	45	3	8	11	67
1894 Year Ending Lady Day	52	1	8	14	75
1899 Year Ending Lady Day	51	0	5	15	71

Finally, as Table 13 indicates, in such a rural area the actual numbers involved were not considerable and so were not judged to be a problem for other inmates. In fact so little were the Guardians concerned with the nature of the pauper lunatics that virtually no separate accommodation was made available for them and they were distributed among the other inmates. In 1869, however, a Day Room on the upper floor was adapted for the use of female lunatics and they normally slept in an Infirmary Ward.

Throughout the Victorian period the average number of lunatics in the Wincanton Workhouse each year was ten. Table 13 does indicate not only the increased significance of the County Asylum at Wells in the latter part of the century but also the on-going importance of kin in a rural area as so many lunatics remained with relatives.

While the Annual Returns to the Commissioners in Lunacy gave the number of lunatics they rarely gave ages in detail. Table 14 shows that three that do may lead to the suggestion that it was not necessarily mental deterioration in old age which propelled people to the Workhouse but the devastating impact of despair with low wages, large families, inadequate accommodation and overwork. In December 1839 the Poor Law Commissioners sanctioned the admission of Thomas Munday, aged forty-two, into the Workhouse without his wife and children,

> "His mind is seriously impaired; and the Medical Officer has recommended a temporary residence in the Workhouse, in order that he may there obtain the quiet and attention of which he stands in need."

Table 14. Ages of Lunatics in Wincanton Union and Workhouse

	In Union		In Workhouse
	1846	1847	1850
Under 10			1
10-19	1	1	0
20-29	6	4	2
30-39	13	10	3
40-49	5	6	4
50-59	6	8	2
60-69	1	2	1
70 and over	0	0	0

It is very apparent that the Wincanton Board were extremely broad in their classification of lunatics and that a few were not properly categorized at all. In 1850 John Laver aged twenty-three was classed as a lunatic as he was deaf and dumb, as was a girl in 1879 even though she had been "taught to knit, read, and sew." In 1869 Jane Brine and Elizabeth Allen were so classed because they suffered from severe epileptic fits; and in 1881 Edward Budgen, much to the surprise of the visiting Commissioner, was so categorized as he was said to be unable to govern his own actions as a result of paralysis caused by an accident. Moral disapproval also played a part for in 1865 Elizabeth Mead aged twenty-three was classed as a lunatic as she had two illegitimate children,

> "she is of weak intellect and entirely devoid of self-control. Upon the subject of her immorality she showed no sense of shame, but complete apathy."

So much depended upon individual interpretation for what was perfectly obvious to one person was not to another. As part of the same visit in 1865 the Commissioner noted, "I have also included Elizabeth Burt who is clearly insane, silly in expression….and rambling and incoherent in conversation." There were always borderline cases which varied in their classification as in 1869 the Commissioner commented,

> "I have requested the Master to add Mary Ann Lucas, who is quite imbecile, and formerly on the list, as was also John Goodfellow, who is stated to be of weak mind."

In 1881 it was noted, "Martha Taverner is an old woman who seems to feel acutely the being considered imbecile. She too seems to me hardly to come within the boundary line." While some inmates may have had mental problems they were certainly able-bodied, for example, the day before the Commissioner's visit in 1869 John Goodfellow absconded and in 1893 James Perrett, classed as an Imbecile, was reported as repeatedly climbing over the wall of the Workhouse yard, which was eight feet high, going into the town and begging. The Local Government Board reminded the Guardians in this instance that they must ensure adequate "provision for his care and control whilst in the workhouse" and that it would be their responsibility if any harm came to him. They suggested that the garden wall could be raised, to which the reply came, "the Guardians do not wish to make the Workhouse look more like a prison than it is at present."

The conditions of the lunatics were monitored more frequently that those of some of the other inmates and certainly of those in a private institution or with relatives, for as well as the annual visit of the Inspector from the Central Poor Law Boards, from 1845 there was also an annual visitation by an Inspector from the Commissioners in Lunacy. The latter used their experience not only to comment on the state of the pauper lunatics but also to make recommendations on their treatment and even classification. Throughout the decades the overwhelming majority of the comments were favourable, for example in 1865 stressing that the rooms "were in the best order and the personal condition of the inmates was very satisfactory", and twenty-three years later, "I can report favourably of their condition and treatment." They often reported that the lunatics "are evidently very kindly treated by the Master." In 1897 it was stated that, "No mechanical restraint is recorded as having been used and no instruments for its use are kept", the implication of course being that such treatment was to be found in other institutions. The visiting Commissioners examined the clothing of the pauper lunatics, the state of their bedding and their diet, all of which generally received favourable comments, even though it was the same as for the remainder of the inmates. The Medical Officer did on occasions recommend additions to the diet for an individual lunatic.

From time to time there were criticisms made such as of the clothing in 1866 and 1872. First it was felt that the epileptic women should have warmer woollen or linsey gowns during the winter and then more generally that the clothing for the lunatics of both sexes was insufficient for winter, especially as the women were wearing cotton gowns. The Commissioner suggested that the men should have either "flannel under waistcoats or outer clothing of woollen material." This may well have been a more general problem within the Workhouse which had not been examined before, and if so, does indicate an unpleasant aspect of life there for all or some of the inmates. The rooms which they used were regarded as satisfactory although on one occasion placing an epileptic man in a room with a stone floor was questioned as was their sleeping in the Infirmary Wards which tended to be over-crowded. The most persistent criticism was reserved for the weekly bathing arrangements. They were probably best summed up by Inspector Irving as a result of his visit in 1894,

> "There are no proper bathing arrangements. The men are bathed in the receiving ward – hot water has to be carried here from the kitchen. The women are bathed in a portable bath and for them both hot and cold water has to be brought by hand."

The Guardians replied that they could not make alterations "without great expense" and they did not perceive the existing arrangements to be an "inconvenience."

To fill their days it was reported in 1858 that "most of them were occupied in some light work," and in 1866, "Many of them are usefully occupied." For exercise they were permitted into the Yards but as this was criticized as lacking any stimulation they were allowed into the garden for a daily walk. The majority, as well as attending the Workhouse Chapel, also attended a Service in the Parish Church each Sunday and by 1897 "those classed as imbeciles go out at intervals beyond the Workhouse grounds." Just occasionally their routine was broken with a treat, for example, in June 1897 the Town Band played for the lunatics as part of the Diamond Jubilee celebrations.

The presence of lunatic paupers in the Workhouse may well have been far from ideal for other inmates at various times. The most serious issues centred around the small number who had a tendency to be violent or exhibit aggressive behaviour which must have terrified some of the other paupers. While the 1834 Act had required that 'dangerous' lunatics should not be detained for more than fourteen days, once the County Asylum was available they should have been sent there directly but a Report in 1861 noted "violent patients are not infrequently sent to the Workhouse previous to their removal to the Asylum" and repeated that they should be sent straight to the Asylum, even though the Master normally placed them under supervision. Possibly on the grounds of cost the Guardians were prepared to retain in their Workhouse those who were just periodically violent. In 1854 Dowling was stated to be "occasionally violent and mischievous" but although the Lunacy Commissioners recommended his removal to a lunatic asylum, the Medical Officer declined to sign the Certificate for removal on the grounds that, "I believe him to be perfectly sane and conscious of all the mischief he occasionally exhibits." In 1869 Jane Brine and Elizabeth Allen, with their epileptic fits, were "at times excited and violent", and in 1890 Caroline Stacey was reported "to be occasionally menacing and she has threatened to strike others with a poker." Not a pleasant environment for other inmates.

In general there appears to have been a greater tendency towards 'dangerous' behaviour by male lunatics compared with female ones and so many more of the former were sent to Wells. The result was that the number of female lunatics in the Workhouse greatly exceeded males. Sixteen annual Reports by the Commissioners in Lunacy gave a total of one hundred and nineteen female lunatics and sixty-five males.

There were also those who were physically offensive which would have impinged on the lives of other paupers. In 1856 George Wines, classed as "an idiot boy", was described as having dirty habits which probably related to bed-wetting as within a year by improving his bedding in an Infirmary Ward the Nurse had managed to cure him of these habits. She was, however, less successful in stopping his tendency to destroy his clothes. In 1886 James A'Court was reported to be of dirty habits which were so bad that the Inspector felt "he is hardly a suitable case for workhouse care except under a paid attendant." At the very least some the lunatics were said to greatly disturb the other inmates especially at night in the Infirmary Wards where they slept.

The Wincanton Board of Guardians appear to have attempted to treat lunatics in their Workhouse in a humane manner judged by the standards of their day. Attitudes in rural areas were sometimes slow to change and for those on Outdoor Relief there was much less monitoring. In 1895 when a Guardian visited a lunatic, Stephen Balch in North Brewham, he discovered him tied to the bed. He was removed to the County Asylum. Once again, however, the Wincanton Board undertook no major innovations or experiments nor did they initiate any new methods of treatment. They were quite prepared to retain in the Workhouse those lunatic paupers who were harmless and who served a useful function; the rest were disposed of, especially to the County Asylum even though it might have been a more expensive proposition. Transference to the Asylum led to one very unfortunate incident in 1883 when the Relieving Officer, Edmund Read, aged seventy, with his youngest daughter were taking a female lunatic to Wincanton Railway Station for the journey to Wells,

> "Near the Station she became restless and troublesome. Mr Read was endeavouring to pacify her, and was putting on one of her shoes, which she had thrown off, when he fell in some kind of a fit, and in a few minutes he had breathed his last."

(16)

7. Children and their Education

a) Treatment

Children under sixteen formed the largest single category in workhouses after 1834: 46.5% of the total in the Wincanton Workhouse in 1837. This percentage was to increase in the 1840s to over 50% and remained at this level until the late 1870s, peaking at over 56% in 1848 and 1855. In the 1880s and 1890s their numbers and as a percentage of the total inmates decreased to around 30% as the role of the Workhouse changed and greater numbers of aged, infirm and sick became resident. There was also a modification in attitude to one which preferred to integrate children into society, rather than keep them in virtual isolation. Decades earlier there had been proposals to allow children to be adopted but these had not always succeeded, for example, when in February 1857 Mary Cos of Castle Cary tried to adopt a nine year old orphan, Margaret Macdonald, the Guardians declined when they discovered the intention was to employ her as a server in the Horse Hair Seating Manufactory there and she would not be able to attend any school. In the 1890s the Wincanton Board became increasingly keen to allow children to be removed or boarded out, although at that period they had no definite policy, preferring to judge each case on its merits. In 1890 William Hunt was provided with clothes and allowed to go to his sister; in April 1891 two children were given into the custody of their stepfather and the following year George Cash was allowed to go to his uncle. In these instances a family relationship was the key factor.

In addition many of the children were from a background which suggested that they could be long term or permanent residents. One Return in 1849 showed that of eighty-one children under sixteen some twenty-six were illegitimate, four had widowed mothers, nineteen were orphans, seventeen were deserted by one or both parents, three were the children of vagrants and twelve of able-bodied parents. As it was likely that nearly half of these children would remain long term or permanently the Guardians had to take a practical and realistic course. At one early stage they even proposed to take into the Workhouse a boy who needed reforming, "his character being such that no person will employ him." In this instance the Poor Law Commissioners agreed, but with reservations, as the family was so large and once again a structured environment was essential.

There was an acceptance by many within the Poor Law System that children could be in their care through no fault of their own but they also adhered to the view that they could not be fed and clothed better than their contemporaries outside of the workhouses as they feared that this would encourage the poor to deposit their children on the parish. Children therefore were subjected to the same regime as the rest of the inmates and for some it was even worse as they could not give notice to leave the House on their own and if they ran away they could be forcibly brought back.

All children under seven years of age were placed in the same Ward as their mother and she had care of them but those over seven were sent to either the boys' or girls' rooms. The Guardians did, however, permit the parents to be with children, if they wished, for half of the dinner period each day in the Entrance Hall, under appropriate supervision. Parents who themselves were not in the Workhouse were initially only permitted to visit their children on Sundays and it was not until 1866 that other times were added, such as Tuesdays and Fridays for fifteen minutes after Supper, in the presence of the Schoolmaster or Schoolmistress. While in this latter case there is some logic in the visiting times as parents would be working during the rest of the week and during the day, the separation must have been hard for the children. In some respects for those whose parents were in the Workhouse with them, it could be even harder for although there could be a short period of daily contact, at other times in the day such as breakfast and supper, they could see each other in the same room but were not permitted to communicate.

Children's diet varied from that of the adults in that cheese did not appear: breakfast each day consisted of four ounces of bread and half a pint of oatmeal porridge; dinner varied more with five ounces of bread and half an ounce of butter on two days, eight ounces of Rice or Suet Pudding on two days and eight or ten ounces of potatoes and vegetables on the other three, with an addition of three ounces of meat on Tuesdays. For Supper on six evenings it was four ounces of bread and half an ounce of butter with half a pint of milk and water but on Thursdays ten ounces of potatoes or peas. There were detailed instructions not only on the quantity for each child but also on the ingredients such as ten ounces of flour and three ounces of suet for every pound of Suet Pudding and twelve ounces of oatmeal to every gallon of water. (See Appendix 1b) Hardly an ideal diet for growing children and no wonder mothers smuggled food out of the Dining Hall for the intervals in between but it was, however, far superior to, and more regular than, that of many children outside of the Workhouse.

All children over seven years of age were expected to work, with girls assisting the able-bodied women with domestic work which included working in the Washhouse. Boys were required to keep their own rooms clean and to work in the garden. Such activities were seen as good training for their future life and also as exercise. For additional exercise all children under fifteen years old were sent out on supervised walks of up to two hours at least twice a week, weather permitting, although by the mid-1870s one School Inspector considered that twice a week was inadequate and recommended that the frequency should be increased. On these walks the children were not permitted to go into the town or enter any house. At times the supervision was somewhat lax as in November 1843 the Guardian for Stoke Trister complained, "that the boys from the Workhouse when walking out for air and exercise last week got into and stole apples from his orchard."

Children were the only group within a workhouse which could be subjected to corporal punishment. The Wincanton Board did not approve of such punishment for girls and from 1842 required the Master from time to time to show the Visiting Committee "every rod or other instrument" which was used to punish children. In

1847 the Poor Law Board banned corporal punishment on girls and older boys, although boys under fourteen years of age could still be beaten by the Master or the Schoolmaster. The Wincanton Board, unlike some other Unions, seem to have adhered to this regulation. In January 1850 the Schoolmaster was admonished when he flogged a boy contrary to these rules and in August 1880 when the then Schoolmaster, Henry Kendall, lost his temper and gave one of the boys a "Severe beating" he was dismissed. A Return in 1873 recorded that no boys had been corporally punished in the half year to 25th March. In the 1890s, however, the Matron appeared to be adopting a harsher line as in November 1891 a complaint was made that she struck and bruised a child. She agreed that, "she had slapped the child with her hand twice because he caused a noise to be made at meal times." A Committee which investigated concluded, "that the whipping was not excessive", but cautioned the Matron to avoid striking such young children. Two years later she gave another boy "6 Strokes on his hand" and again the Guardians decided there was no cause for complaint as the "boy had not been unduly chastised." Initially children could be subjected to other punishments such as being confined in a dark room during the night, although this was banned in 1847. In 1881 the Schoolmaster was cautioned for his actions when he gave a boy a cold bath after he had wet his bed.

The regime under which the children lived could be harsh for in December 1880 an allegation was made by Cornelius Bidgood, an adult pauper, that,

> "the little boys are huddled together up in a long room on Saturdays without firing to heat of any descriptions with a older boy to inforce silence from 1 o'clock till 9 o'clock Sunday morning."

How long this had been happening was not specified and although the Guardians produced evidence to attempt to discredit Bidgood the Local Government Board investigated and found that there was a basis for the complaint. They advised the Guardians that the practice must cease.

Rules, regulations and punishments were not necessarily a sufficient deterrent for when a School Inspector visited in July 1883 he found, "The boys at the time of my visit most unruly." In fact in the following month the behaviour of John Carp, aged eleven years, was so bad that Magistrates ordered him to be sent to the Somersetshire Certified Industrial Home for Boys at Bath until he was sixteen years of age. In the 1890s the Matron was faced with several difficult girls, a situation which may in part be explained by the removal of the last resident Schoolmistress and the Industrial Trainer proved not to be an adequate substitute. On a number of occasions in 1894 and 1897 the Matron brought the daughter of Louisa Forward before the Board as "She was a naughty girl and often had to be punished." She frequently refused to do her work and would not obey the Industrial Trainer so the Matron reported she "could not do anything with her." On each occasion the girl promised to be better in the future. More serious was the behaviour of Louisa Hodges in 1895 and 1896 as she was described by the Matron as a ringleader who made "the other children disobey the Trainer and Matron." By January 1896 the position had deteriorated so much that the Matron found she could do nothing with her and so she was sent to the Bath Industrial School, at a cost of 7s per week.

Until the 1890s the children wore the same regulation Workhouse clothes as the rest of the inmates and the officers were instructed to ensure that they were kept clean once they had been admitted. To that end each child, whether they liked it or not, was required to have a regular bath. For some children who had experienced only cottages without any water supply, this regulation may have come as an unpleasant shock. In 1881 when it was found that after their baths boys were being put into a cold room, Inspector Courtney suggested a fireplace be added. Once again it is not possible to determine for how long this practice had existed. Inspector Preston-Thomas was generally very sceptical about the cleanliness of boys, especially in the Wincanton Workhouse where he considered the bathing arrangements to be bad. While he accepted that hands and faces could be clean boys he alleged were often "dirty underneath." As a result of having some of the boys stripped he was able to report that he "found their skins very clean", a fact he attributed to a very good Matron. (17)

Children who were the particular responsibility of the Guardians, such as orphans and the deserted, were often sent out to service or apprenticed. Before 1834 it had been the common practice to apprentice children, especially boys, as soon as possible to remove them from parish responsibility. It was usual for them to be accompanied with a sum of up to £10 for the employer. After 1834 this practice was officially forbidden although sending children out as apprentices continued and the Wincanton Board appear to have disregarded the Central Board on the issue of payment. In August 1848 John Way, aged eleven years, was apprenticed for seven years to Richard Chick, a Hairdresser in Wincanton, with a premium of £6, that is £4 in money and clothing to the value of £2. In September 1850 James Stacey, an orphan, was apprenticed to a shoemaker, William Hooper in Wincanton, with the same premium. In April 1888 Elizabeth Ann James, a cripple girl, was apprenticed for two years as a Dressmaker with Miss King and in this instance the Guardians agreed to pay £16 a year for her lodging, maintenance and clothing. At the very end of the century in February 1899 Lionel White, described as "an orphan illegitimate & destitute", was sent to the Bath Industrial School for training. The Guardians appear to have continued to monitor treatment, for example, when they discovered in August 1855 from Charles Lacey that, while he was satisfied as an apprentice, he was not attending the Wincanton Sunday School, they ordered his Master to ensure that he attended regularly in future. Not all placements were successful as the Guardians received a report in August 1862 that Jeremiah Henry Read had absconded after three years from his Master, George Hill a Shoemaker in Castle Cary.

There was also some interest throughout the period in leaving the Workhouse and going into the Armed Forces, particularly the Navy and in a few cases to serve an apprenticeship there. In December 1849 George Huchens entered the Royal Navy as a Naval Apprentice for seven years on HMS 'Impregnable' at Devonport, the cost of his outfit being £5. The 1881 Census revealed that three boys, Arthur Green aged twelve, John James aged fourteen and Henry Thomas aged thirteen, were residents of the Industrial School Ship 'Formidable' in Bristol. In April 1895 James Bond went to sea and the following year F. Everett was sent to the training ship 'Arethusa'. Interest in the military may be one reason why there was such an emphasis upon Drill for the boys in the Workhouse.

Far more children were sent out to domestic service and the Poor Law Commissioners were convinced that the test of a good education or industrial training in the workhouse was the number of children "so trained who are taken into honest and useful industrial courses, and remain in them as good servants or good workmen." The Wincanton Board sent children out to Service under different arrangements: in 1836 Fanny Hill was sent into the service of Mrs John Hooper of South Brewham with everything found but no wages; more usual was the arrangement for "Board, Lodging, Clothing and Washing" along with a small sum in cash, such as 4d a week to Margaret Macdonald in 1859 and 9d a week to Julia Hill in 1863. The children went out to Service with the clothes in which they stood up and little else and such was the destitution of Ann Mead in 1852 that the Guardians had to spend £1 5s 0d on purchasing the clothes themselves. From August 1896 they did give them a wooden box to store anything they might receive.

By October 1859 it had become clear to the Guardians that children were being taken out as servants and then returned "at the end of several months servitude without any payment of wages and often having worn out the clothing taken with them on leaving the house." Two years later when Thomas Flower of Buckhorn Weston returned Margaret MacDonald without any wages being paid they took more determined action and applied to the Magistrates for a summons. In June 1863 when Mr Sims of West Bourton did the same to Julia Hill he too was summonsed.

Far more serious was that from time to time the children were assaulted by their employers who presumably were anticipating docile, cheap labour and found instead sometimes difficult children with no experience and few appropriate skills. In August 1858 James Longman of Dimmer Farm, Castle Cary, was fined £5 by magistrates after he assaulted Keziah Forward aged thirteen by whipping her so much that she ran away and back to the Workhouse "with marks of blows on her person." In April 1859 Eliza Hill was allegedly assaulted by Mr and Mrs Thomas Dowding of Cucklington, after she had been transferred to them by Mr Godwin, a butcher of Buckhorn Weston, without the knowledge of the Guardians. In this instance they decided to take no further action. In August 1872 Mr Gatehouse of Penselwood had to explain to Justices an allegation of ill-treatment made by a girl called Curtis and after his evidence once again no further action was taken. Some children disliked their position so much for whatever reason that they simply ran away, such as a boy called Spratling from Mr Cary of Charlton Horethorn in 1892 and Mrs Everett's daughter did the same in 1895.

On the other hand some placements appear to have worked satisfactorily, for example, in January 1900 Alfred Reardon aged fourteen was sent to Mr How, a Schoolmaster in Wincanton, where he remained a year and his employer was reported to be pleased with him. He then transferred to Mr Mackey, a Cheesemaker at Castle Cary, with a salary of 2s 6d a week. In September 1899 Georgina Doughty was sent for six months to Mrs Hannam, a Grocer's wife in Wincanton, who was reported to be "very satisfied." At the end of the period a situation was found for the girl in Bournemouth where her new employer was also reported to be well pleased with her.

It is impossible to ascertain exactly how many boys and girls returned from Service but two surviving Returns give some indication. A Return in 1861 showed that between 1851 and 1860 twenty-four boys and thirty-six girls had been sent out to Service and of these no boys and ten girls had been returned through "misconduct" and three boys and seven girls for "other reasons", a total of some 33%. A later Return revealed a lower rate as of four boys and two girls sent out to Service in 1884 three boys and both girls had proved satisfactory. Some observers blamed the inadequate education in the workhouses for the failure rate while others attributed it to ill-health as the children were suddenly faced with up to sixteen hours a day of manual labour. In 1892 Eliza Maidment returned to the House in such an emaciated state that at one point it was considered to be starvation, but the Medical Officer would not certify to that effect and "considered Mrs Drew looked well after the child while she had been under her care."

The apparent failure rate at times amongst the girls was particularly high when compared with Somerset as a whole where it was about 23%. This may suggest that the industrial training in the Wincanton Workhouse was, as School Inspector Ruddock commented, more designed to diminish periods of compulsory idleness than train them for any specific employment. What many of the Wincanton Board failed to realise was that, although assistance with household chores from seven years old for girls might help the domestic economy of their Workhouse, it had little long-term social or educational value. Ideal domestic servants were not created from girls who had no concept of private property, never having any possessions of their own, and for whom even the simplest family routines such as laying a fire or a table were unknown. They could at least scrub. There were obvious failures, such as Jemima Jeffries, born in 1859, who was sent out to three different employers between 1870 and 1872 and was sent back each time, before finally joining her mother in Bath for another situation. (18)

Children were amongst the first to experience the gradual liberalization in attitude towards the inmates of workhouses, partly because of the desire to integrate them more fully with their contemporaries and partly through humanitarian sentiments which occasionally bordered on pity. As with other inmates children enjoyed a special New Year dinner from 1836 and in 1841 the first mention is made of children being given a book each as a present. By the 1860s the children were receiving annual presents and those apprenticed out by the Guardians were allowed to return to enjoy the Christmas festivities, which later in the century included a Christmas Tree. In the 1870s a day-trip to the seaside became established as an annual event, usually to Burnham-on-Sea on the railway, but in the 1890s occasionally to

Bournmouth. At the same period the children were also given a treat of tea at a country house, such as that of Mrs Wyndham Mildmay of Queen Camel in 1891. By far the most established was the visit to the house of T.E. Rogers, for many years the Vice-Chairman of the Board of Guardians, at Yarlington where they were treated to sandwiches, cake, tea and fruit. These annual visits started in 1870 and continued for the rest of the century. When subscriptions were raised there were other trips out such as to Stourton Tower in August 1873 which included refreshments and games.

Local celebrations were another occasion to treat the children, for example, in 1856 they were permitted to leave the Workhouse to celebrate the end of the Crimean War with local inhabitants. Over forty years later they celebrated the Diamond Jubilee of Queen Victoria with local residents and were even allowed to be out until 9 o'clock in the evening. There were other ad hoc trips such as to a circus in May 1892 and in November to hear Handbell Ringers, an experience repeated in November 1897. Sometimes the treat came to them in the Workhouse such as a gift by Mr Eden of 420 oranges in January 1899.

As the local Vicar was also the Chaplain of the Workhouse there remained a close connection between the Parish Church and the children. As early as November 1855 the Chaplain had successfully requested that boys with good voices should be allowed to sing in the Church Choir. In the 1890s there were requests that the children should be permitted to attend a range of Services, such as a Christmas one in 1891, a Flower Service in June 1892, an afternoon Easter Service in 1893 and a Good Friday Service in 1896. In addition in the 1890s there was an annual invitation for the children to attend the Sunday School Treat.

Other organizations also took an interest in the children, so for example in May 1896 they were permitted to attend the local Friendly Society's Fete. In April 1888 Mrs Marriott, as a representative of the Girls' Friendly Society which was a Diocesan organisation, was given permission to visit the Workhouse to help girls who were fit and able for Service. The following year she was allowed to take the girls to meetings held in Bruton on the strict understanding that such girls could not become members. In 1897 the Guardians declined to sanction the formation of a branch of the Society in the Workhouse but relented two years later under pressure from the Lady Visitors. The aim of the Society was very clear, "Young Women and Girls as Members, are banded together to help and encourage one another in Purity of Life, and faithfulness to their Station." The concept of knowing one's place in life remained strong at the end of the nineteenth century. Another way to encourage leading a good life was through abstinence from alcohol and from 1889 the children were allowed to attend Temperance Lectures in Wincanton, at the instigation of the Chaplain, and even to enrol as members of the Church of England Juvenile Temperance Association, "provided they are not permitted to take the pledge of total abstinence." (19)

One of the great dangers for children who were long-term residents in the Workhouse was increasing institutionalisation which could lead to a lifetime of dependence. More integration into society would, it was believed, help to decrease this risk but such integration meant that they had to be suitably educated and this was to remain during the period 1834 to 1900 the prime concern of the Guardians in relation to the children in their care.

b) Education

The Poor Law Commissioners were adamant that,
> "The child is dependent on the boards of guardians for more than maintenance: it must be trained in industry, in correct moral habits, and in religion, and must be fitted to discharge the duties of its station in life."

They were convinced that if pauper education could achieve these objectives then social stability would be attained, the vicious circle of hereditary pauperism broken and the labouring classes inculcated with industrious habits. On a more practical basis, Assistant Commissioner Weale in the West Country believed that,

> "the children should be taught to perform such domestic and other works as will be useful to them in after life. To knit a stocking, to plat a hat or bonnet, to mend a shoe, to repair a coat, are useful arts."

By the 1870s there was a shift in emphasis to provide an education which would make the pauper children self-supporting, "It is to the extinguishing of the pauper spirit by the creation of a rightful sense of self-respect that we must look."

The possibility of long-term benefits in relation to self-reliance, industriousness and social improvement from pauper education certainly appealed to rural guardians but, while they approved of the moral and industrious aspects, they expressed concerns that an intellectual education might educate them above their station in life. A more educated workforce could be more mobile and that would have implications for a farming community. There was therefore reluctance to consider subjects such as Geography and it did not appear in the Wincanton Workhouse Schools until 1852. By the 1860s, however, many farmers recognised that new methods and machines required better- educated labourers. Nevertheless in 1898 T.E. Rogers complained,

> "that hardly any of the rising generation of our rustic youth take kindly to farm work. The education they are receiving wholly unfits them for any such work. They – the pick of them – look out for employment in the police, or especially on the railway, where they are their own masters, just as the girls seek to qualify as dressmakers rather than as domestic servants."

Although the Poor Law Report of 1834 made little mention of education there were already a number of schools in the thirty-nine parishes which were to comprise the Wincanton Union. In the thirty-eight parishes which provided information in 1833 (only Penselwood did not) three parishes had no school, five had just a Sunday School and thirty had both a Day School and Sunday School. In all 1,887 children attended these Days Schools and 2,577 the Sunday Schools, 9% and 12% of the total population respectively These Returns, however must be treated with caution as they do not indicate if it was different children attending Sunday and Day Schools or whether there was an overlap and they do not indicate the background of the children, so, for example, they included boarding schools in Bruton, Castle Cary, Horsington and Wincanton which were for children from middle class families. Some of the schools operated more like a child-minding service as both parents needed to work The overall impression created was that the education for the labouring class in the area was much neglected. In 1837 Assistant Commissioner Weale was in no doubt,

> "the education of the peasantry and the lower order of artisans is in the County in such a degraded state that it is impossible to devise a system for the Workhouse which will not be more attractive and useful."

The Poor Law Commissioners required each workhouse to employ a Schoolmaster and a Schoolmistress to provide a minimum of three hours of schooling a day in the 3Rs, along with the principles of the Christian religion, and to undertake industrial training "as shall fit them for service, and train them in habits of usefulness, industry, and virtue." The Wincanton Board certainly appeared to comply as on 1st July 1836 they resolved,

> "that until the appointment of a Schoolmaster and Schoolmistress all the Boys and Girls who are inmates of the Workhouse shall be sent to the Wincanton National School."

As the numbers were small economic factors also influenced their decision. It is nevertheless an interesting interim measure given that for most of the rest of the century the children were to be educated in virtual isolation in the Workhouse.

The Guardians, however, were soon forced to re-think, partly as the National School proved inadequate and partly because attendance was at the discretion of the Master and Matron who were more concerned with the domestic work in the House. The result was that in April 1837 the Chaplain reported that the children were not being properly instructed and this criticism prompted the Guardians to advertise for a middle-aged female who would teach on the National System. As there were no Workhouse School Inspectors before 1846, it was the Chaplain who examined the children and his role in this respect was crucial as his position in society allowed him to place pressure on the farmer-Guardians. In addition it also became apparent to them that a better system of supervision of the children was required when they were not in school.

The decision to appoint just a Schoolmistress was taken on the grounds of cost as there were only twenty-eight children under sixteen years of age in the Workhouse at that time and not all of these were old enough to attend a school. They also felt that a Schoolmistress could supervise the girls at other times, the boys being supervised by other officers, most notably the Porter. By 1847 it was clear that the Schoolmistress could not cope so a Schoolmaster was employed instead, but the first two of these also proved unsatisfactory. Faced with an increase in numbers and under severe criticism from the Chaplain in December 1849 the Guardians reluctantly resolved to employ a teacher of each sex. It had taken the Wincanton Board thirteen years to implement the requirement which the Central Board had laid down in 1836.

The increase in the number of children in the Workhouse in the 1870s indicates that they experienced the impact of the campaign against Outdoor Relief in the same way as adults. By the mid-1880s the numbers had dropped significantly and in the last six years of its existence the Workhouse School averaged forty-seven children.

Table 15.   Average Number of Children attending Wincanton Workhouse Schools

Half Year ending Lady Day	Boys	Girls	Total
1851	25	31	56
1856	30	29	59
1861	28	18	46
1866	22	16	38
1871	29	45	74
1876	31	49	80
1881	23	43	66
1886	26	20	46
1891	21	26	47

For all of the children three main areas were of particular importance in providing them with an education in their isolated environment. The first was the curriculum which initially in all workhouse schools was very restricted as it consisted of the 3Rs and Religious Knowledge. The Wincanton Board insisted that the books used in their school should be selected from the list published by the Society for Promoting Christian Knowledge and used in the National Schools. Subsequent Ledgers show that National Society Books were purchased most years along with, for example, £7 19s 0d spent on Christian Knowledge Society Testaments in December 1852. Such an education was extremely elementary but would have compared favourably with that available to the children of the poor outside of the Workhouse.

In the 1850s and 1860s there was a broadening of the curriculum, largely as a result of the pressure of the Inspectorate for Workhouse Schools established in 1846. Wincanton does not appear to have been particularly rapid in its adoption of new areas, although Geography first appeared in 1852. By the mid-1860s the children were being examined in Religious Knowledge, Reading, Spelling, Penmanship, Arithmetic, Geography and History. After

1870 curriculum innovation in the Wincanton Workhouse Schools was negligible, except for more use of Object Cards, at a time when, under the rigorous scrutiny of the new Inspectorate for Schools, elementary Schools in the country as a whole were improving steadily to meet the demands of an increasingly complex society. Certainly what the children were taught was examined thoroughly, initially by the Chaplain and then from 1846 by the Inspectors and at times some of the results were very good, for example in 1881 of the forty-seven children examined thirty-eight passed in all the Subject Standards and of these twenty were in Standards I and II out of six. (20)

The second area of importance for the children was the physical working conditions and the educational facilities. The original Schoolroom near the back of the House had the usual ten-inch wide deal seats around the wall. There were two tables each twelve feet long, two feet wide and two feet three inches high, along with four forms each twelve feet long eight inches wide and with the seat fifteen inches from the floor. There was also one other form for the younger children which had a seat six inches wide and was lower being twelve inches from the ground. In 1852 the Guardians were forced to build a sitting room for the new Schoolmaster and a second schoolroom to accommodate the boys. It was constructed over a single storey building in the Boys' Yard and cost them £140 18s 0d. This left the girls in the original Schoolroom between the Infirmaries and which was judged by Inspector Ruddock to be, "very objectionable, both as regards the health of the children and the comfort of the children." No immediate action was taken.

By early 1870 as part of a broader plan to improve classification and provide more accommodation for the sick, the Guardians had devised a scheme to remove the children completely from the Workhouse. They wished to construct a separate building for them in three parallel blocks in the southern part of the garden in front of the Workhouse. One block would contain two schoolrooms and the other two blocks would house the dormitories and accommodation for the Schoolmaster and the Schoolmistress, "The Guardians consider by removing the children from the present Workhouse great permanent good may be looked for." The Central Board was unconvinced and criticized the Plans broadly in terms of size and cost and then in a multitude of details. After several months of correspondence the Guardians conceded and decided on just one building with two new Schoolrooms, one of which would also serve as the Chapel. By December 1871 the building "used as School and Chapel on the Ground detached in front of the house, Common fireplace there in Brick, Stone and Slated," was insured for £300 and the furniture and fittings for a further £25. In January 1872 School Inspector T.B. Browne commented, "The Guardians have built very good Schoolrooms." The Day Rooms and dormitories of the children, however, remained within the main building. It was unfortunate that the Guardians had decided on change at a time when nationally the campaign against Outdoor Relief was being launched and a much stricter regime being advocated within workhouses. This new building marked an improvement in the physical conditions of the children but they remained encompassed within a Workhouse which offered little opportunity for imaginative development.

The facilities within the Schoolrooms were limited so that in August 1852 School Inspector Ruddock was very critical of the use of flat tables rather than single sloping writing desks. On this occasion there was a swift response and by December the Guardians were able to report that these desks had been obtained and were in use. Ruddock was also critical of the scope of the books and apparatus available and this criticism, along with the creation of the additional Schoolroom, led the Guardians in October of the same year to draw up what was probably their largest ever Order consisting of some 182 new books, mainly centred on Reading, English Grammar, Etymology and Arithmetic but also including for the first time twenty-four Compendium of Geography, along with two Maps, one of England and one of the World. Subsequent inspections seem to suggest that these maps were the only visual stimulus in the Schoolrooms as no mention was made of pictures. Each of the rooms had a blackboard and the children were provided with slates on which to write. In May 1878 the Guardians decided to purchase a

Harmonium for the School at a cost not exceeding six guineas, to be used for Services as well.

The third area of importance for the children, and probably the most crucial in a residential situation, was the calibre of the teachers, especially as some of the children were orphans or deserted and many of the others had little contact with their parents. The influence of the teachers could be considerable but a problem which was to bedevil workhouse schools for much of the century was how to maintain a regular supply of efficient, suitably trained and qualified schoolmasters and schoolmistresses. In 1864 School Inspector T.B. Browne lamented, "The notion is not yet eradicated that a person fit for nothing else may still be fit to teach pauper children." The first applicants for the Wincanton Workhouse School were paupers and as late as 1869 the salary had to be increased because there were no candidates. Other early Schoolmistresses were not qualified, being related to the Master and Matron, first a daughter and then a niece. (21) From 1850 there was some improvement as may be seen from Table 16. This was partly the result of a government grant being introduced from 1846 towards the salary of a teacher, dependent upon efficiency, and partly from the effects of a pupil-teacher scheme requiring five years of training.

In at least seven cases the teacher had received training and had previous experience but others did not, for amongst those appointed were an assistant in the Post Office, a Coach Maker, a Joiner, a Stone Cutter, and two men who had served in the Navy. The Guardians had hoped to attract teachers of experience and maturity to give stability but the low salary and poor working conditions meant that that proved to be impossible. Out of a total of forty-four teachers appointed after 1837 only three were over thirty-five: a Schoolmaster aged fifty-three and two Schoolmistresses aged thirty-six and fifty-seven. Twenty-eight were aged between twenty and twenty-nine and two were under twenty years of age. Many of them remained in post for a very short time.

Table 16.   Experience and Qualifications of Teachers

Total number of Teachers appointed 1850-1890	34
Trained in a College	6
Pupil Teachers	9
Previous experience in National or Board Schools	8
Previous experience in Workhouse Schools	12
Previous experience in a Sunday School	1
Previous experience unspecified	3
No details given	2

In such circumstances the state of the School and the education of the children varied considerably through the decades. In the early years the emphasis in most workhouses was to comply with the requirements of the Poor Law Commissioners. Change came with the School Inspectorate and the parliamentary grant after 1846 but the Wincanton Board were slow to implement recommendations. The result was that between 1847 and 1853 Inspector Ruddock produced a series of critical reports after his visits. In 1849 he declared, "I cannot speak favourably of this school," and in 1851, "Very indifferent schools; the children are ill-instructed and not under good control." The Chaplain was also dissatisfied in 1849 when it was reported to the Guardians,

> "He regrets being obliged to state that the progress of the children has been by no means as satisfactory as he could have wished."

In 1853 the Schoolmaster, Daniel Chambers, received a final warning not only on the instruction of the children but also on broader issues relating to them. "You are not sufficiently attentive to neatness and cleanliness, either as regards the School-room or the children." It had the desired effect as the Annual Reports for the remainder of the 1850s and into the 1860s traced gradual improvements. Even Ruddock was able to comment in 1861, "Visited the Schools

– they are in an excellent condition & highly commendable to the teachers."

In the late 1860s there were problems associated with the rapid turnover of Schoolmistresses and their quality. Inspector Browne found "the girls in a low state, and very deficient in arithmetic" in 1867 and recommended that the Schoolmistress "be warned that improvement will be expected." He found the situation the same the following year and in 1869 noted, "the girls are in a low state, ignorant and inattentive." Once again he felt that the Schoolmistress should be warned and on this occasion it did lead to some improvement by the time of his next visit in the following year.

While the Annual Reports on the Schools remained very favourable throughout the 1880s, it was in the 1870s that they seemed to have reached a peak under Maria Ingram and William Childs, the Stone Cutter. In 1874, for example, Inspector Clutterbuck commented,

> "This is an excellent school. Both boys and girls were considerably above the average in intelligence. I found that they had a very fair amount of miscellaneous knowledge which showed the real interest both teachers take in the progress of the children, but what stuck me more than anything else was the joyousness……..very unusual in pauper schools."

Such comments are remarkable as just a few years before in 1866 the children were referred to as "more than unusually dull" and two years earlier it was reported that they "did not show much intelligence in either school." To add to their problems while the teachers had a core of children who were long-term residents there was also a significant fluctuating population. At one extreme these were known as "Ins and Outs" because of the frequency with which they were admitted and discharged from the Workhouse. A good example of this category were the Morgan children who entered and left the Wincanton Workhouse on nineteen different occasions between January 1870 and September 1872. Such activity caused major disruption to children's education and yet Ingram and Childs seem to have overcome this.

After 1871 the Local Government Board began to place less emphasis upon workhouse children being educated in isolation as numbers dwindled, the supply of good teachers remained a problem and the dangers of institutionalisation became better understood. The Wincanton Board were slow to change and as late as 1909 their Chaplain commented, "The children are bright and well cared for and distinctly benefit mentally and physically by their residence in the Workhouse." The Guardians took their first hesitant step towards an alteration in July 1883 when they considered a motion to send the children to the local Board School but although it was defeated the very fact that they were discussing change was an important development. To a certain extent it was being forced upon them as the number of children was decreasing and discipline was very poor especially in the boys' school and was once again severely criticised by the Inspector. They decided instead to re-establish after more than thirty years a mixed school under the control of a Schoolmistress and to appoint an Industrial Trainer to look after the boys when they were not in school.

Numbers continued to decline slowly and when in May 1891 there were only thirty-five children in the School, the Guardians decided it had become uneconomical. They established a Committee to review the situation and it recommended that the children should attend the local Board School at an agreed cost of 2d per child per week. By Michaelmas it had cost them £10 2s 0d which they judged to be economically appropriate and they accepted that some longer term expenditure was necessary in the form of new clothing for the children, but only as their existing "uniform dress becomes worn out." They also decided to replace the male Industrial Trainer with a female one to look after the girls and as in the earliest days of the Workhouse the task of looking after the boys fell to the Porter.

The move to an outside school was a marked success as not only were the children well received in the Board School as they were clean, punctual and regular in their attendance but also as the Visiting Committee noted in March 1895, "that much good has arisen from doing so, as they seem happier, brighter and more fitted to fight the battles of life than when closely shut out from contact with other children."

While this comment endorsed their decision, by implication it contained criticism of the policy that the Guardians had pursued for decades. (22)

While intellectual and moral education was required, of equal importance, and for many of the rural Guardians of supreme importance, was the Industrial Training. Many believed that manual labour would remove harmful earlier influences in their lives and so they would become useful labourers no longer dependent on the Poor Law. Small numbers, however, in rural workhouses meant that it was uneconomical to employ a specialist and so this burden was often passed to the Schoolteachers. From 1837 onwards the Schoolmistress in the Wincanton Workhouse was required to instruct the girls in needlework and knitting, which would include making some of their own clothes. From 1891 this responsibility passed to a female industrial trainer who was paid £15 a year and who assisted the Matron when the girls were in school. In addition in the 1850s there had been a Maid of All Work and it was intended that girls will "from time to time be placed under her to learn Cooking, and general household work." At the same time an Inspector suggested that a small building be erected where "they may be taught to wash and get up their own linens and clothing so as to better qualify them, for service." The idea was rejected as it was felt that there was rarely a sufficient number of girls of the appropriate age in the Workhouse.

The Schoolmaster was expected to supervise the boys at work in the garden and in cleaning their rooms. In 1843 shoemaking was introduced but it appears to have been short-lived, probably as a result once again of small numbers. In July 1883 faced with no Schoolmaster and little work the Guardians resolved to employ an Industrial Trainer in Tailoring at a salary of £20 a year who was to have charge of the boys out of school hours, which was generally about two hours a day and all day on Saturday. In 1890 drilling the boys was added to his duties. The aim of the training seems to have been to make the boys proficient in production and repairs for the own needs and to avoid expenditure, rather than as a trade, one which was already over-supplied. Most of the boys after all were destined to be labourers, except perhaps the few who were successful as apprentices. One newspaper did suggest in 1872 that bread might be baked in the Workhouse and this would provide employment and instruction for the boys but it was not followed up by the Guardians.

Industrial Training did not usually occur before ten years of age so the numbers involved at any one time were quite small. While the average number in the Schools in the late 1870s and early 1880s was seventy children an average of about twenty-four were receiving Industrial Training as well. In many Reports the Inspectors noted that the boys had little regular work, except in the garden, with odd ones being used to clean boots and knives. In November 1890 the Local Government Board even refused to sanction the salary of the Industrial Trainer on the grounds that there were only six boys, "but none under bona fide instruction" as they were too young to do anything other that "merely mend or patch old clothes." The work of the girls, however, later in the 1890s was much praised, "The industrial training of the girls is excellent. The specimens of needlework, knitting & patching were very creditable." The female Industrial Trainer was praised by T.E. Rogers when he noted in the Visitors' Book in January 1894,

> "Having had the opportunity this morning of seeing all the girls after their dinner in charge of the Industrial Trainer, I was much pleased by their clean, cheerful & contented appearance. They all seemed perfectly happy & well cared for."

This is a particularly interesting observation, coming as it does in the mid-1890s at a time when the Matron was experiencing such trouble with some of the girls. It may show that they could create the appropriate impression when the occasion arose, such as a visit by the Vice-Chairman of the Board of Guardians.

The effectiveness of the Workhouse education in Wincanton is difficult to assess. Throughout the 1860s and 1870s the children's performance in their annual examination by an Inspector was usually classed as "Fair". In the 1880s the system of reporting results changed and indicated that between 54% and 94% of those entered passed in the three basic subjects of Reading, Writing and Arithmetic. Teaching was of course generally mechanical with its rote learning which did not encourage any independent thinking. In the nineteenth century this would have been seen as very appropriate for their station in life. From the 1860s there was some concern that children brought up in the workhouse would see it as their home and remain or return there in later life. This does not seem to have been the case in Wincanton for of the twenty-seven children under fourteen years of age who were admitted in 1836 and 1837, and remained at least one year, none was in the Workhouse thirty or sixty years later. A Parliamentary Return in 1861 found that none of the seven paupers in this Workhouse who had been there more than five years had been educated in a workhouse school. This evidence is too limited for any definite conclusion but in the 1870s Inspector Browne found that in the West Country as a whole very few inmates were educated in a workhouse school, just twenty-five in 1872 and a number of these were elderly so may have been admitted for other reasons. Such statistics may suggest that the education and training provided did allow the children to become independent labourers in later life.

The Wincanton Board of Guardians complied with the law in relation to the education of the children but they were certainly not innovators or supporters of rapid change: developments which occurred were usually as a result of pressure from the Inspectorate. In one respect the education provided placed the workhouse children in a potentially more advantageous position than that of those outside of the Workhouse. From the very beginning of the system, education for children on Indoor Relief was compulsory, a situation which did not occur for all children until after 1880.

For many children in the workhouse life must have been monotonous, uninspiring, strict, but above all, lacking close human relationships. On the other hand, a somewhat romanticized view developed, expressed by Inspector Clutterbuck in 1886,

"I go as far as to assert that for many little desolate pauper children no home in the world could be found better than some rural workhouses in my own district, where Master, Matron, and teacher…..are alike united in their efforts to launch the frail little bark well equipped in every respect for its life voyage." (23)

8. Life for the Unwanted

a) Bastardy

One group of able-bodied that experienced the displeasure of the Guardians was women pregnant with, or the mothers of, a bastard child. Before 1834 much of the blame for such a pregnancy was placed upon the female, although to avoid suffering the economic burden, parishes invariably tried to ascertain the father so that he could be forced to pay a sum each week to the mother to support the child. Failure to find the father meant that the child became a potential burden to the parish until he or she could be apprenticed. It did lead to some inhuman practices such as dumping a pregnant unmarried female over the parish boundary before she could give birth. Assistant Commissioner Chapman certainly found that in the West Country there were many ratepayers in favour of greater severity when dealing with this category, a view supported by Henry Hobhouse of Hadspen who replied to the Questions from the Commissioners on behalf of the Hundred of Bruton, although he acknowledged, "I could suggest a change; but no legislator would be hard-hearted enough to adopt it."

The 1834 Act aimed to place the economic consequences of illegitimacy firmly upon the mother as a way of improving morals and it certainly appears to have been successful as by 1837 Somerset as a whole recorded a 46% decrease in illegitimacy. In September 1838 the Wincanton Board banned all Outdoor Relief to "women pregnant with Bastard Children" and ordered them to the Workhouse. This measure had a pronounced effect as before 1834 in one parish alone there were thirteen bastards on Outdoor Relief but by 1840 there were just twenty-three from the whole Union resident in the Workhouse which accounted in 1843 for 2.5% of the total relief granted.

While a decrease in numbers was maintained throughout the century, bastard children continued to be born. By 1853 some 195 such children had been born in the Wincanton Workhouse since 1834, averaging about ten a year. This figure remained the same for 1860 but declined to four in 1861 before rising to eight in 1862. Between 1870 and 1873 thirty-eight children were born in the House and twenty-two between 1890 and 1892. In 1899 there were just five. For most of the period to accommodate childbirth there was a small Ward with two Lying-In beds available, increased to three in 1896, and the Annual Reports for the 1880s and 1890s indicate that such figures were generally sufficient.

Once in the Workhouse the pregnant females and mothers of bastard children were required to perform the ordinary household work for as long as they were able to do so but this policy was abandoned in 1853 under pressure from the Poor Law Board. The Guardians then decided to place them in a separate room to pick wool while their children were placed in an infant ward. They did, however, have access to their children at breakfast, dinner and supper times and in addition for half an hour at 10 o'clock in the morning and between 2 o'clock and 3 o'clock in the afternoon each day for the purpose of feeding. As classification was poor in the House it was not unusual for a girl who had possibly been seduced and then abandoned, but whose life until that point had been good, to be placed in the same Lying-In Ward or Day Room with women who had had several illegitimate children and whose behaviour was classed as immoral. Various Inspectors criticized this situation but nothing was done.

Some of the pregnant females were reduced to absolute destitution, for example in December 1837 Sophia Ball and her baby were admitted to the Workhouse when they were found destitute and begging in the streets of Wincanton by Henry Legg, one of the Relieving Officers. In 1853 Sarah Edwards, a single woman, who had lived in the Workhouse for nearly four years after having a male child, was described as "perfectly destitute" and when she asked to leave the House had no clothes for the child or any money to purchase them, so the Guardians granted her 21s to buy the child clothes. Many years later bastardy could return to haunt the elderly as in March 1853 Richard Mogg, "born a bastard 78 years ago in the parish of Wincanton" was ordered to the Workhouse from Taunton as Wincanton was his place of Settlement, even though he had not lived there for most of his life and knew no-one there.

In general attitudes to unmarried mothers remained harsh in rural areas in the nineteenth century. In 1854 the Guardians had no hesitation in classing all of them as "of dissolute and abandoned habits." In 1865 Elizabeth Mead was categorized as a "lunatic" as she had had two illegitimate children before the age of twenty-three. As late as 1910 the Chaplain commented,

> "As to the women who, being practically ordinary prostitutes, come into the Workhouse regularly for their confinements..........I should like to see some more stringent measures taken with such women, to punish and perhaps to reform them, and to protect the ratepayers."

Occasionally there were glimpses of a more humane approach as in the case of Ann Pearce in October 1853. She had been "seduced and abandoned by a Young Man at Sherborne" and being reduced to destitution abandoned the baby when about one month old at the Workhouse gate. She was quickly apprehended but when the Guardians heard her story they decided that "no public good would result from a prosecution." She was duly admonished and transferred with the child to Sherborne Workhouse. Sixteen years earlier in 1837 another child had been found abandoned:

> "A female child found at the door of G. Clewett at 5 o'clock on the morning of 5 August 1837 near the South Turnpike gate in the parish of Wincanton."

For her it started a series of positive events. She was taken to the Workhouse and named, not unsurprisingly, Annie Southgate. When baptised the Chairman of the Board, John Rogers, stood as her sponsor and she was adopted by the Sealeys, the Master and Matron of the Workhouse. When she grew up she trained as a teacher and became the Schoolmistress in the House where she met and subsequently married the Schoolmaster, James Foord. They were then appointed Master and Matron of the Andover Workhouse. (24)

b) Vagrants

From the establishment of the Poor Law in 1601 the able-bodied itinerant undeserving poor, referred to as "sturdy rogues and vagabonds", were sent to Houses of Correction after a whipping. This group continued to cause concern throughout the Victorian period, by then usually called "casuals" or "vagrants" as they were generally able-bodied, unemployed, rootless and frequently perceived as dangerous or lawless. Surprisingly therefore the 1834 Act did not mention them but by 1837 the Poor Law Commissioners recommended that they be given shelter in return for performing a set task and treated like other inmates. The various economic crises in the 1840s necessitated this policy to be amended. By 1841 their numbers had increased so much that the Central Board suggested that conditions for them needed to be tightened up to discourage them from returning:

> "These are the mendicant vagrants, who are known to be generally persons of dissolute character, to lead habitually a life of laziness and imposture and not infrequently to resort to intimidation and pilfering."

By 1848 they had to admit that this policy had not worked and that it was up to Relieving Officers to investigate each case more carefully to establish real destitution and to make a distinction between those who were genuinely travelling around the country to seek work and those who were not.

In the decades which followed a range of other rules and regulations were added, for example in 1871 no casual was permitted to leave a workhouse before 11 am on the morning of the day after he arrived and only then after completing the task set. A second visit within a month would result in a full day's hard labour and detention until 9 am on the third day. From 1882 all casuals had to perform a full day's work and then leave on the third day but as this penalized genuine work-seekers, in the 1890s those who completed their task on the second day were permitted to leave early in the morning of the third day, at 5.30 am in summer and 6 am in winter.

The Wincanton Board adopted an admission procedure which was broadly similar to that for other inmates, with a certificate being issued by the Relieving Officer or, if necessary, by the Master at any time between 6 am and 9 pm. All vagrants had to be "thoroughly cleansed" before being placed in the small Vagrant Wards, a male one being twenty-one feet three inches long by nine feet wide, accommodating twelve men, and a female one sixteen feet four inches long by eight feet wide for up to four women. Both Wards were on the south side of the Workhouse with access from the outside so that the vagrants did not have to pass through other parts of the House to reach them. On entry they were searched and if any money or effects were discovered they had to leave immediately or face arrest under the Vagrancy Acts. One difference was that they retained their own clothes and were not given the standard Workhouse dress, a source of considerable disappointment to a few.

As early as 1848 the Poor Law Board advised Boards of Guardians that some areas had appointed a local police officer as an Assistant Relieving Officer to deal with vagrants. Possibly because of a prevailing suspicion of the police it was only very slowly adopted and so the idea was pursued again by the Central Board in the late 1860s. In August 1870 the Wincanton Board passed a resolution that vagrants "might with advantage be placed entirely under the Police", but they do not appear to have acted upon it. It is only from 1883 that they appointed the local Superintendent of Police on a salary of £10 a year as the Assistant Relieving Officer for Tramps.

The sleeping arrangements for the vagrants were basic so it cannot have been a pleasant experience as there were no beds but they slept between partitions two feet high with a hard straw or reed-filled mattress and a rug to cover them. Even worse it was reported in 1869,

> "there is a w. closet in the corner of each ward quite open to the wards except for a small wooden screen & the ventilation of the wards are insufficient."

Their diet too was very restricted as it consisted generally of six ounces of bread and two ounces of cheese for breakfast and six ounces of bread and one and a half pints of gruel for supper. For those who remained for a full day in the 1880s and 1890s there was a further six ounces of bread with either one and a half ounces of cheese or one pint of soup for dinner.

In return for this accommodation and food all able-bodied vagrants were required to work. To begin with the Wincanton Board was quite lenient as in 1842 they required just one hour of labour "before partaking of any Meal." For men this was cracking stones or crushing bones and for women "scrubbing the female yard, or floors of the day-rooms and the entrance hall." By January 1844 the time involved had been extended to four hours after breakfast in keeping with the requirements of the Poor Law Commissioners, and a more specific and amended requirement introduced in the case of females and the partially disabled:

> "Every able-bodied Male to crush 20 lbs of Bones or crack 28 lbs of Stones to a fine gravel for Walks, and every able-bodied female, or partially disabled Male to pick ½ lb of Oakum."

In 1846 the Guardians were reporting problems as bone-crushing had been banned and oakum picking ceased because "of the difficulty of effecting a sale of the article and of the heavy loss sustained thereon when sold." They were left with men cracking a larger amount of stones and women scrubbing the Day Rooms and Entrance Hall. The Central Board had reservations in relation to women, "the admission of Vagrant women, detailed to work, into the House seems objectionable." Nearly fifty years later in April 1895 Inspector Courtenay was also horrified when he found a tramp washing the floors of the Men's bedroom, and even though he was informed that this was an exceptional case as there was a shortage of labour, he commented in the Visitors' Book. "It is most undesirable that tramps should be brought into the Workhouse proper." In November 1846 the Wincanton Board reported to the Poor Law Commissioners that they had decided to reduce the amount of stone to be cracked by the men from 56 lbs to 40 lbs and that women were to pick 15 lbs of straw for plaiting.

Various Reports by Inspectors for the next five decades indicate that the system remained the same, with the additional requirement that when a male vagrant was detained for a full day one hundredweight of stone had to be cracked and a female one had to pick oakum. A proposal to introduce a Corn Crusher in 1889 was rejected. From the mid-1860s, however, doubts began to be expressed by some of the Inspectors concerning enforcement, for example in 1865 Gulson commented,

> "I greatly doubt, however, whether this requirement of work is regularly enforced by all the Masters of workhouses. I think, in some instances, they are too glad to get rid of vagrants without the trouble of strictly requiring the task of work which ought to be rigidly exacted."

How far the Wincanton Board enforced all the appropriate regulations is impossible to determine. Certainly there was some concern by 1893 as in November the Visiting Committee noted that, "Vagrants should crack more stone." In January 1896 one Guardian believed that harder stone should be purchased as there were so many able-bodied casuals in the House. In April of that year a Committee Report on Vagrancy found that the Board of Guardians strictly adhered to Central Board orders, "so far as possible", but two years later the Master reported that the rules of the Local Government Board "were carried out to the letter."

The only surviving statistics relating to vagrant labour date from 1910 when between 16th April and 28th May one hundred and fifty-eight vagrants, of whom one hundred and twenty-five were adult males and twenty-nine adult females, were admitted to the Wincanton

Workhouse. Of these fifty-two (some 33%) were set no work: thirty-six because it was Sunday, three were too old, one had a bad hand, seven were pregnant, four were not fit and one had just one arm. Of the remainder eighty-three cracked stone, sixteen cleaned, five washed, one cleaned windows and one refused to do anything and so was taken into custody and received seven days with hard labour. A certain degree of discretion and even leniency towards various categories may have been prevalent in the enforcement of the rules. On the other hand, the Guardians had no hesitation in prosecuting able-bodied vagrants who refused to work, reaching a peak in 1896 with nine such cases. The usual punishment was seven days with hard labour in Shepton Mallet Gaol, although a few received ten or fourteen days.

It is not possible to assess the overall number of vagrants who visited the Wincanton Workhouse as through the decades methods of reporting numbers changed, sometimes a count on a designated day, sometimes on the night preceding an Inspector's visit, sometimes the total for a whole year. In 1845 some 372 were relieved during the year, 544 the following year and, as the economic crisis developed, 1,384 in 1847. The numbers declined to 469 in 1850, 488 the next year and by 1853 was just 195. Even in the crisis years of the late 1840s the average number of vagrants was less than four a night. Day counts in the 1870s and 1880s recorded between one and eight each time. Regular day counts on the 1st of January and 1st July in the early 1890s saw a decrease to between one and five each time but 1894 and 1895 produced fifteen and fourteen respectively, these latter figures coinciding with a perceived depression in both industry and agriculture and at a time when the Wincanton Board were becoming concerned about the work being performed.

The overwhelming majority of the vagrants who visited Wincanton were male, for example in the half year to Lady Day 1865 there were one hundred and eighty males, fifteen females and six children and in ten day Returns from 1st July 1890 to 1st January 1895 there was just one female. On rare occasions the male accommodation was insufficient for the numbers, for example on 29th

October 1881 there were twenty-four males, on 1st January 1894 fifteen and on 1st January 1895 fourteen. The 1890 statistics also indicate the seasonal nature of the visits as they were much greater on 1st January, for example on 1st July1893 and 1st July 1894 there were no vagrants at all and just one on 1st July 1891 and 1st July 1892.

In real terms, therefore, the number of vagrants was small but they were continuous and appeared large alongside other admissions as may be seen from Table 17.

Table 17.   Vagrant Admissions 1889-1893

	Number of Vagrants	Average Number of Vagrants each night	Total Admissions	Vagrant Admissions as % of Total Admissions
Sept.1889	169	5.6	184	91.8
Sept.1890	84	2.8	104	80.8
Sept.1891	75	2.5	91	82.4
Sept.1892	146	4.8	152	96.0
Sept.1893	231	7.7	242	95.5

The length of stay by the vagrants was minimal and although in total 705 were admitted in the five months above, all were discharged within the same period. The mid-1890s witnessed a pronounced economic slowdown which was seen by many people as a depression and it is not surprising therefore that more men were unemployed and some were moving around the country to seek work. Just one Admission and Discharge Book for Casuals has survived and this indicates that of one hundred and forty-five admitted, ninety-nine or 63% were classed as labourers, along with nine charwomen and one servant. The remainder covered a wide range of occupations including three bricklayers, two painters, firemen and tailors, as well as a stone cutter, stableman, groom, collar maker, shoe maker, baker, glover and carpenter.

For much of the Victorian period the attitude of the Wincanton Board of Guardians towards the vagrants was, to say the least, highly critical. Faced with an increase in numbers in the late 1840s the Clerk, Robert Clarke, was instructed to write to the Poor Law Board on behalf of the Guardians,

> "That a great portion of such wayfarers are professional mendicants wandering about the country from Union House to Union house, in order to obtain food and lodging…I beg to add, that a few hours in the Stocks, and an occasional whipping of an incorrigible rogue by the parish constable, under an order of a justice of the peace, would, in my opinion, be a most efficacious and inexpensive punishment."

The same critical sentiment was also present in a letter sent in May 1863,

"I beg to state that the Board of Guardians are again pestered here with an ever increasing number of vagrants, chiefly single men under 50 years of age and mostly able-bodied." At the end of the century some Guardians remained hostile as in March 1893 T.E. Rogers "remarked that his opinion was that very few who tramped the country were really in search of work, and said if they did they could easily get employment." Two years later he declared, "nine out of 10 of them are habitual loafers."

There were signs, however, that attitudes were changing, albeit very slowly. In April 1894 the Guardians agreed to accept some books and Wall Cards from the Tramps' Mission. One Guardian went so far as to state that, "He firmly held that their treatment of the tramps was harsh, cruel, unkind and unjust." In the 1890s this was almost a lone voice as resolutions he proposed found only one other supporter. One local publication did at least try to take a slightly more light-hearted view:

> "They Say, That Tramps will be searched, bathed, detained two days, and required to break 10 cwt of Stone at the Wincanton Workhouse That as a further inducement to patronise that hospitable establishment it is proposed to include free vaccination. That suitable light work will be found for

lady-tramps – they being required to pick at least 12 lbs of oakum."

The presence of vagrants in the Wincanton Workhouse did create some problems for the Master and Matron, in November 1862, for example, George Lee was charged before Magistrates, who were also Guardians, often Charles Barton and T.E. Rogers, with disorderly conduct and received twenty-one days in Shepton Mallet Gaol. In November 1870 Charles Edwards received seven days with hard labour for misbehaviour in the Workhouse and George Adams and Henry Prince fourteen days each with hard labour also for misbehaviour in January 1871. Occasionally a vagrant was charged with insubordination if he refused to do the task allotted, such as Christian Walker, "a German", in April 1886 and he too received seven days with hard labour. It was much more common for vagrants to destroy their own clothes in the Workhouse in the hope of receiving new ones and that too usually resulted in seven or fourteen days with hard labour, as Adam Wilson of Manchester and Alfred Sims of Newhaven found in June 1868, William Francis, Henry Williams and Frederick Hillier in November 1870 and Thomas Morgan and William Hayes in February 1886. In fact between 1st February 1884 and 3rd March 1886 nine vagrants were successfully prosecuted for this offence. George Bennett may well have expressed the views of other vagrants when he "said he was very sorry but there was no other way of getting clothes, and his old clothes were really indecent." The Porter, on the other hand, told the Magistrates that tearing up clothes was a way of escaping their morning's work and in May 1881 Bennett was accordingly sentenced to fourteen days with hard labour.

One interesting innovation, presumably designed to stop the destruction of clothes, to save money and to cause maximum humiliation was used in 1863, having operated earlier in the Yeovil Union. In October of that year three tramps, John Stone, George Walker and Robert Casson, were brought before magistrates in a "Union suit", having destroyed their own clothes. The Master claimed that he could not afford to keep providing clothes and requested that they be placed in sacks,

"An Order was made that they be placed in sacks, and taken to gaol for a fortnight. The men vowed they would never submit to a sack being put over their heads, and said they had broken their own clothes because they were too filthy and ragged to be worn. They were taken to the lock-up, where three new sack-bags were procured, arm-holes and head-holes cut in them, and they were gently slipped over the head of each prisoner, and thus, amidst the laughter of the crowd, they were driven, in an open vehicle, to Shepton Mallet."

How many times this was done or for how long is not recorded.

On rare occasions a notable character emerged amongst the tramps. On 2nd February 1846 Dame Burton died in the Workhouse aged ninety-five years. She was "known as the Gypsy Queen of the West", had eleven children and some seventy grandchildren and great grandchildren. She and her husband had been brought to the House from Henstridge "where they were found on one of the coldest days of that severe winter, within their tent almost exhausted." (25) Her husband, Harry Burton the 'King of the Gypsies', died in the workhouse in July of the following year aged ninety-four.

9. Offences, Crimes and Punishment

a) Offences

The Poor Law Commissioners insisted that strict discipline must be maintained in the workhouses as this was seen as one aspect of deterrence. In the years after 1834 they issued rules and regulations which covered every moment and activity of the pauper day, from early rising to early retiring. The maintenance of discipline was a difficult matter in a workhouse as inevitably these rules and regulations caused resentment and irritation and in addition some of the inmates were unused to such restrictions and communal living. A fluctuating population was more difficult to control than the more stable one found in other institutions such as asylums and some of the inmates undoubtedly had mild to severe mental health problems.

The Wincanton Board followed rigidly the Orders of the Central Board and soon had a long list of offences which fell into two broad categories: disorderly and refractory. Amongst offences deemed disorderly were making a noise when silence was required, using obscene or profane language, threatening another person, refusing to work, playing cards and disobeying an order from an official. Refractory ones included insulting the Master or Matron, assaulting any person, being drunk, damaging Guardian property and committing an act of indecency.

Throughout the nineteenth century clothes remained an issue. Up to the early 1850s inmates absconding with Workhouse clothes was the problem, for example, in June 1842 John Willis left the House with Workhouse clothes which he subsequently sold to Henry Sandy and Isaac Vining. All were caught and either imprisoned or fined. The following month two boys, Cane and Thompson, absconded with Union clothes but were caught and sent back. Absconding and selling the clothes had become so organised by young lads by 1850 that the Guardians decided to mark the clothes in a concealed place. The result was that absconding with clothes significantly declined although still occurred as was recorded in 1851 when Elizabeth Longman, "a pauper of weak intellect," disappeared. She was subsequently found dead in a plantation of Knoyle Down Farm in Wiltshire. In July 1857 James Stacey was sentenced to twenty-one days with hard labour for absconding "taking with him a Waistcoat, shirt and a pair of Stockings." He had already served three weeks in August 1852 for a similar offence.

By the mid-1860s the commonest problem in relation to clothes was inmates destroying either their own or Union ones. Such a situation had occurred before as in August 1840 the Master reported, "the wilful destruction of wearing apparel by Paupers in the house", and was ordered to keep careful lists when clothes were given out or changed. The majority of those involved in tearing up their own clothes were vagrants who hoped to obtain better ones but others were ordinary inmates such as Ann Wilson and Alfred Sims in June 1868, George Webb in March 1870 who also argued that his own clothes were rags, and James Woodforde in November 1881. Each was sent to Shepton Mallet Gaol for periods of seven or fourteen days.

Damage occurred within workhouses themselves and in some parts of the country it was seen as a protest against the Workhouse System itself. There is no evidence for this in Wincanton as most of the episodes seem to relate to a specific grievance usually affecting an individual. In January 1841 John Hutchings "destroyed the refractory Ward door" when he was locked in there for another offence. The result was that the Guardians decided to have the doors of the Refractory Wards lined with iron to prevent a similar occurrence. In November 1853 James Stacey served six weeks with hard labour for damaging a Mantle piece in the Workhouse. In June 1872 John Gould, who was regarded as a persistent troublemaker, tore up three bed sheets in a fit of rage which led to one month in prison. Richard Lewis, a long-term inmate, was another persistent offender in a number of areas, as far as the authorities were concerned. In

November 1888 he caused damage valued at 15s to a ceiling and roof in the Workhouse for which he received six weeks with hard labour. In March 1891 he "damaged the floor of the bedroom by scraping his boots over it", and in September 1894 received fourteen days with hard labour for unspecified, "Wilful damage."

The Ledgers and Minute Books indicate that the services of a joiner and glazier were in constant demand at a level which would seem to have far surpassed accidental damage, normal wear and tear and deterioration through age. Every month, for example between July 1857 and June 1858 T. Francis, a glazier, submitted bills which ranged between 1s 9d and £6 7s 8d, in total £13 15s 5d. In fact in 1881 John Gould spent fourteen days in prison for smashing twelve squares of glass. Potentially the most serious incident occurred two year earlier when the store-room door was set on fire during the night. Theft was the obvious cause and as all the outside doors were locked two inmates were suspected but there was insufficient evidence to proceed. It was reported, "The panels of the door were burnt away, and damage to the extent of about £2 done."

As so many of the inmates were in the Workhouse as a result of destitution, for some the temptation to steal was too great, as has already been seen in the case of clothes and the store-room but there were many other instances. The first decade was to witness stealing of items both inside and outside of the House. In May 1838 William Ashford was prosecuted for stealing a pair of shoes from the stores, as well as absconding in Union clothes. A far more extensive theft occurred in June 1842 when fourteen out of thirty pairs of trousers were stolen from the same stores and as no inmates were prosecuted the Master himself was held responsible for negligence and had to pay the cost of the trousers which amounted to £4. These two incidents suggest not only individual desperation but also more organised activity.

Charles Willis appeared particularly inept as a thief as he was committed to jail for stealing a pan inside the Workhouse in January 1844, having the previous March served another sentence for gaining access to the Men's Yard over the wall and stealing a quantity of bones which were to be crushed. In 1839 Charles Francis and William Roper were sentenced to three months when found in the Workhouse gardens attempting to steal potatoes. Of especial interest outside of the Workhouse was the copper wire on which clothes were hung in the Drying Ground at the back of the House. In March 1841 about fifty yards of this wire was stolen along with a mason's trowel but despite offering a reward of a Guinea no one was caught. The Guardians were more successful the following year when Thomas Read, a pauper, stole some copper wire in September and in November at the Wells Sessions he was sentenced to ten years transportation, having been previously convicted of a felony. The same punishment was inflicted on Henry Ridwood, aged forty-one, in 1847 when he too stole some copper wire.

As all the able-bodied were required to work, refusal to do so was regarded as unacceptable. Cases of such refusal occur throughout the decades after 1834 but relatively few were recorded, possibly as in the early days they were classed as 'insubordination' rather than refusal to work. Cases brought in front of the magistrates involving able-bodied adults such as vagrants usually resulted in a sentence of seven days with hard labour in Shepton Mallet Gaol, as Christian Walker found in April 1866 and Thomas Leadbeater in September 1897. February 1896 must have been a difficult period as on the 14th of that month eight casual paupers refused to work and each received seven days with hard labour. Most of the regular inmates who reached the prosecution stage for refusal to work seem to have been female, such as Eliza Ann Parsons in May 1882, Louisa Forward, a thirty-year old servant from Cucklington in July 1893 and Annie Hill, a twenty-seven year old charwoman from Yarlington in February 1895. Occasionally there were men such as Edward Combe, a fifty-nine year old labourer from North Cheriton. Most received seven days with hard labour but Jane Kiddle, aged forty, for some reason received twenty-one days with hard labour in October 1856. Other paupers who were not regular offenders were either locked in the Refractory Ward for a period of time on bread and water, as happened to Chamberlain in January 1892, or received a verbal warning from the Board of Guardians as in the case of Bracher in March 1898. Verbal warnings were usually given to children who failed to do their work, such as B. Forward.

Acts of violence and physical assaults seem to have been very sporadic in the Wincanton Workhouse. In a number of instances being required to undertake a task was the starting point, for example, when a vagrant, George Thompson, was allotted his work in October 1868 he refused, ran off, but was caught by the Porter whom he knocked down and kicked several times in the ribs. For this offence he was sentenced to three weeks with hard labour at Shepton Mallet. In October 1893 Ernest Ridout, aged sixty-two, received fourteen days with hard labour for "unlawfully striking another inmate". In May 1895 a lad called Thomas Herbert, aged sixteen, refused to work and then kicked a male pauper, John Cross, which led to a visit to the magistrates' court and seven days with hard labour.

Other assaults were recorded but no hint given of causation, especially if they were between paupers, but living in close proximity for such long periods may have had some bearing. In April 1878 Maria Hewitt was sentenced to twenty-one days with hard labour for an assault upon an infant child named George Mead. In March 1896 it was reported to the Board that Hannah Curtis had struck Sarah Pickford, which resulted in her being locked up for twelve hours on bread and water. The year before Annie Hill had hit Eliza Trim on the head with a stool after having her hair pulled, "The girl was told she must not give way to her temper." There may have been a sexual element in May 1893 when Elizabeth Chamberlain complained that Alfred Clothier "had assaulted her in the dining Hall in a very indecent manner." Despite Clothier's denials he was taken before magistrates and sentenced to twenty-one days with hard labour.

Physical assaults upon the officers in the Workhouse were also rare. One came to light in February 1841 when Charles Willis complained that the Schoolmistress had flogged his ten-year old son, Edward. Several pauper witnesses gave evidence to the Board that the boy had not been punished improperly as he had received a slap on the side of the face. One pauper commented, "If my child behaved as Willis' child did I should have punished it as the Schoolmistress did." It emerged that the child had deliberately kicked her. In June 1872 John Gould, who was reported to be "of a very violent disposition" and subject to fits, threatened to stab the Nurse with a knife "and became so violent that he had to be put in a straight jacket." He received a sentence of one month. This is one of the very few references which have survived of a means of physical restraint being available and used in the Workhouse. In May 1893 Ernest Ridout was sentenced to seven days with hard labour for assaulting the Porter, William Roodhouse, and in November 1897 George Yates received one calendar month for assaulting and beating a later Porter, Ben Mount. A very small number of inmates may have had a problem with either their own temper or authority. In December 1895 Eliza Trim, a domestic servant from Wincanton aged twenty-four, assaulted the Matron, Selina Barnes, and received seven days with hard labour and the following year she assaulted the Cook, Mrs Dymock, when refusing to light the fire in the laundry. She was sent back to prison for another seven days.

An unpleasant episode occurred in 1874 which involved three inmates, Richard Lewis, Joseph Foot and William Mead. It started when Lewis complained about his soup, became abusive, refused to leave the Dining Hall and was violent when the Porter and Master tried to expel him. Foot joined in to help Lewis, ran after the Master, threatened him and struck the Porter. At the same time "Mead got a stone hammer and threatened to beat the Master's brains out with it." Each was sentenced to six weeks with hard labour but on hearing this "Lewis and Foot violently resisted the police and it required the aid of six or seven constables to hand bolt them." Their sentences were increased to two months.

Verbal assaults were much more common than physical ones, sometimes between inmates, although few of these were officially reported, and sometimes directed against the officers. In April 1894 one pauper Louisa Forward complained that another, Eliza Trim, had "called her abusive names on several occasions." Trim was warned not to use bad language again. Insolence towards the officers was particularly prevalent in the 1890s, possibly as the result of a series of staff changes and the removal of the Schoolmistress. In January 1892 both the Matron and the Cook reported a pauper female, Chamberlain, as being insolent and in March the Matron made the same complaint against two other women, Parsons and Forward. The usual punishment was confinement on bread and water for periods of up to twenty-four hours. A few instances were taken more seriously and in these cases inmates ended up in front of the magistrates: in April 1889 Charles Morris, aged twenty-three, was sentenced to seven days with hard labour for threatening the Porter; in October 1899 John Balch, aged sixty-six, received the same for abusive language toward the Male Attendant, H. Grant, his age in this instance did not save him. Another punishment could be a warning if the incident was judged not to be too serious so when the Master reported a male pauper Lemon for insolence in August 1893 he just received a warning, which may also have taken in account the fact that he was aged and infirm. The same happened to another aged and infirm pauper, John Balch in February 1895 when the Nurse complained that his language had been both abusive and obscene, this time his age saved him.

When Charles Willis failed to have action taken against the Schoolmistress in 1841, he used "abusive language" to the Master which earned him three hours in the Refractory Ward. The Visiting Committee noted in May 1893 that, "George Bottle has been making use of unbecoming language to the officers & others," and three years later the Male Attendant, Smart, complained that Allen, a male pauper, had used bad language. In August 1844 Thomas Cox was ordered to leave the Workhouse when he was found "guilty of uttering unwarrantable insinuations relative to the Schoolmistress," especially as he appeared to have a pension which he could use to maintain himself.

As there were so many rules and regulations it was inevitable that paupers would be in breach of them from time to time, especially as some of the inmates would resent either being there or some aspect of their treatment. Unfortunately in many instances a broad word such as 'disorderly' or 'misbehaviour' was used which gave no indication of what actually happened: William White, aged thirty-three, was sentenced to ten days with hard labour in January 1847; James Stacey, aged fifty-six, to twenty-one days in January 1853 and another fourteen days with hard labour in May; John Hamblin and Joseph Robins received fourteen days and ten days respectively in January 1854; Charles Edwards seven days for misbehaviour in November 1870 and George Shire fourteen days a year later. Between June 1873 and October 1874 five more cases were heard. In November 1862 George Lee received twenty-one days for disorderly conduct and in July 1893 Louisa Forward was taken in front of magistrates for "Misbehaviour & Disorderly conduct," with no explanation being given. Court papers and the Guardians' Minute Books clearly indicate that through the decades the magistrates received a constant stream of inmates from the Workhouse on this type of charge.

Just occasionally a glimpse was given of the actions behind the charges, In July 1886 Richard Lewis was once again charged with misbehaviour and since becoming an inmate in 1871 it was alleged that he "has often caused much trouble and annoyance." On this occasion he had thrown his soup on the floor shouting, "This is some of Barnes's and Barton's robbery." (Barnes was the Master and Barton Chairman of the Board.) Lewis interrupted the Court proceedings at this point to declare that he had not said that at all but rather, "I said Barnes and Barton are two thieves and murderers." It was also alleged that he had tried to kick open a door but it was locked. For all this he was sentenced to six weeks with hard labour. Three years later he was back on the disorderly conduct charge when he threatened the Master and Porter.

Acts of indecency were regarded as being refractory and so in September 1836 Jonah Thompson was committed for one month "for indecently exposing his person to a female in the house." He followed this up six years later by committing the refractory offence of returning drunk to the Workhouse after being granted a day's leave of absence and for this he was placed in the Refractory Ward for twelve hours. Being absent from the Workhouse without permission could lead to imprisonment as happened to Luke Cannon in July 1881 when he was sentenced to ten days with hard labour. In January 1890 Joseph Everett, a labourer aged twenty-nine, received fourteen days for the same offence, by this time it was recorded that he had already twenty-six previous convictions.

In all these cases it was just individuals or two or three inmates involved but on two occasions the disobedience was more widespread. In both instances, however, it related to a specific grievance rather than any attempt to undermine the system or the Workhouse. In February 1841 all the able-bodied men occupied the Old Men's Day Room and refused to work, "alleging that their gruel for breakfast on that day was not good." The Clerk refused to listen until the men returned to work and sent the Master to fetch the Constables. On hearing this the men returned to their tasks and the Clerk sampled the gruel which he found to be very good. In July 1877 the Porter, David Jones, who was under threat of dismissal, went so far as to allege that, "the House is very often nearly in a Mutiny." He claimed that the Master treated some of the inmates too harshly but the Guardians could find no evidence for this and no general unrest surfaced. (26)

b) Punishments

The Poor Law Commissioners directed that any pauper found guilty of an offence categorized as 'disorderly' should be deprived of their normal diet for up to forty-eight hours and receive instead bread and water. For refractory offences the pauper was to be confined in a separate room, usually referred to as the Refractory Ward, with or without a change to their diet. Cases had to be recorded in log books which were shown weekly to the Board of Guardians and more serious cases taken in front of magistrates. For those receiving medical care, who were under twelve or above sixty years of age the sanction of the Medical Officer had to be obtained and corporal punishment could only be inflicted on children under fourteen by the Master or Schoolmaster.

The Wincanton Board issued their own Rules and Regulations which broadly followed those prescribed by the Poor Law Commissioners. As early as June 1836 they resolved that for a first offence a pauper should "be fed of Bread and Water for the space of one day" and for a second and subsequent offences be placed in the Refractory Ward for up to twenty-four hours and then, if necessary, taken before a local magistrate. The exact period in the Refractory Ward was left to the discretion of the Master, "having an especial regard to the health of the Pauper, the state of the weather and the nature of the offence." When the new Workhouse was completed they reiterated these Rules and Regulations in July 1838. The reference to the weather is interesting and probably derives from the fact that there was no form of heating in the Refractory Wards.

Wincanton Workhouse had two Refractory Wards or Cells, one for males and one for females, both of which had the usual deal seats around the edge and no other furniture. The original building specification required that there was "on the outside a strong Padlock and Staples." The male Ward, which opened directly from the southern side of the Men's Yard next to the stone breaking cell, was some fourteen feet long by six feet six inches wide. The female Ward was in the north-west corner of the Able-Bodied Women's Yard, just beyond the women's three W.C.s and was some eleven feet six inches long at its maximum extent and eight feet wide, with a very small window, presumably with bars. A Plan of 1898 does not show a window in the walls of the male Ward so it is possible that some light entered through a small aperture in the door. The Guardians obviously intended to keep these paupers usefully employed as in January 1847 the Clerk was instructed to purchase "half a Ton of Oakum for the occasional employment of Able-bodied Paupers reported disorderly and refractory by the Master." They also required the Master to bring before them each week all those who were reported disorderly and refractory so that they could warn them about the consequences of their actions.

The Wincanton Board added a further regulation in May 1842

relating to disorderly and refractory paupers which contained an element of humiliation, "Every such Pauper shall eat his Meals, during two days, standing at a table in the dining hall, facing the other Paupers and wearing a cap with the word disorderly or refractory printed or written thereon in legible Characters." How long this particular practice continued is not clear. Certainly deprivation of the normal diet remained the standard punishment for decades, for example, when a girl made an unfounded allegation against the Schoolmistress in May 1866 it was ordered that, "she be deprived of her meat dinners for one week." A Return in 1872 gave "stopping food" as a punishment for paupers refusing to do their work.

The Guardians appear to have conformed to the requirements on corporal punishment as references to abuses in this area are extremely rare. One did occur, however, in October 1843 when William Hiscock complained about the punishment inflicted upon his son and as a result of an investigation by the Board the Master was admonished. They were of course prepared to sanction physical restraints for inmates perceived at times to be dangerous to themselves or others so for example by 1872 they possessed a strait jacket which in that year was used on John Gould and in March 1897 they purchased a pair of handcuffs to restrain a violent tramp, reported in a local newspaper to be six pairs.

The destruction of so many of the relevant books makes it impossible to determine the number of paupers who were judged to be disorderly and/or refractory and how many were subsequently charged in the local magistrates' court. One Return, which covered the period from March 1835 to March 1842, shows that thirty-two inmates from Wincanton Workhouse were committed for a range of offences, see Table 18a. The period of detention imposed by the Justices of the Peace may be seen in Table 18b.

Table 18a.   Inmates committed to Prison, 1835-1842

	Under 20 years of age	Over 20 years of age
Misbehaviour, Drunken & Disorderly Conduct, Wilful damage, refusal to work	2	8
Assault and breach of the peace	1	0
Deserting or Deserting taking Union clothing	13	7
Theft	0	1
Total	16	16

Table 18b.   Periods of Detention 1835-1842

Discharged	0
14 days and under	4
1 month and under	10
2 months and under	14
3 months and under	3
6 months and under	1
Over 6 months	0
Total	32

A Return for 1852 indicated that five inmates were imprisoned for offences in the Workhouse so the number per year appears to have remained fairly constant.

The Poor Law Commissioners insisted upon strict discipline within workhouses and the evidence suggests that the Wincanton Board complied in this area. They had no hesitation in taking offenders before local magistrates where, as Table 18b. shows over 56% received a sentence of one month or more, compared with 48% for Somerset as a whole, both of which were much greater than the national figure of 21%. This may suggest that either West County magistrates were more severe in their sentences than elsewhere or that far more less serious offences were being taken to the courts in other parts of the country. (27)

In the Wincanton Union the composition of the Board of Guardians meant that the inmates were often tried and sentenced by some of the same men who had sent them for trial, most notably for over forty years the Chairman and Vice Chairman of the Board, Charles Barton and T.E. Rogers, who were both ex-officio members of the Board as they were local magistrates. As the Guardians regularly dispatched paupers to the magistrates' court, there is no reason to suppose that they allowed their Workhouse officers any degree of leniency in the enforcement of internal punishments. Such attitudes may be seen as part of social control by which the poor were reminded that there was a strict hierarchy and any deviation from the required behaviour would not be tolerated. On the other hand, there is no evidence to suggest that the officers in this House were excessively severe or in any organized way deliberately abused their authority. Rules and regulations were in place and in this area they were prepared to enforce them to the letter.

10. Sex and Cruelty

a) Sex

An important feature of the New Poor Law was the classification of paupers in the workhouses which led not only to the separation of children from their parents but also to the separation of the sexes. It was immediately apparent to those involved in the new system that it would be economically impossible to construct an institution at that time which gave each married couple a separate room. In addition, of course, the authorities did not want to encourage the paupers to have more children who would themselves became chargeable to the Poor Rates and for morality's sake unmarried men and women had to be segregated.

It soon became clear, however, that, probably through the inexperience of the architects with this new type of building, the designs for the workhouses were inadequate for rigid segregation: Day Rooms for boys and girls frequently had windows which overlooked the yards of the men and women and contact could take place in the Dining Hall, in spite of the rule of silence. For the first thirty years or so of its existence little was said about the classification in the Wincanton Workhouse but as attitudes at the centre began to change for the next thirty years there was almost annual criticism of the arrangements in this House, but there was also the resigned acceptance that little could be done without major rebuilding which the ratepayers would not contemplate. From time to time there was also the suggestion that the Master, and possibly some of the Guardians themselves, were none too concerned about rigid classification for all groups, for example, in February 1850 the Poor Law Board reprimanded the Master for his lack of "the enforcement of proper classification."

By the end of the nineteenth century the concern expressed repeatedly by the Inspectors was not that there was contact between the sexes but that the lack of classification led to the demoralization of those who to that point had led blameless lives. In 1895 Inspector Courtenay stressed that the Guardians must find ways of separating "deserted women of good character and young women with their first children from the idle, dissolute and ill-conditioned inmates." By 1898 Inspector Preston-Thomas felt that most Boards of Guardians in his area had been attempting "to keep young girls who have not 'lost their character' or those who have come to be delivered of a first child, from the more depraved and hardened women." Such separation in the Wincanton Workhouse was far from successful for in 1909 the Chaplain complained that the moral life of the children was "distinctly bad." He believed that, "The girls cannot be kept separate enough from the women, young and old, whose conversation and way of looking at life is often demoralizing, nor the boys from the men." He went on to lament that as a result, "the proportion of children who turn out well is disappointing," although he also in part attributed this to "hereditary tendencies." The only somewhat limited action which the Guardians had taken as early as 1866 was to order that the door between the Girls' and Women's Yards be kept locked.

In addition to this theoretical contamination there was in rare instances what was judged to be inappropriate physical contact. In January 1850 the Master had to report to the Board of Guardians that Harriet Short, a long time inmate, had become pregnant by Joseph Coles, a married inmate. Upon investigation the Board found that the two had been alone in an outbuilding where straw for the beds was stored when the former went there to have some mattresses filled. Coles blamed the incident entirely upon Short but in the end it was the Master who was criticized for allowing them to be together in such a place without adequate supervision.

More frequently reported were relationships between an inmate and an officer. As early as December 1840 a former inmate, Mary Ann Thomas, who was in the Shepton Mallet House of Correction awaiting trial for larceny, alleged that while she was in the Workhouse, the Master "had had improper connexion with her." The

Master, supported by the Matron, strenuously denied the allegation and another inmate stated that while Thomas had originally claimed that the Master "had taken liberties with her," she later denied that she had ever said so. The Board decided that the accusation was "wholly untrue and a vile fabrication." An allegation against the Schoolmaster, Benjamin Sims, in 1872 had more substance when it was claimed that a woman had been in his bedroom on more than one occasion when he was there. Sims did not deny the charge and was allowed to resign.

Accusations against the Porters were more common and all proved to be correct, which may have called into question the policy of appointing only single men, a policy which did not vary until 1891. In April 1855 the Porter, David King, was accused of having a single mother, Sarah Parsons, in his bedroom and also of meeting her at the New Inn in Wincanton. While he admitted the latter he denied the former but as the Board saw no reason to doubt the evidence of two pauper witnesses he was dismissed. A later Porter, George Stone, had already left the Guardians' employment when Sarah Jane Davis gave birth to an illegitimate child and claimed that Stone was the father.

In November 1876 another Porter, David Jones, was dismissed for "direct disobedience" as he had been ordered to bring a pregnant pauper, Maria Hewitt, to the Boardroom. She refused to go and he declined to force her but when the Relieving Officers went to get her she came without any trouble. Jones had had what the Guardians called "an improper intimacy" with her, the result of which was an illegitimate child. In February 1877 the Board initiated proceedings against Jones to compel him to maintain the child and 2s a week was fixed. Jones however did not go quietly and in the months which followed he made a series of allegations against the Master, none of which were substantiated by the Local Government Board, relying heavily upon the observations of the Guardians. Another Porter, Harry Norris, resigned in August 1891 when the Matron reported that Eliza Jane Parsons had been found in his bedroom at 9.30 pm. Parsons's punishment was to be confined for twenty-four hours on bread and water.

At this point the Guardians decided to appoint a Porter who was married, with his wife becoming the Cook. It did not always prove possible to maintain this arrangement in the 1890s and one subsequent single Porter, Mitchell, was appointed in November 1894 but he too was dismissed in March 1895 for improper sexual relations, this time with the single Cook, Alice Weare. Both of them were found by the Matron in the early morning outside of the Porter's bedroom door in their nightclothes and it was also discovered that the Cook's bed had not been slept in. The Cook was also dismissed and another married couple appointed.

One other incident of supposed sexual misconduct related to the first Master, Simeon Gulley. In 1837 as the health of the Matron, Susan Gulley, started to deteriorate she was granted leave of absence for one month in July to undertake sea-bathing, which was recommended by the Medical Officer of the Workhouse. It proved unsuccessful and in October she died. For six weeks Mary Ann James acted as Matron and then in December Hannah Avis, a widow who was the only candidate, was appointed on a three months' trial. Early in March 1838 the Guardians heard reports "derogatory to the Master of the Workhouse in reference to Miss Baker of Wincanton." A Committee was established to investigate and decided that the Master should be admonished, that Miss Baker should not visit him in the Workhouse, "that the conduct of the Master had been highly indiscreet and reprehensible but they had no evidence of an circumstance criminality." Three months later Gulley resigned when he married Miss Baker. As the acting Matron could not write legibly the Board decided to advertize for a married couple as Master and Matron. Gulley must have been extremely dissatisfied with the actions of the Guardians, partly because there was no evidence that he had started another relationship while his wife was alive and he only began seeing Miss Baker when he was a widower, and partly as he was not permitted to continue as Master with his second wife as the new Matron even though they applied for the posts. Before the new Master and Matron, the Sealeys, could take office Gulley made some allegations "prejudicial to the moral Character of James

Sealey." When the Board investigated these they were found to be groundless. Over a year later in November 1839 Gulley presented the Guardians with a bill for provisions he claimed he had purchased between May 1836 and May 1838. As the Clerk could find no record of such purchases the Board declined to pay him anything.

b) Cruelty

There were periodic allegations of ill-treatment in the Wincanton Workhouse, significantly from inmates rather than from any of the Guardians, Visitors or local residents. As has been seen, cases of alleged assault occurred throughout the nineteenth century and the corporal punishment inflicted upon the boys up to fourteen years of age, may also fall into this category, as does placing a child in a cold bath for bed-wetting. After a stillborn child was born an allegation was made against the Matron in November 1891 that she had overworked a pregnant woman but when the complaint was investigated the Guardians found that there were no grounds for it. The death by scalding of a three- year old boy, Ernest White, in the same year was due more to neglect rather than to deliberate cruelty. The Guardians found that there was no system in place to test the temperature of the water and that the sole care of the bath rested with an imbecile. The Coroner concluded that due care had not been taken but the events irritated the local press as the Guardians refused to disclose the results of their investigation or admit the press to their meetings.

In the months following his dismissal late in 1876 the Porter, David Jones made a series of allegations against the Master, John Barnes. Some related to him staying out until the early hours of the morning and others that he kept thirty to forty pigeons at the Workhouse which consumed about a quart of peas a day that he took from the stores. Much more serious were the allegations which related to cruelty:

> "The Master was often very cruel to some of the Inmates in keeping them in the Receiving Ward locked up for a day or

two after the Medical Officer had passed them to some other part of the House."

He claimed that the Guardians did not know that was happening as they did not visit the Workhouse frequently enough. He then proceeded to cite specific examples, "in one case the Master ordered me to hit a Man's Eyes out because the man did not obey his orders soon enough." In a letter the following month, " Also that the Master was very cruel to the Inmates. Some of the Boys he used to kick about shamefully. A boy of the name of Henry Mead was ill treated very much by him." This boy in fact complained to magistrates but on being told to produce witnesses did not proceed with the allegation. The Local Government Board asked the Guardians to comment and in the light of their response took no action.

This case of David Jones illustrates very clearly one of the two ways in which allegations of ill treatment were dealt with, namely a letter straight to the Central Board. Invariably the Central Board would pass a copy of the letter to the Guardians and require their observations. Generally the Guardians tended to denigrate the character of the writer, whether officer or inmate, and on most occasions this approach worked as the matter was taken no further. This hostile reaction from the Guardians is probably an indication of the Board's determination to manage its own affairs and not to allow undue interference from a central authority. In some cases the reputation of a particular inmate was so bad that the Guardians did not need to go into any detail, so for example, when Richard Lewis alleged in August 1895 that the Matron had struck a boy with a stick and "laid violent hands on a cripple woman Elizabeth Lancaster," the Clerk made a simple reply, "there were no grounds, that Lewis is not in any way worthy of credit."

The second way in which an allegation of ill treatment was dealt with was through an internal complaint made directly to the Board of Guardians. In these cases almost invariably the Board would investigate: some of the allegations they found groundless, often based upon motives of revenge or spite; whereas some they found proved and took prompt, if not drastic action, for example in 1850 when the Schoolmaster, Frederick Cox, flogged a boy in breach of the regulations he was admonished. In other instances they investigated and found insufficient evidence to proceed, for example in May 1893 Samuel Whitlock claimed that the Master had assaulted him, used abusive language and was drunk. The Board investigated the charges and "found that they could not be supported by any satisfactory evidence."

There appear to have been no cases of deliberate ill treatment in the Wincanton Workhouse. When ill treatment did occur it was usually the result of negligence or the momentary loss of control which resulted from living and working in such an institution. All were expected to follow a rigid code of discipline, although at times this does appear to have been implemented with some degree of laxity, especially in the area of classification. The Guardians may not have been over-rigorous in their inspection of the House and so the possibility of the ill treatment of some inmates by others was always there. The number of such cases which manifested themselves in assaults remained very small. (28)

11. Religion and Death

a) Religion

In some areas of the country, such as East Anglia, religion was a source of contention in workhouses but this does not seem to have been the case in Wincanton where the Board of Guardians, while remaining staunchly Church of England, permitted contact with other churches. Non-Conformity was well established in this part of Somerset, especially with the Independents (later Congregationalists) and Methodists. The Religious Census of 1851 showed that there was a total of thirty-three Non-Conformist chapels in twenty-two out of the thirty-nine parishes in the Union and together accounted for some 35.7% of all seats in places of worship. On a day-count in 1851 Non-Conformists accounted for 35.6% of attendance.

With such a non-conformist presence in the area, the Wincanton Board decided in 1836 to allow both a clergyman of the Church of England and a Licensed Minister access to the old Poorhouse. The following year the Poor Law Commissioners made it perfectly clear that they disapproved of the practice of allowing paupers to attend the local church once a chaplain had been appointed but the Wincanton Board decided to ignore this recommendation so that, when the new Workhouse was opened in 1838, they resolved, "all such Paupers as are able shall attend divine worship in the Parish Church of Wincanton at least once every Sunday", although this did exclude the able-bodied males and females as it was feared that good behaviour might not always be achieved with them. The other inmates had to be accompanied either by the Master or the Matron. The Board amended this resolution in 1842 by adding Christmas Day and Good Friday to the attendance list. To ensure the "observance of order and decorum" the Paupers were lined up in the Workhouse grounds before passing through the outer gate. They were required to be in the Church five minutes before the service commenced and were not permitted to leave until the rest of the congregation had departed. They were to be seen to be part of the community but they had to know their place. Significantly at the same time Non-Conformists, or Dissenters as they were usually called, were permitted "to attend public worship at any dissenting chapel in the neighbourhood of the Workhouse", provided that they took with them a certificate to be signed by the Minister or a Deacon of the Chapel, indicating time of arrival and of departure. Permission for attendance at other churches also included Roman Catholics and by the late 1850s Roman Catholic priests could be admitted to the Workhouse to give instruction, if a request was submitted.

In fact very few Non-Conformist or Roman Catholics were in the Workhouse at any one time in relation to the number who were recorded as being members of the Church of England. Table 19 gives an indication for a sample number of years.

Until a Creed Register was introduced in 1869 figures are taken from Admission and Discharge Books, along with various Returns and Reports. The figures give general trends but are at times misleading as a pauper might be admitted and discharged more than once in a year. There was, for example, only one Deist, Richard Lewis, who was admitted on three separate occasions during 1890.

Statistics reveal that of the 1,270 paupers admitted between January 1870 and December 1873, 89% professed to be members of the Church of England, 10.6% Protestant Dissenters and 0.4% Roman Catholics. Percentages for admission from January 1890 to December 1892 were similar with 89.3% Church of England, 9.9% Protestant Dissenters and 0.8% Roman Catholic. These percentages for denominations other than the Church of England are much lower than for England and Wales, which was, for example, 20.8% in 1875. Groups such as the Independents and Methodists encouraged a work ethic amongst their members and as these groups were strong in the Wincanton Union it may help to explain the difference. In addition they were also more adept at ministering to their own members in time of need through a highly developed communal spirit and this may also have helped to keep their members out of the Workhouse.

Table 19. Religious Beliefs of those admitted to the Workhouse

Religion	1836	1837	1838	1861	1866	1870	1875	1880	1885	1890	1895
Church of England	148	187	224	96	120	329	218	215	105	162	134
Baptist	1		1			2	3	3	3		
Methodist						7	4				
Roman Catholic						1	3		3	2	
Independent						3	3	3	3		4
Wesleyan Methodist							30	22	3	15	17
Primitive Methodist							2	1	1	2	
Presbyterian							1				
Salvation Army									1		
Deist										3	1

With so many paupers professing to be members of the Church of England the Wincanton Board had no hesitation in appointing as their first Chaplain the Vicar of Wincanton, the Revd. William Carpenter, at a salary of £25 a year, increased to £40 a year when the new Workhouse was completed in 1838 and to £50 in 1872. As the Guardians considered the proximity of a clergyman to be important almost without exception successive Vicars of Wincanton , or their curates, became the Chaplain to the Workhouse for the rest of the century. In very rare instances they went further afield, for example, between September 1872 and June 1873 the Rector of North Cheriton, the Revd. Thomas Gatehouse, acted as Chaplain.

The duties of the Chaplain were carefully laid down so that from 1838 he was required

> "to read the full divine Service and preach a sermon to the Paupers in the Workhouse every Sunday morning commencing at Nine or before eleven and also every Thursday afternoon in every week commencing at two or by three."

Services were held in the Dining Hall until the completion of the new Schoolroom block in 1871 when they transferred there. By the mid-1860s it was recorded that the Chaplain also visited on Tuesdays. The Poor Law Commissioners required the Chaplain to superintend the moral and religious state of the inmates, to direct the religious instruction of the children, and to administer spiritual counsel and comfort to the aged, infirm and sick. Such a requirement meant a few additional visits and a Return for 1880 indicated that the Wincanton Chaplain visited the Workhouse on average thirteen times each month, staying approximately fifty-five minutes each time. This number of visits was very similar to those of Chaplains for the other Unions in Somerset but in those workhouses the visits lasted just over an hour. This suggests that the spiritual attention given to the inmates was generally very limited, although in the 1840s the Chaplain was not slow to point out the deficiencies in the education the children were receiving.

Relations between the Board of Guardians and the Chaplain seem to have remained good throughout the period except on odd occasions. Twice in the 1880s for example the Guardians felt the need to draw to the attention of the Chaplain his failure to visit the Workhouse sufficiently and to remind him that his duties were laid down by the Local Government Board. The most serious dispute arose in January 1897 when, as a result of falling numbers, as an economy measure and possibly as the result of an increase in the number of Non-Conformist Guardians, it was proposed to reduce the salary of the new Chaplain, the Revd. Walter Farrer, to £30. Farrer refused to accept, undertook some research which revealed that in the whole of the West Country only one Union in Dorset paid such a low salary. It was then suggested that volunteers, including Non-Conformists could serve as unpaid chaplains. This suggestion produced a furious debate which culminated in the resignation of T.E. Rogers, the Vice-Chairman, who was also the Chancellor of Wells Cathedral, declaring,

> "Chaplains of public institutions are always clergymen of the Church of England. To have any others would be a great injury to the inmates of the house, a direct dereliction of duty and an improper act on the part of the guardians."

At this point Revd. Farrer accepted the appointment at a salary of £40 a year.

How much spiritual comfort the inmates derived from the Chaplain is impossible to determine and how far some of the latter understood what it was like to be reduced to poverty is very debateable. Certainly the remarks that Farrer was to make to the Royal Commission in 1909 about various groups were less than charitable. It is clear that the continuing influence of the Church of England was manifest in this rural area but the Wincanton Board were remarkably tolerant of other denominations and prepared to permit diversity in practice so that with this enlightened attitude religious conflict was avoided. (29)

b) Death

There is no evidence that the Chaplain was called into the Workhouse to minister to the dying. As increasingly it was the aged who became resident there, death was to be expected on a regular basis. As no Register of Deaths has survived from before 1866 there is little evidence on the number of those who died in the Workhouse in its first thirty years. Annual Financial Statements for the three years ending Lady Day 1853, however, refer to sixty-four deaths, of which twenty-six were males, twelve females and twenty-six children, giving an average of twenty-one a year. In the period 1866 to 1900 inclusive there were 665 deaths which gave a slightly lower average of nineteen a year, which may be considered not excessive given the age and physical condition of many of those who entered the Workhouse. As might be expected the winter months of January and February witnessed the greatest number of deaths with a total of eighty-five in January and eighty-four in February, representing 25.4% of all deaths in the thirty-five years covered. August and September saw the least number of deaths with thirty-nine and thirty-seven respectively.

Of the twenty-eight who died in the Workhouse in 1900 and 1901, 23 (82.1%) were over sixty. Table 20 gives a breakdown of deaths by age group and indicates the importance of the Workhouse as a place for many of the aged to end their days. It must have been a very depressing experience for many of them entering an institution which they knew they would not leave alive.

The Table below shows that while 8.7% were under ten years of age at death, some 66.8% were over sixty and 19.8% over eighty. One of the two stillborn births was in November 1891 when an allegation was made that the Matron overworked the mother but upon investigation there were found to be no grounds for the complaint. At least seven of the deaths were not actually in the Workhouse as the dead bodies were brought there by the local police, as happened in the cases of Henry Brine and Charles Parsons in August 1871, William

Rex in January 1880 and Sophia Duckett in May 1889. Two others, Charles Francis in April 1872 and Ann Roper in October 1879 were brought there after being killed on the railway. The most unpleasant and serious case came in April 1883 when James Wadman aged seven was brought to the House dead. Shortly afterwards an Inquest Jury returned a verdict of "wilful murder" by his father Albin Wadman.

Table 20. Ages on death in Wincanton Workhouse 1866-1900

At birth	2
Under 3 months	22
3 months and under 1 year	12
1 year to 9 years	22
10 - 19 years	20
20 - 29 "	15
30 - 39 "	32
40 - 49 "	50
50 - 59 "	46
60 - 69 "	104
70 - 79 "	208
80 - 89 "	118
90 - 99 "	13
100 and over	1
Total	665

Those who were dying in the Workhouse during the first twenty years of its existence were left in the Infirmary Wards, which must have very distressing for them and for the other inmates. It was not until March 1858 that the Guardians ordered,

> "that in future when any Patient in the Hospital be pronounced by the Medical Officer to be in such a state that death is likely soon to ensure that such Patient be removed to the inner ward."

After death the body was removed to the Mortuary which was a small building eleven feet long by eight feet wide built against the western boundary wall. It seems to have been well-maintained for one Visitor found it in February 1898 to be "clean & in every way well appointed."

For the vast majority of those who died in the Workhouse there followed a simple pauper's funeral. A small number of bodies, however, were removed by relatives and friends for burial: five in the 1870s, fourteen in the 1880s and seventeen in the 1890s, possibly suggesting that it was becoming increasingly unacceptable to receive such a funeral. Until 1857 the policy of the Guardians was to bury all who died in the Workhouse in the Churchyard of Wincanton Parish Church but in that year the Vicar and Churchwardens complained that,

> "The number of burials from the Workhouse in the Parish Churchyard have so crowded the ground as to render it almost impossible to continue the system."

The Guardians sought legal advice from the Poor Law Board and as a result of this amended their system: for those who died in the Workhouse but were chargeable to a particular parish the body was to be taken back to that parish and buried there at its expense. A Contract was awarded to transport the body, for example, in December 1888 Mr Mead presented the lowest tender of 2s 6d to places within three miles, 4s to places three to six miles away and 7s 6d to those over six miles distant. The vast majority of burials passed off smoothly although there were occasional problems, such as in September 1896 when it was found that the grave dug at Charlton Horethorne for Edwin Lanning was six inches too short as a result of the Porter giving the wrong measurement to the Master.

For those chargeable to the parish of Wincanton or to the Common Fund of the Union, their final resting place continued to be the Churchyard, and later the Cemetery of Wincanton, transported there first by a local contractor and later in the Workhouse's own horse-drawn Hearse which was purchased for £25 in November 1866 and which cost £3 12s 0d to repair in April 1878. At the end of the century the change in the nature of the House and its consequent lack of able-bodied men created problems at funerals. In May 1896 one Guardian, R. Hutchings, reported that while it was customary for four able-bodied inmates to act as bearers for a total payment of 1s, on a number of occasions it was observed,

> "that they were scarcely strong enough to carry a corpse from the bier to the grave, and in lowering the coffin to the grave the bands had almost slipped from the bearers' hands."

For added strength the Guardians ordered the Porter and the Male Attendant to assist. It proved not to be an adequate solution as three years later the Chaplain complained of "the weakness of the bearers sent with funerals from the house." On this occasion the Guardians decided that if necessary the Master could seek and pay for outside help.

The poignancy of some deaths in the Workhouse may best be illustrated by a newspaper report concerning one boy who died in June 1896,

> "John Perry, a boy of 13, who was a great favourite in the Workhouse, and who had been ill for some time past, having died was buried......the Matron and 12 boys and girls followed body to grave."

For this funeral, as for all pauper burials, the Passing Bell was rung.

The number of deaths each year obviously affected the overall cost, so for example the total expended on Workhouse funerals in 1855 was £20 19s 0d whereas ten years later it was £10 6s 0d. The average cost per head also varied slightly so that in the 1840s and 1850s it was between 13s and 14s but by the mid-1860s had decreased to between 10s and 11s, part of which may be explained by the provision of their own hearse.

While many of the deaths in the Workhouse were related to old age or from a clearly discernible disease, such as a death from smallpox in January 1840, occasionally the nature of the death meant that an Inquest became necessary. These occurrences throw some light upon various aspects of workhouse life and treatment. One of the commonest verdicts on sudden death was, "Visitation of God": a verdict which was returned in April 1850 on John Hansford when he was found dead in one of the Water Closets; the same verdict was given for Emmanuel Martin aged seventy when he "died somewhat suddenly in one of the courtyards." In the case of the latter, the Coroner, Dr. J. Wybrants, took the opportunity to comment that since he had become Coroner "it was the first inquest that he had held on an inmate of the House, which showed how well it had been conducted." Managing those classed as lunatics was always difficult and in April 1873 Frederick Hannam, a forty-eight year old lunatic, died when he stuffed his allowance of seven ounces of bread into his mouth, "choked accidentally while eating" was the verdict.

Temporary insanity was the verdict returned on John Parsons in March 1869 when he left the Infirmary Ward and hung himself with a bed sheet and handkerchief from the iron bars on the windows in the staircase. The Guardians informed the Poor Law Board that,

> "The unfortunate man was addicted to drink and over and over again has been committed by the Justices to the Gaol for drunkenness spending most of his time either in Gaol or this Workhouse."

In this case there is just the hint that if Parsons had been monitored more closely, especially by the Nurse, his untimely death might have been avoided. In February 1885 when Andrew Coleman aged seventy-eight, who had been in the Workhouse for many years after being a Well-sinker in Castle Cary, died the verdict eventually returned was heart disease and so natural causes. At the time of his death he was being treated for eczema of the legs by being given arsenic and both the Nurse and the Medical Officer had to testify that he was not given too much. Nearly fifty years before in November 1836 when Richard Luffman aged eighty-four died shortly after leaving the Workhouse, a local doctor, Mr Parsons, alleged that he "had died from exhaustion for want of more solid food." The Inquest Jury, however, expressed their view that the dietary was satisfactory and returned a verdict of "Visitation of God." In all these cases the Workhouse and its officers had managed to avoid criticism and blame.

There were a very small number of instances when the Workhouse and its system could not escape direct criticism. One was on the death by scalding of Ernest White in 1891 (see above) which was an obvious case of neglect. The Workhouse had also by implication been criticized in December 1853 after the death of John Barnard aged forty-eight in Shepton Mallet Gaol, where he had been sent for seven days with hard labour for refusing to work in the Workhouse. Various prison officials testified that he was in a very poor state when he arrived and the Surgeon stated that he appeared to have had a diseased liver and jaundice and died from dysentery. The Master of the Workhouse, James Sealey, testified that the Visiting Committee considered him to be an impostor. The Workhouse Medical Officer, William Brunton, while agreeing that he was "weak and poorly", did not consider him genuinely ill. He came to the conclusion,

> "that it was a case of pure destitution, that he was weak and destitute from want of the necessaries of life. I could find no trace of disease about him."

The Inquest Jury did not agree and returned a verdict that he had died from dysentery "accelerated by exposure to cold and want of the proper necessaries of life previous to imprisonment." The failure of the Medical Officer to detect any disease may suggest a lack of thoroughness in the way in which new inmates were assessed upon admission.

Death was an ever-present reality in any workhouse given the physical condition of many of those admitted. For some inmates it must have been a devastating experience in the period before their death if they remained in control of their mental faculties. Either left in an Infirmary Ward or alone in an inner ward, they were separated from family and friends for there is no evidence to suggest that visitors were permitted at that time. At least they received some degree of care, had food, shelter, warmth and a bed, which could not have been guaranteed for some of them if they had faced death outside of the House. For some families the prospect of a pauper's funeral was seen as a disgrace, something to be avoided if possible, and there was an increasing trend to try and claim the body and arrange interment elsewhere. (30)

12. Special Days

One of the key themes of life in the Workhouse was the rigid enforcement of a multitude of rules and regulations which led to a monotonous existence for the inmates. Virtually every minute of every day was accounted for, day in and day out, week in and week out. Any variation in routine was therefore extremely welcome and one of the most important of these from the point of view of the paupers was an alteration in the diet for a special occasion. (see above)

Visits by friends or relatives constituted a welcome change but such visits were strictly limited and were thus perceived by the inmates as yet another restriction imposed upon them. When all the paupers were lodged in the old Wincanton Poorhouse in 1836 visitors were permitted only on Thursdays but once the new Workhouse was opened Monday was added. On both days visiting was allowed between 10 am and 3 pm, always in the Entrance Hall and in the presence of the Master, Matron or Porter, the exception being that no visitors were allowed to see any inmate who was undergoing punishment for being disorderly or refractory. At all other times the Porter was under strict instructions not to admit any visitors to the House except with the permission of the Master or Matron. The Porter was also given the power to search any one entering the Workhouse who was suspected "of having possession of any Spirits or prohibited article." It was forbidden for letters or notes to be sent to inmates unless sanctioned by the Master and the result of this was that on one occasion the Nurse was reprimanded in October 1839 when she passed a note to a girl from the second Mrs Gulley.

The monotony could also be broken by obtaining leave of absence which the Master could grant "for any urgent or special reason" for a period of up to twenty-four hours. The Workhouse was not a prison and so most categories of paupers could leave on giving notice to the Master and performing any required task but as many of the inmates were there through destitution, they had no where else to go. In most cases, therefore, this leave of absence allowed a pauper the opportunity to seek employment, find a cottage and so be discharged from the Workhouse altogether. Unless they had been granted such leave of absence the Porter was required to prevent other paupers from exiting. For the majority of those who availed themselves of the system, it worked well but problems did occur such as a small minority who absconded, often in Workhouse clothes, or like Jonah Thompson in April 1842 returned drunk. Leave of absence was not meant to be a day out for the inmates and so in October 1844 the Master was criticized by the Guardians for granting such leave to two able-bodied paupers on Wincanton Fair Day.

It is very noticeable that the liberalization in attitude towards some categories of paupers mainly occurs in the last twenty years or so of the nineteenth century but the tradition of celebrating Christmas and the New Year started much earlier. From 1836 the diet was amended for either Christmas Day or New Year's Day and in 1841, after being examined by the Chaplain, each child received "a suitable book" from money subscribed by two Guardians. This seems to be the first reference to any present being given to the children. By 1860 there was a large Christmas Tree provided each year which was hung with several dozen variegated lamps. "The tree, too, was profusely hung with useful and instructive articles for every inmate to have something." The following year it was reported that children who had been sent out as apprentices or servants were permitted to return to enjoy the treat. All of this was provided as a result of private subscriptions. By the late 1860s the children were receiving toys and sweets sent in by local residents as an account of the day in 1869 indicates:

> "A hamper was sent from the neighbourhood of Bruton, from a 'clergyman's wife and children' to the chaplain of the union, containing tea and sugar for the old women, and lots of toys and sweets for the children. To this kind and acceptable present, Mr Fitzgerald, of Maperton-house, and other friends made an addition, and it was decided to have a Christmas

tree……..The dining- room appropriated for the display had been most tastefully decorated and converted for the occasion into quite a fairy place, lit up with coloured lights, and a grand show of toys, apples, nuts &c……In the evening, a magic lantern exhibition took place, interspersed with readings, songs, and music."

By the 1890s the celebrations and treats appear to have become more extensive but still relied upon "numerous subscribers" or gifts from individuals. An entry in the Visitors' Book for 2nd January 1895 gives an indication of the items involved.

"The Annual Christmas Tree and treat to the little ones, and Inmates was given on New Year's Day, when a large quantity of toys &c were distributed, each old woman was presented with a woollen shawl & pocket Handkerchief and the men a woollen comforter & and ounce of tobacco."

On Christmas Day 1897 each male received a quarter of a pound of tobacco and each female half a pound of tea and a pound of sugar, while the children were given sweets, cards, toys and scrap books. In addition entertainment had become incorporated into the day. On 2nd January 1895 the Town Band played music in the evening and several local inhabitants gave a concert in the Schoolroom. During the New Year's Day Party in 1897 the elderly in the Infirmary were entertained by Miss B. Hoskins on the violin and by a choir of lady visitors. There was also entertainment for the children with songs and recitations. At New Year 1899 the children were entertained with a Punch and Judy Show. Such seasonal treats and entertainment must have provided a welcome break from the general monotonous life in the Workhouse.

Linked with special occasions was the increased provision of items such as tobacco, snuff, tea and sugar, and even alcohol. At Christmas 1859 there is a reference to "snuff, tobacco and pipes" after the dinner, with the men being given the tobacco and the women the snuff. The snuff seems gradually to have been replaced with tea and sugar for the women and also for the sick in the Infirmary Wards and throughout the 1890s this was the standard practice, so that, for example, in January 1899 the men received one ounce of tobacco, the women tea and sugar and a cup and saucer as well. In January 1878 "Each man had a pint of ale and ½ pint do the women", and in addition, "Mr Pitman of North Cadbury and Mr Plomer of Wincanton gave some cider." The provision of alcohol continued, for example, on Christmas Day 1897, "Each male adult was supplied with a pint of porter, and each female adult with half-a-pint." While the inmates may have been delighted the temperance lobby must have seen it differently.

By the end of the nineteenth century the celebration of external events also relieved the tedium of daily routine in the Workhouse. In July 1893 one Guardian recorded "the excellent treat" given to the inmates on the Royal Wedding Day, although its nature was not specified. The Diamond Jubilee of Queen Victoria in 1897 led to more festivities with a roast dinner with tarts and blanc-mange washed down with a quantity of porter. After the meal there were speeches, Three Cheers and a rendition of 'God Save the Queen', then the inmates dispersed, "the men 'to burn their idol' (tobacco) and the women to enjoy their tea and sugar." Later in the day a large tea was followed by games for the children until at 8.30 pm they all adjourned to their bedrooms.

While children had long been given a treat by being taken to the seaside each year, it was only in the late 1890s that trips out seem to have been extended to other inmates. In September 1898, for example, Mr C. Shaw of West Hill took twenty-four inmates, mainly aged and infirm but still able-bodied, to Stourton in a brake and three waggonettes. Once there they were provided with bread, cheese and tea and then, "They rambled about enjoying their tobacco until five o'clock, when they sat down to a capital tea of cake and bread and butter."

One of the major problems for those who were past work was that there was little to do in the Workhouse during the long hours of the day. There were few attempts made to provide any intellectual stimulation, even if, in the early days of the Workhouse, many of the aged could read and failing eyesight also prevented such activities. Nevertheless some small attempts were made to encourage reading, but within strict limits. In 1842 one of the Rules and Regulations of the Workhouse required that only books or printed material from the Society for Promoting Christian Knowledge "be allowed to circulate or to be read aloud amongst the inmates." There was always the fear that some sort of subversive material might be obtained, such as the "Book of the Bastilles" or copies of "The Poor Man's Guardian" newspaper. The following year the Chaplain suggested that a library be established and this was soon accomplished with the books being placed under lock and key by the Master and the Chaplain was asked to superintend their circulation. No evidence has survived on how many books there were, what titles and the extent of their use. In the 1890s gifts of books were more common with Mr Portman thanked "for his handsome present of books" in November 1890 and Mrs Watling for her gift of books in June 1897. Magazines and newspapers began to appear in the late 1890s when Mrs Bailward, the wife of a Guardian, gave a collection of "Graphics" in March 1898 and the following year it was reported that she had placed a box at Templecombe Station "for the collection of newspapers for the use of the inmates of the Workhouse."

Other odd treats are recorded, for example on one occasion when the children were entertained by T.E. Rogers at Yarlington, each one received 6d, and in 1894 two local clergymen gave a magic lantern show for the inmates. For those who provided or organized the treats for the inmates it represents a continuation of the philanthropic tradition which had a long history in this part of Somerset. While there may well have been elements of social control and social superiority implicit in their actions, for many of the donors it was a demonstration of their Christian charity and humanitarianism, especially towards vulnerable groups such as the elderly and the children. Such occasions were undoubtedly much appreciated by the inmates as it relieved the daily tedium and visitors such as T.E. Rogers in the 1890s commented upon their "cheerful & contented appearance. They all seemed perfectly happy & well cared for." Mrs Emma

Bracher reported that, "All seemed happy & comfortable." Both of these were of course Guardians. While such treats were welcome they were relatively few and far between in each year and for most of the days there was just the strict, unrelenting, repetitive regime. (31)

13. Inmates thoughts on their lives

Guardians, officers and visitors may have believed that the inmates were happy and contented but that was not always the perspective of the paupers themselves. Every aspect of the Workhouse life received complaints at some time or another but given the length of the period under consideration, the number was relatively few. The expectation was that if a pauper had a complaint it would be made at the weekly Board Meeting, to an individual Guardian, to the Visiting Committee or by letter to the Guardians: all of which would have been very daunting for the majority of the inmates. It may well be therefore that despite general grumbling amongst the paupers nothing was said officially. Just occasionally a letter was sent directly to the Central Board but their usual policy was to send it back to the Guardians and not to interfere. From time to time an articulate pauper emerged and that person was usually regarded as a nuisance and efforts made to discredit him or her. (See for example the letter of G. Gould, Appendix 2b) When complaints were received almost invariably the Guardians did investigate but the impression created is that they started with a degree of scepticism. In December 1894 one Guardian, R. Hutchings, noted in the Visitors' Book, "Complaints from the Inmates have been very few and after thorough investigation have been found generally of a very frivolous character."

Food generated complaints throughout the century with the quality of the bread provided being prominent, especially in the early years and the state of the butter in the 1890s. In May 1881 John Gould alleged that his diet had been reduced to dry bread, potatoes and water and a decade later Richard Lewis complained that his pudding was not fit to eat and two years after that that he had not received his treacle with his pudding, the Matron replying that he had been given sugar instead as apples had been put in his pudding. In November 1872 Jane Sergeant wrote directly to the Local

Government Board on a number of issues including, "that the meat that we get hear is not holesome to eat", and that inmates were not treated equally. (See letters in Appendix 2)

For those who had experienced the old system pre-1834 the new Workhouse came as a most unwelcome shock and therefore complaints about the work involved, the amount and nature of the food, and the rules and regulations were common in the first few years of the new system but were usually made as the pauper left the House and were taken no further. In the 1860s there were a number of complaints that clean linen was not distributed regularly and in 1895 one widow complained that her late husband had been kept too long in the Receiving Ward with no fire and the window open.

Needless to say another area which attracted complaints was the conduct of the officers in the Workhouse. The Minutes and Correspondence files of the Wincanton Board clearly indicate that they were prepared to investigate various alleged offences but in sixty years it averaged less than one a year and some of their investigations were very perfunctory affairs. It is impossible to assess if the reported cases represented the total of alleged offences committed as many of the paupers would have been reluctant to complain for fear of making their situation worse. The Guardians also recognised that most of the officers were in a higher social position than the inmates and therefore tended to accept the word of the principal officers when allegations were made. There is no evidence to suggest that the Guardians approved of some of the offences alleged to have been committed as a way of discouraging would-be applicants. When the Board found a good officer there is an element of protection provided as a reward for loyalty.

Complaints of many different types against the Master surfaced throughout the period, for example in January 1841 he was accused of confining Elizabeth Cuff in the Refractory Ward for too long and making her work on a Sunday, both of these charges proved unfounded. In August 1843 he was accused of burying paupers without shrouds but an enquiry to Robert Cross, the undertaker, proved this likewise to be unfounded. In 1882 the Master was accused of shutting boys in rooms but an investigation found that it was "made without sufficient cause." In May 1893 Samuel Whitlock alleged that the Master assaulted him but the Guardians could find no satisfactory evidence. Allegations were also made against the Matron, such as by Maria Day in April 1843 that she kept the wine ordered for the sick and cut up sheets to make tablecloths. In this case the Visiting Committee found the charges to be without any basis

Allegations against the Schoolteachers tended to centre around physical and verbal abuse, such as the unfounded claim by Charles Willis against the Schoolmistress in February 1841 that she had flogged his son. Some charges were proved correct, such as the claim in July 1881 that the Schoolmaster had given a boy a cold bath after bed-wetting which led to a caution. A complaint made by the pauper Cook, Mary Ann Cross, in July 1851 that the Schoolmaster, Frederick Cox, had used "abusive and improper language" led to an investigation by the Poor Law Board and Cox was forced to write a letter of apology, expressing his "sincere shame and sorrow." It appeared that the Cook normally cleaned a passage by the kitchen at 9 am and locked a door which prevented the boys reaching their Schoolroom. One morning he stopped her doing so and claimed that she abused him, which led him to exclaim, "it is a pretty thing for me to be abused and ruled by a set of whores." He was cautioned, "for the future so to govern your temper that you may not again make use of improper language." This case does illustrate the tensions which could be created in an enclosed institution by seemingly small incidents.

One of the more serious complaints was made in March 1884 when it was alleged that the Industrial Trainer struck at least two boys with a stick and his fist. The original letter of complaint was written by one of the boys, Solomon Dewfall (See Appendix 2c) The Local Government Board recommended to the Guardians that the Industrial Trainer, Albert Worthington who had been appointed against their advice, should be dismissed. The Guardians at first replied that they had received no complaint and then that as Worthington had not been permitted to defend himself they would not call upon him to resign. The Central Board agreed to an inquiry after the School Inspector, J.C. Clutterbuck, reported in July that while the appointment was not turning out very satisfactorily, "there is no tangible ground for getting rid of the man." A month later Inspector Courtenay held the official Inquiry and recommended that as there was so much conflicting evidence Worthington should be reprimanded, which duly happened in September.

Undoubtedly the most prolific complainer was Richard Lewis, usually referred to as a blind man. In July 1877 the Board agreed that he should receive 1s a day on being admitted to Guy's Hospital in London for treatment to his eyes and he was also sent again in March 1880. At some stage prior to May 1882 he was in the Exeter Blind Institution but, according to Courtenay, "from which he was sent away for misconduct." Food featured in many of his complaints, which included not only those about his puddings and lack of treacle but also throwing his soup on the floor in protest. He also alleged that American bacon was being purchased in 1882 rather than British. Alleged assaults appear in a number of his letters in the 1890s, including that the Matron "had struck of boy with a stick and that she had laid violent hands on a cripple woman Eliza Lancashire & that a Tramp had cut the ear off a boy." The Board's conclusion was that there was no evidence for any of this. In addition a number of his allegations contained sexual implications (See letters from Lewis in Appendix 2d) Over the years he wrote many letters directly to the Local Government Board complaining about a range of issues: that women were forced to work on Sundays, that boys worked and scrubbed until 8 pm, that the Master cursed and threatened inmates, that potatoes were not washed, that a boy was forced to do the cooking, that a carpenter was employed for months making picture frames that the poor did not want and that Yard doors were locked so that adequate exercise was not possible. Having the doors unlocked was one of his few successes.

Although his poem written in 1884 (See Appendix 3) shows that he was highly critical of authority and the social classes above him, it was only towards the very end of the 1880s and during the 1890s that he becomes increasingly hostile, even though he had been abusive to the Master from his admission in 1871. In April 1892 he claimed that, "Barton and his Tory Gentlemen are worse than the heathens of 2000 Years ago", having on a previous occasion called Barton and Barnes 'thieves and murderers.' An outburst in front of magistrates in November 1889 was reported in the local press when Lewis was sentenced to twenty-one days with hard labour for disorderly conduct,

> "You know there is no tribunal to whom a pauper can appeal; but the time will come when you will have to answer for your wicked cruelty to a tribunal. I do not care for you and I would not flinch if you ordered my being burnt in the Market Place."

Undoubtedly many Board Meetings and Court Sessions were enlivened by Lewis's comments and behaviour but it also meant that the vast majority of his allegations were ignored or investigated superficially. Inspectors felt that many of his complaints were motivated by "malice & spite" and in April 1897 Inspector Preston-Thomas commented,

> "the old men are worried and terrorized by a blind man Lewis who is of abominable character & whose repeated imprisonments have not improved him."

By the time of his sentence of fourteen days with hard labour in September 1894 for "wilful damage" he had fourteen previous convictions. In that year he was described as a forty-two year old basket maker, born in West Chinnock who was five feet seven inches tall with brown hair. It was claimed that he could not read or write, although during previous Court appearances he was said to be able to do both but imperfectly. His letters, assuming he wrote them himself, would suggest this was an understatement. The Wincanton Board regarded him as "troublesome" although a local newspaper considered that he "is endowed with much intelligence and a wonderful memory."

While the Workhouse was distressing for many of the poor, it may have been particularly so for those who had experienced a different way of life or who had obtained some education and achieved advancement. One inmate in 1881 for example was John Merrill, a seventy-nine year old Surgeon born in Madras Presidency, East Indies. The absence of any intellectual stimulation must have been especially hard to bear. One such man was James Walter, a native of Wincanton, born in 1797, and who followed his father as a plasterer and tiler. At some stage he moved to work in London and in 1838 was Librarian to the Episcopal Bishop attached to the British Embassy in Paris. At this time he wrote and published a number of poems, such as "Ben-hadad", dedicated to Lady Fullerton. In 1847 he was back in Wincanton where he was seen walking badly, possibly as the result of some kind of paralysis, which may have been caused by a stroke, staying with friends and trying to earn money by giving a series of Shakespearean Readings. This plan failed and in November 1847 he entered the Workhouse and from there he penned a letter to a local friend, William Winter. (See Appendix 4) In this letter he wrote that he found the other inmates "neither learned nor witty…..have no curiosity, no ideality." He also believed that "they are malignant, envious and slanderous as incarnate fiends." After ten weeks his friends provided him with some money and local tradition relates that he returned to Paris and may have died fighting in the 1848 Revolution. (32)

The few surviving letters from pauper inmates paint a vivid picture of some aspects of Workhouse life and it is a great pity that there are not more. A lack of adequate literacy must have been a considerable barrier for some inmates and fear of the consequences for others. The impression created is that they were not well received by the Guardians as they represented a potential threat to the status quo. As far as many of them were concerned the paupers had to know their place.

14. Life for some Workhouse Officers

With so much attention focussed on the lives of the paupers in a workhouse it is easy to forget that some of the officers experienced an unusual existence as well. While the Medical Officer and Chaplain were part-time and lived outside of the workhouse, full-time employees such as the Master, Matron, Schoolteachers and Porter were also resident within the institution. For them too there were long hours, specified duties and little stimulating contact with the outside world. In fact permitting a friend, relative or visitor to remain with them in the workhouse without permission once the outer gates were locked at night was punishable by instant dismissal, a similar fate awaited them if they remained out of the House overnight. The lifestyle imposed, along with low salaries in a small rural workhouse, meant that it was not always possible to attract and retain well-qualified or trained people for the various posts, a fact which created a number of problems in the Wincanton Workhouse.

a) Master and Matron

These two officers were the key figures in the smooth day-to-day operation of the Workhouse and for that reason the Poor Law Commissioners and their successors recommended a married couple. As the Central Boards lacked the powers of compulsion, on five occasions throughout the Victorian period the Wincanton Board of Guardians did not fill these posts with a married couple, a decision which created a range of difficulties.

Every aspect of the management of the Workhouse, no matter how small and apparently insignificant, was the responsibility of the Master and Matron, with the former bearing the majority share. In the General Order containing Workhouse Rules published by the Poor

Law Commissioners in 1842 there was a list of twenty-six duties imposed upon the Master and fourteen upon the Matron. Amongst other duties the Master had complete oversight of all matters relating to male paupers, admitted all paupers, enforced work, checked male wards for cleanliness, oversaw meals, checked male wards at 9 pm in summer and 8 pm in winter to ensure that the paupers were in bed and all fires and lights were extinguished, dealt with the Medical Officer, kept accounts and other books, had charge of provisions and even said prayers before and after meals. The Matron was responsible for all matters relating to female paupers and children under seven years of age, superintended the making and mending of all clothes, ensured that clean linen and clothes were provided to inmates each week, directed all washing, oversaw the care of the sick and checked the female and children's wards at night at the same time as the Master visited the male wards.

To emphasize their key role, to enable them to perform it efficiently and gain rapid access to all parts of the Workhouse, their accommodation was at the centre of the building, at the point where the different wings met. Immediately above the Dining Hall was their sitting room and the Master's Office. Adjacent to these and protruding into each of the wings was the Clothes Store, their own kitchen, a bedroom and additional sitting room. On the second floor above their joint sitting room and the office were three additional rooms for use as bedrooms. From the rooms on both floors windows looked over each of the four Yards and a series of doors and staircases gave instant access to all parts of the House.

For much of the period these two officers seem to have performed their duties to the general satisfaction of the Board of Guardians. When William and Elizabeth Bird left in 1871 after five years' service to move to a similar post at St Albans, a local newspaper commented, "it is impossible to speak of them too highly, and it is with great regret that their services will be lost." In March 1895 the Visiting Committee reported, "that great praise is due to the Matron for the very efficient state and management of the House in all its departments."

157

On the other hand if either of these officers became lax or were negligent it could have far-reaching consequences for the management of the establishment. In some cases the Guardians dealt with the matter quickly but in others it appears to have reached a serious state before they took any effective action, which may suggest that their own supervision of the officers was not always as rigorous as it should have been. In addition they did at times display a marked reluctance to accept the advice of the Central Board in matters concerning their officers, which in itself confirms their desire to manage their own affairs without what they perceived to be central interference. In July 1839 the Master, James Sealey, allowed his keys to the Provision Store to be given to a pauper inmate and as a result the supply of potatoes depleted rapidly and for which the Master was admonished and required to improve his procedures. In 1850 it was reported, also in relation to Sealey, that,

> "Great dissatisfaction prevails among the Guardians on account of the Master's want of care, both as to the enforcement of proper classification and of a good day's work by the able-bodied men in the Workhouse."

Once again the Master was cautioned but it may be that given the poor design of the building, which made adequate classification impossible, it was not entirely his fault. It was acknowledged, however, that for a number of years the House had been "satisfactorily managed." The following year Sealey was once again admonished, this time for deviating from the dietary.

By 1865 there were concerns about the management of the Master, Andrew Hopkins, the former Schoolmaster,

> "In the opinion of this Board the Master of this Workhouse has not done his duty and that the general management of the Workhouse has been for sometime past in an unsatisfactory state."

Yet a month later following his resignation the Board gave him an open testimonial, "we found him kind to the inmates and especially attentive and humane to the children and generally punctual and careful in carrying out the duties of his office." From the evidence it is impossible to determine if the responsibility of managing the

Workhouse was beyond Hopkins or whether his more humanitarian style of management was not in keeping with the methods favoured by the majority of the Guardians. At the same time they informed Anna Pike, who had been the Matron since February 1864 that she "was not so efficient in carrying out the duties of the House", so she too resigned, allowing the Guardians to appoint a married couple.

The only other significant issues relating to the performance of duties by the Matron centred around Mrs Sealey. As early as February 1854 one Inspector had endorsed a letter requesting an increase in the salary of the Matron, "The Matron of Wincanton WH is not an efficient person in the situation." After the death of her husband in 1857 she continued as Matron but clearly did not get on with the new Master, Hopkins, as she claimed, "The present Master has not treated me well," but Inspector Gulson noted, "the Matron is impatient of control & much more to blame than the Master." A few months later he went so far as to suggest, "the time is now come when the interests of the Establishment require another Matron," but the Guardians decided to permit her to continue in post. In June 1859 she and the Nurse were discovered to have been absenting themselves from the House without leave, for which they were both admonished. By the early 1860s she was also suffering ill-health, what the Medical Officer called "deeply seated disease of the Liver," so much so that during attacks she was incapable of performing her duties. In 1863 allegations began to emerge that she had ignored the condition of sick children and these along with her continued ill-health led to her resignation in January 1864.

After the resignations of Andrew Hopkins and Anna Pike the married couple of Thomas and Matilda Flower, who had been the Assistant Master and sub-Matron of the Greenwich Workhouse, were not a great success. In just over a year they resigned after complaints from the other officers. Inspector Gulson noted,

> "The Master lost the confidence of the B. of Gds in consequence of his staying out late at night. The Matron was accused by the Smistress of using improper language toward her & thus weakening her authority with the Children."

The Workhouse was obviously at a very low ebb as the Schoolmistress resigned on the same day as the Master and Matron and the Porter was dismissed. William and Elizabeth Bird, schoolteachers from the Birmingham Workhouse restored stability.

In 1871 the Birds were replaced by John and Margaret Barnes, he being a former policeman in Newcastle-upon-Tyne, and they remained effective until the death of Mrs Barnes in February 1890 at which time the Guardians recorded, "their grateful recognition of her faithful services during the long period she has held office of Matron." The Guardians reappointed John Barnes along with Louisa Barwell, the Schoolmistress, as Matron. As this arrangement opened up the possibility of another period of difficult management, the Local Government Board informed the Guardians that they would prefer a married couple and asked them to reconsider but they stood firm. The Central Board finally agreed on the understanding that if one of them left, both positions should be vacated and a married couple appointed. When the Matron resigned the following year the Guardians simply ignored the agreement and appointed Selina MacPetrie as Matron.

On this occasion the anticipated difficulties did not materialize as six months later the Master, aged 65, and Matron, aged 31, married, being granted four days leave of absence. In September 1896 John Barnes died having "faithfully discharged the important and responsible duties of Master of this Workhouse for a period of 26 years." The Central Board demanded the appointment of a married couple but again the Guardians ignored it especially as they perceived the Matron to be "an excellent disciplinarian who shows great firmness and kindness in the treatment of the Inmates." They appointed Bishop Kennett, who was the Assistant Master in Hasting Workhouse and before that a Booking Clerk on the South Eastern Railway. Two years later he and Mrs Barnes married.

In their positions both the Master and the Matron were prime targets for a wide range of allegations: some were frivolous and others motivated by the spirit of revenge. Various Masters, as has been seen, were accused of assault, cruelty to inmates, mistreating boys, improper language, lack of morals, breaches of rules, staying out late, keeping pigeons and not providing burial shrouds. The Matron faced allegations such as assault, failure to provide clean linen, stealing wine, and cutting up sheets. The vast majority of these accusations proved to be groundless. In addition the officers, and especially the Master, could face abusive language and being assaulted, for example, the Guardians gave James Sealey four guineas in November 1841 to pursue his case against James Whedon for assault "whilst in the discharge of his duty."

For this lifestyle the officers received a low salary in a small rural workhouse. It was originally fixed at £30 a year for the Master and £20 for the Matron, increased to a joint salary of £57 in 1854, £65 in 1865, £80 in 1866, £85 in 1871 and £95 in 1878, being £55 for the Master and £40 for the Matron. They also benefited from full board and lodging with washing, heating and lighting, which taken together was a significant addition. There was occasionally in the early years the opportunity for nepotism as in June 1839 Amelia Sealey, the daughter of the Master and Matron was appointed the Schoolmistress. Four years later their niece, Ann Cains, was granted permission to reside temporarily in the Workhouse "to learn straw work." The following year she assisted the Master during the illness of the Matron and a few months later in February 1845 was appointed the Schoolmistress, a position she occupied with limited success until October 1847. (33)

b) The Schoolteachers

Although the Schoolteachers were crucial to the education of the Workhouse children, the problem of maintaining a regular supply of efficient, suitably trained and qualified Schoolmasters and Schoolmistresses was one which was to bedevil workhouse schools for much of the century. The first applicants which the Wincanton Workhouse attracted were paupers and as late as 1868 the salary had to be increased as there were no candidates, while other early Schoolmistresses were unqualified, being merely the daughter and then the niece of the Master and Matron, with Amelia Sealey being recorded as fifteen years old in the 1841 Census. Nevertheless from about 1850 the level of qualification and experience did increase, partly as a result of the payment of a grant towards workhouse teachers' salaries dependent upon efficiency, and partly as a result of the pupil-teacher scheme introduced in 1846 which provided five years of training.

The nature of the salary offered and the working conditions meant that the Guardians failed to attract the mature, middle-aged schoolmistresses which they initially required and as Table 21 indicates the majority were in their twenties and Table 22 that their period of tenure was short.

Table 21.   Age of Schoolteachers on appointment

Age	Schoolmaster	Schoolmistress
Under 20	1	1
20-24	9	9
25-29	4	6
30-34	3	1
Over 35	1	2
Not specified	2	5
Total	20	24

Table 22.   Duration of tenure of Schoolteachers

Duration	Schoolmaster	Schoolmistress
Under 6 months	5	8
6 months to 1 year	4	1
1-1½ years	4	3
1½- 2 years	2	1
2-4 years	3	6
Over 4 years	2	4
Longest period	8 years 3 months	9 years 8 months
Shortest period	4 months	1 month

Six main reasons may be advanced to explain the short period in office of most of the teachers. The first was the low nature of the salaries offered. The Schoolmaster's salary increased from £20 to £45 a year by 1875 and the Schoolmistress's from just £8 in 1836 to £40 in 1875, decreasing to £35 in 1883 when the number of children was reduced, even though from that year she had responsibility for the education of the boys as well. These salaries, while in keeping with those paid in other workhouse schools in the county were often below those in some elementary schools. In 1852 when the Workhouse teachers were receiving approximately £20 each, the Schoolmaster in Bruton National School was paid £35 a year and the Schoolmistress £32 10s 0d. There was a pronounced reluctance in some farming communities to pay adequate salaries, as one comment in 1871 revealed: "What! £50 a year for a Schoolmaster! Why that's enough for a pa'son." In addition, however, the Schoolteachers received furnished accommodation, usually a sitting room and a separate bedroom, full board, heating, lighting and washing. The rations were at all times the same as for the Master and Matron. Some of the Schoolteachers took advantage of the offer of 1s a week in lieu of the ration of beer. Such remuneration might have been acceptable had it not been for other considerations.

Second, the conditions of employment were not conducive to lengthy residence. Their duties were specified as, "To instruct the boys and girls.......To regulate the discipline and organization of the school, and the industrial and moral training of the children." Like the Master and Matron the Schoolteachers were required to be resident in the Workhouse and could not stay out over-night. They were circumscribed by petty rules and regulations, for example, in November 1855 when the Schoolmaster, William Godfree, requested to be allowed to spend his evenings with the Schoolmistress in her sitting room the Board refused "such request deeming it highly improper," schoolteachers after all were required to be single. At times the physical working conditions could be unpleasant with, for example, the girls' schoolroom at one stage next to the Infirmary Wards. The teachers were also responsible for the children outside of school hours during the years when no alternative provision was made, and were concerned with their manners and appearance, "To keep them clean in their persons, and orderly and decorous in their conduct."

The job was, therefore, time-consuming and grinding so that not surprisingly ill-health was a common feature: three Schoolmistresses and one Schoolmaster resigned specifically through ill-health between 1867 and 1886. Numerous references to grants of days or weeks for convalescence appear in the Minutes, for example, in March 1878 the Schoolmaster, William Childs, was granted two weeks leave for ill-health and Matilda Townsend six weeks "in consequence of ill-health" in July 1886. During the illnesses of the Master or Matron the Schoolteachers were expected to assist with their duties as well as to perform their normal ones, which placed a severe strain on Ann Southgate in the early 1860s with the various periods of illness of the Matron, Mrs Sealey.

Third, in addition to the physical disadvantages of the occupation, there were practically no opportunities for intellectual or professional improvement. Many teachers had little chance of enhancing their qualifications as permission to attend outside educational establishments was non-existent in the Wincanton Union. Most of the Guardians saw little need for any innovations for the type of child in their schools. In practical terms it meant that there was little chance of improving the level of Certificate granted. For some of the teachers with limited ability to begin with the incessant requirements and multiplicity of duties meant their qualifications remained static: Ann Southgate remained on Probation Division I for nine years and Emma Curtis resigned in June 1852 when she was informed that her Probation Division I could not be altered. James Foord actually went down from Competency I to Competency III before rising again to Competency II. Only five schoolteachers had their Certificate level raised and these were all in the period 1873 to 1888 when the fruits of better training were being experienced. For the remaining sixteen teachers whose Certificate level was given, there was no change.

Fourth, on noting the rapid turnover of schoolteachers in his District in 1881, Dr Clutterbuck commented, "these changes have, for the most part, taken place in small unions, in which the teacher's office is too often regarded as a mere stepping stone to some post in a public elementary school."

Table 23.   Teachers moving to other Appointments

Reason for leaving 1837-1891	Schoolmaster	Schoolmistress
Appointment in a National or Parochial School	3	1
Appointment in another Workhouse School	1	2
Appointment in a Board School	0	1
Unspecified School appointment	1	0

Movement within the education system obviously played a part for some teachers leaving the Wincanton Workhouse schools as Table 23 shows.

Fifth, many of the schoolteachers objected to being subordinate to the Master and Matron, to whom intellectually they were often superior. This situation was considered in a Report in 1841 but there is no evidence that any significant action was taken and the result was that friction could develop. In 1852 Inspector Gulson had to explain in detail the respective duties of the Matron and Schoolmistress and caution the Matron about her future conduct towards the latter. In August 1866 Elizabeth Tustin resigned because of the opposition she had encountered from the Matron.

Sixth, and finally, there was a sense of isolation in the dreary, monotonous existence of a rural workhouse where so many of the Guardians had little interest in the education of pauper children. Any infringement of the rules could lead to instant dismissal as Daniel Chambers experienced in 1855 when an inmate was reported to have been in his bedroom. Nevertheless, even in such austere surroundings, or perhaps because of them, romance did manage to flourish for between 1856 and 1876 three of the Schoolmasters resigned to marry their female counterpart and one of each sex resigned to marry an outsider. Considering the difficulty in procuring good teachers, it was short-sighted of the Guardians to adhere rigidly to their policy of employing only single adults in these positions, as they undoubtedly lost very able teachers, notably William Childs and Maria Ingram in 1876, both of whom achieved Certificate Efficiency III. Under their control the Inspector in 1874 found in the School that there was above average intelligence, a wide knowledge and "joyousness." He concluded, "This is an excellent school."

Table 24. Reasons for resignation of teachers 1837-1891

Reason	Schoolmaster	Schoolmistress
Incompetent	3	5
Ill-health	1	3
To marry	4	4
Another school appointment	5	4
To become Master of the Workhouse	1	
Certificate not improved		1
Severe coach accident		1
Disagreement with the Matron		1
Private reasons		1
Inmate in bedroom	1	
Beating a boy	1	
Died in office	1	
None given	3	3

Given the problems of teacher supply, what remains remarkable in the Workhouse is not the limited nature of the education which the children experienced, but the fact that they received one at all, and one which at times the various Inspectors could praise. (34)

c) The Porter

The position of the porter was regarded as of lesser importance than that of a number of the other Workhouse officers, mainly because the salary tended to be low and in the early years some of the porters were recruited from the paupers in the Workhouse itself. In these cases they were paid no salary at all but in November 1838 the Guardians did agree to provide "a suit of clothes and a change of linen and stockings." No specific qualifications were required, although each Porter had to be able to read and write as he kept various registers. The primary duties of the Porter centred around security for he had to ensure that those entering the Workhouse had permission to do so, to search all paupers and goods entering or leaving the house to "prevent the admission of any spirituous or fermented liquors, or other articles contrary to law." He also kept a record of all those entering and leaving the Workhouse and was responsible for locking the gates and outer doors at night, initially 6 pm in winter and 9 pm in summer, handing the keys to the Master and opening up in the morning.

In an attempt to attract better candidates, for these duties the Porter received £8 a year from 1842, which rose to £12 a decade later and £14 in 1853 when it was discovered that the salary of Porters in most of the neighbouring Unions was higher. It increased to £16 in 1857 when the then Porter, Champion Latcham, undertook to shave and cut the hair of the inmates as required. It continued an upward trend to £20 in 1867 and £25 in 1874, when the increase was forced on the Guardians as they were unable to attract a suitable candidate so the existing Porter, David Jones, agreed to withdraw his resignation. It reached a peak of £28 in 1879 when the reasons specified for the increase were that more Vagrants had led to additional work and the Guardians were very satisfied with the performance of William Stowe. When he left in 1887 the salary reverted to £25 and remained at that level for the rest of the century. In addition the Porter received full board and lodging with heating, lighting and washing. He had a separate room off the Entrance Hall, along side the Receiving Ward so that he had immediate access to the front door. One complaint emerged about conditions in October 1851 when the Porter, Henry Carew, stated that he was using the same bedding as the paupers and the Guardians agreed "that proper bedding be set apart." Occasionally a Porter decided to accept 1s in lieu of beer such as Stowe in March 1878.

For the majority of the period the Porters were required to be single, although one was a widower with no children. This requirement was not relaxed until the 1890s when in October 1891 William Roundhouse was appointed Porter and his wife the Cook. In October 1895 the married Porter and Cook, Frederick and Caroline Dymock were permitted to have "one evening a fortnight out from 6.30 to 9.30." Married couples, however, were still not the invariable rule as Arthur Mitchell, the Porter from November 1894 was single, but it was the fact that he had the Cook, Alice Weare, in his bedroom that led to his dismissal in March 1895.

More than thirty men filled the office of Porter between 1836 and 1900 and of these the overwhelming majority were aged between twenty and forty, with an average age of just over thirty. The oldest was probably a pauper, Henry Fleetwood who was 64 in 1841. Approximately half of them served for less than one year, with George Davis, a shoemaker by trade, lasting just one month in 1844 before he was dismissed as incapable and Charles Colborne occupying the post for two months in 1871 until he resigned being "tired of work." The longest serving Porter was William Stowe who remained some ten years and seven months, having previously been in charge of the imbeciles in the Bristol Workhouse and who had been born in Newfoundland. In total seven Porters had previous experience in a Workhouse and the remainder came from a variety of backgrounds, such as seven who had been in the Army, including Champion Latcham who had been "wounded before Sebastopol", two were tailors and one a shoemaker. More unusually one had been a silk picker and another the Manager of a Temperance Hotel in Wells.

The Guardians did not always succeed with an appointment, for example in September 1853 they proposed to appoint James Lee as Porter, a former Schoolmaster in the Bethnell Green and East Grinstead Workhouses, but as two references suggested that he was not capable and tended to become intoxicated, the Poor Law Board refused to sanction the appointment. On this occasion, one of very few, the Guardians bowed to central pressure and appointed John Terrell, who had previously assisted his father as a road contractor.

Porters sometimes faced the brunt of the anger and frustration of the inmates and cases of verbal and physical abuse did occur as the activities of Richard Lewis and his friends clearly showed. In addition they were not always highly regarded by the other officers, for example, in July 1892 both the Porter and the Cook complained that the Master and Matron did not treat them in a proper manner and after an investigation the Matron was cautioned by the Board.

Porters resigned for a variety of reasons, one to become Master of another Workhouse, one to join the Police and one to be married. With the other officers the Guardians tended to allow resignation rather than initiate dismissal proceedings but in the case of the Porters they were not so meticulous. In all some nine were dismissed: three of these, David King, David Jones and Harry Norris were for improper relations with inmates and one, Arthur Mitchell with the Cook; three more, William Withridge, Thomas Curtis and William Williams, for drunkenness; George Davis for being incapable and George Gibbs in 1866 for making false entries in his Porter's Book and giving his keys to paupers while he went out.

Other Porters came close to dismissal such as William Dymock in July 1896 when complaints were made about his "strong and unbecoming language." Henry Carew received a final warning in November 1857 after he had been discovered "distributing in the Workhouse the mischievous tracts of Prince, the head of the Establishment known by the name of 'The Abode of Love' near Taunton." He appeared to have had a large number of these tracts in his possession, which were subsequently destroyed. Just one Porter, Frank Barber, died in office in April 1870 from an unspecified cause, after completing one year and one month in the post.

For the officers life in the Workhouse could be as tedious,

isolated and monotonous as it was for some of the inmates. Within the institution so much of their time was prescribed by duties, rules and regulations. Generally they maintained the support of their employers, despite periodic attempts by the Central Boards to interfere. Except in the case of Porters there was a pronounced tendency to allow resignation rather than enforce dismissal, even if at times the removal of a key officer earlier, such as the Matron in 1863, would have been to their advantage. Resignations allowed testimonials to be given so that the person concerned would have an opportunity to obtain another post: in one way this could be seen as passing on a potential problem, but in another it displayed some concern for the officer and the realisation that in a different situation there might be a greater chance of success. The tensions and divisions created by the failure to have a married couple at all times as Master and Matron, and the occasional ill-health of the latter, led to the occurrence in 1863 which threatened the disciplined structure of part of the House as both the boys and girls were ignored at night. In October 1863 it came to the attention of the Board that,

> "for several months past the Schoolmaster had abandoned the boys at night and removed to a distant part of the house to sleep in the same bed with the Master......that the Matron and the Schoolmistress had done the same thing, and that the girls had been left by themselves at night."

All were warned and threatened with dismissal if it happened again. That this situation had existed for several months once again does raise a question as to the degree of close scrutiny exercised by the Guardians. (35)

15. Odds and Ends

a) Classification

The Report of 1834 into the operation of the Poor Law recommended that there should be at least four classes of paupers so that,

> "Each class might thus receive an appropriate treatment; the old might enjoy their indulgences without torment from the boisterous; the children be educated, and the able-bodied subjected to such courses of labour and discipline as will repel the indolent and vicious."

In practice, however, largely as a result of cost, this did not happen and all inmates were placed together in one general workhouse where the Poor Law Commissioners required the seven categories. They did not in their classification list specify any category for the sick, lying-in cases, lunatics, infants or vagrants and so these could be mixed with other inmates, although the latter were soon separated. Above all, there was no segregation by character or conduct, either past or present. In such a system it meant that the various groups could be brought into contact when undertaking the ordinary work of the House or at meal times.

The plan of the Wincanton Workhouse was totally inadequate in respect of classification, largely as a result of architects' inexperience. While the Central Board might exhort the Guardians to maintain rigid classification to ensure decency and for administrative reasons, there was in reality little that could be done at Wincanton, even if the Guardians saw it as a priority which is unlikely as the impression created during more than the first twenty-five years is that they were not over-concerned, unless a specific issue arose, as there were very few references to classification in that period. The fundamental problem was that the positioning of the yards allowed physical and verbal contact between different categories, mainly through the windows but also through doors if they were not locked. The solution would have been significant alterations or rebuilding but for economic reasons that was out of the question.

Various Inspectors had no difficulty in identifying the problem: in May 1869 Colonel Ward noted, "The classification is rendered very incomplete from the several classes having only one yard in common." In 1887 Inspector Courtenay repeated his analysis,

> "as I have often stated before the plan of the Workhouse is faulty, as owing to the different wards overlooking the Yards there is communication between the children and adult inmates."

Eight year later he once again noted the problem but also indicated that attitudes may have been changing: the accommodation was

> "only divided by small yards so that everything which goes on in one can be at once known by the inmates of another, for instance, the boys' yard is practically in communication with the men's apartments. There is no way in which this can be altered except by building an entirely new Workhouse, which would be considered favourably by the Guardians."

He was probably being over-optimistic as in the short term nothing happened.

The Guardians did make some small improvements during the century for as early as December 1846 they divided the able-bodied women's day room "for the better classification of female paupers", probably to isolate unmarried mothers. In 1870 they expressed the hope that building a new Schoolroom outside of the main Workhouse would "enable them to appropriate the rooms and yards to the better classification of the inmates," but their scaled-down final plan limited its effectiveness in this respect. The simple expedient of ensuring that doors were locked had some effect, for example, in May 1866 the Guardians ordered that, "the door leading from the Girls' Yard to the Women's Yard be always kept locked." In 1893 it was reported that the door from the Men's Yard which led to an area where vagrants cracked stone was kept locked when the vagrants were there but unlocked when they left so that there was a greater space for the men to exercise, one of the successful outcomes of Richard Lewis's complaints. That arrangement, however, did allow for the possibility of men gaining access to the garden and being able to climb over the wall.

Gradually national attitudes began to change and as early as the 1860s more emphasis was placed on separating women of "good and bad character", as it was expressed, and of trying to remove those whose malevolence made the lives of others miserable, but it was not until the liberalization of the 1890s that Inspectors regularly highlighted the issue. In October 1895 Inspector Courtenay recommended that Boards of Guardians should endeavour "to separate the old and respectable inmates, widows and deserted women of good character, and the young women with their first children from the idle, dissolute and ill-conditioned inmates." He did, however, accept that in small rural workhouses such as Wincanton, this would be extremely difficult to achieve. In 1898 Inspector Preston-Thomas returned to the same theme when he suggested that those of previous good character should have separate wards and other privileges such as newspapers and more visits but he too openly despaired of such refinements being implemented in his "backward" West Country workhouses. His visits to Wincanton certainly confirmed his opinions for there, "In the house he found the classification amongst the worst, the girls being insufficiently kept from the women; and he also found that the imbeciles were kept with the old men in one yard."

Significant alterations to the buildings in the early twentieth century did mean that by May 1902 he was able to report that the Workhouse "has been much improved by the recent alterations & additions." It was not however a complete solution as in 1909 the Chaplain was still able to complain that the girls had too much contact with the women and the boys with the men. (36)

b) Segregation

The Poor Law Commissioners envisaged that through their classification system there would be segregation, partly by age and certainly by sex, as not only did they wish to avoid paupers producing more children but also the cost of providing separate small rooms, particularly bedrooms, would have been prohibitive from their perspective. The separation of husband from wife and children from their parents remained one of the most hated aspects of the Workhouse System throughout the Victorian period as it deprived them of normal relationships. The number of families with children which could be affected was large as may be seen from Table 25.

Table 25. Children admitted to the Workhouse with parent(s)

	1837-8	1870-1
Children admitted with both parents	93	33
Children admitted with mother only	91	65
Children admitted with father only	13	4
Total	197	102
% of total admissions	30.6	13.2

Children of course could see their parents for a short period at dinner times and any visitors at designated times, which also allowed husbands and wives to meet under supervision. As the general classification at Wincanton was so poor, the rigid segregation envisaged by the Commissioners was more theoretical than practical but even so the policy of segregation remained distasteful to the pauper inmates. There was little justification for the strict maintenance of the system as the century progressed and the nature of the workhouses changed so that they were no longer institutions for disciplining the adult able-bodied labourers.

c) Rules, Regulations and Routine

Every aspect of life in the Workhouse was governed by Rules and Regulations, many of which were produced by the Central Board and adopted by Boards of Guardians, who in addition could introduce bye-laws of their own. In 1842 the Poor Law Commissioners issued a comprehensive list of rules which included silence at meal times, no obscene or profane language, no threatening or striking another person, no cards or games of chance and no entering any part of the Workhouse that was not designated their area. All inmates were required to "duly cleanse his or her person, not to drink or smoke or commit an act of indecency." Robert Clarke, the first Clerk of the Wincanton Board, was absolutely convinced that a rigid system was required,

> "it is equally indispensable that the internal arrangements be strict and un-relaxing, for if the house be once permitted to be used with as much freedom as the Cottage, or anything approaching thereto, either by the young or old, I am satisfied by daily experience that it will not produce the objects intended, that it will fail to be a test of destitution."

At the beginning of each day the Workhouse bell was rung, generally at 5.45 am both in winter and summer, although there were slight variations at different times such as 6.30 am in April 1898 and for the following five months. When the Workhouse was constructed it included a square open-sided brick Bell Turret which was some ten feet tall at its highest point and three feet ten inches wide. It was capped with sloping stones and contained a bell which was fifty-six pounds in weight. The turret was built above the wall which was between the scullery and the staircase which led to the Master's and Matron's rooms, just outside of the Dining Hall. From the bell a rope extended down to the ground floor at this point. As well as beginning the day, the bell was used to summon the inmates to each meal, to call the children to the schoolroom and to mark the end of the day when the paupers went to their dormitories. Every day half an hour after the morning bell was rung the Master and Matron visited each

Ward, except those of the aged and infirm, for the roll call. The aged and infirm, along with children under seven, were permitted half an hour extra in bed. At the end of each day the Master and Matron visited their respective Wards at nine o'clock in the summer and eight o'clock in the winter to ensure that all the paupers were in bed and that all lights and fires were extinguished. On one occasion when the Matron failed to do this in August 1852 a candle did actually cause a small fire.

Everything with which the inmates came into contact that could be marked was as in 1841 the Guardians ordered, "All the Goods, Chattels, Furniture, Clothes, Linen, Wearing apparel, tools, utensils, materials, and things capable of being marked be forthwith, and at all times hereafter, marked."

While this action was designed to prevent theft, it also had the effect of intensifying the depersonalisation which the inmates experienced for as a result of the process nothing which they came across was personal to them. Similarly their freedom of movement was restricted, which must at various times in the day, have left some of them feeling that they were in a prison. All the Ward doors were fitted with two nine-inch bolts and so the last thing each pauper heard at night was the sliding of these bolts. The Front Door with its lock and bolts was kept locked at all times with the Porter holding the keys during the day and the Master at night. In addition all external doors to the Yards had locks and bolts. The presence of locks with a common key did create some problems for as early as October 1839 it was decided to change the locks on the doors to the yards as "inconvenience" had been caused by a common pass key. Twenty years later it was resolved to change the locks and have separate keys for the Male and Female side of the house "that will not pass each other," because, "there being many Keys in the house that will pass the same lock and many locks so much worn as to be opened without any key at all."

Within the institution there was the recognition that some attempt had to be made at hygiene, even though the relationship between dirt and disease was not fully understood. On entering the Wincanton

Workhouse there was the compulsory bath, followed by the removal of the pauper's own clothes for fumigation if necessary and washing, to be replaced with the standard workhouse clothes. Each week a change of linen was arranged under the direction of the Matron, "To see that every pauper in the Workhouse has clean linen and stockings once a week, and that all the beds be kept in a clean and wholesome state." That requirement alone ensured that the able-bodied women employed in the laundry were kept busy and that the drying ground, which sloped away to the west of the Workhouse and on which Robert Garratt had erected twenty oak posts linked with copper wire in May 1839, was well used. For those paupers who were resident for more than a week there were baths which were at least fortnightly in the summer and once a month in the winter, but this pattern did seem to vary. In addition the failure to provide fixed baths in some parts of the House meant that almost on a daily basis many gallons of hot water were carried in buckets around the building.

To prevent sharp objects such as scissors and razors remaining in the hands of the inmates, to aid the elderly men and to maintain a reasonable appearance male paupers were shaved and hair was cut from time to time. For many years a local barber, R. Chick, attended the Workhouse on a regular basis and, for example, in December 1837 was paid £1 11s 5¼d for his services, £2 5s 6d in June 1838 and in July 1852 just 11s 8d. From 1857 this function was performed for a while by the Porter, although at some stage the services of an external barber were resumed for in October 1904 it was noted that the Union barber had completed 500 visits to the Workhouse, "That his 'operations' there total over 25,000." (37)

d) Safety and Comfort (?)

For the comfort of the Guardians, officers and inmates some form of heating was required. The Board Room had a large fireplace and the rooms of the officers were supplied with "neat Cottage Grates with side hobs – strong fire irons of the very best make and plain pattern."

The Fire Insurance Policy of April 1838 indicated that the remainder of the rooms were heated by common fireplaces or by steam pipes which came from a boiler in the cellar under the kitchen, the building being insured for £2,000. In February 1844 it was noted that the steam apparatus in the cellar had ceased to be used and the boiler removed. Rooms, which had previously been heated by this method, were in future to be warmed by Hendersons Aerothermus Stoves. A few of these were soon removed for an unspecified reason as in October 1850 the Guardians decided to replace them with open fire places in the Old Men's and Able-bodied Men's Day Rooms. By 1871 most of the house had common fireplaces, although one hot air stove remained in the Dining Hall and rooms that were used to store documents were heated with hot water pipes to remove the danger of fire. Not all the fireplaces were effective for in September 1894 the Visiting Committee recommended that a stove be placed in the Infirmary Ward instead of the fireplace "which is badly constructed and sends out no heat."

Even before the inmates moved into the new Workhouse a construction problem had emerged with the chimneys. The original specifications required all of them to rise four feet above the slates on the roof but this proved to be inadequate for when a trial was held in August 1838 they caused smoke to fill all the rooms. William Atyeo was paid £6 10s 0d to raise six of the chimneys four feet, which seems to have cured the problem. From the mid-1870s the Guardians were purchasing annually 180 tons of Radstock coal at prices which ranged from 13s 3s to 18s 6d a ton. No complaints appear to have been recorded about the level of heating so this may be one area which the inmates appreciated, especially as some came from damp cottages and were so destitute that they could not afford heating.

Considering that there was an increasing number of open fireplaces, a large number of locked doors and some windows with bars, there was a marked lack of concern about the danger of fire. The number of incidents of fire which were recorded was very few: in August 1852 a girl named Foyle was given a candle to go to bed but the Matron did not check that it had been extinguished and the result was that bedding to the value of £1 4s 4d was destroyed by fire in the Girls' Bedroom; in 1879 there was fire damage to a storeroom door which appeared to have been deliberate arson, although the culprits were never caught. It was only in the 1890s that more attention was paid to fire precautions. In his Report for 1890 Inspector Courtenay listed, "a portable Fire Engine, five buckets hanging in the Front Hall and a hydrant with a constant supply of water." By the time of his visit a year later he was able to report that, "a constant supply of water has now been laid on to all parts of the house." It was also noted that there was a Volunteer Fire Brigade in Wincanton and that they frequently visited the Workhouse for practice.

In 1894 the Local Government Board pointed out in a letter to the Guardians that in the event of fire it would be extremely difficult to escape from the central rooms, especially those of the Master and Matron, and recommended action be taken to remedy this. Their letter was not well received,

> "that from the construction and past history of the Workhouse they regard the danger from fire as infinitesimal, but even should one occur, there is in the town an efficient fire brigade possessing the necessary appliance for saving both life and property."

They went on to point out that the majority of the Guardians and ratepayers were more remote from the fire brigade and had no fire escapes in their houses. Their reply concluded,

> "they consider it rather hard that they should be called upon to provide superfluous appliances for the Workhouse when adequate precautions have already been taken."

At the same time, however, they adopted a recommendation from the Visiting Committee that a fire-escape costing £1 10s be installed. This consisted of "a rope and pulley…so that the Master can let himself to the ground in case of fire." Pressure from the Central Board continued and in 1896 Inspector Courtenay as able to report that the Guardians were "contemplating placing fire escape staircases at each end of the main building", but as so often was the case nothing happened in the short term.

While the Workhouse had enjoyed a good supply of water, first from its own well and then after 1875 from the Town Water Works, the Guardians paid relatively little attention initially to more than basic sanitation provision. Although Edwin Chadwick's study of public health published in 1842 helped to change attitudes, in rural areas, such as around Wincanton, for several decades many of the cottages of independent labourers had little if any sanitation and reports from their own Medical Officers of Health in the 1870s and 1880s continued to reveal the same situation. Little wonder, therefore, that the Guardians were slow to introduce improvements, especially as Inspectors such as Gulson found their arrangements satisfactory in the 1850s and 1860s. His comments after a visit on 13th November 1861 were typical,

> "I have been over the Workhouse, and have found all parts of it in excellent order, and I do not think that there is a cleaner, or more comfortable, or better-ordered Workhouse in the county, than that of the Wincanton Union."

The original building specifications required the construction of urinals for the men and boys, divisions being made by Keinton stone slabs three feet six inches high and one foot wide for men and three feet high and ten inches wide for boys. A small number of water closets were built, each with a wooden enclosure made from one and a quarter inch thick elm, "strongly fixed with proper holes and lids." They were flushed with water stored in three deal tanks, one holding 250 gallons and other two fifty gallons each. The contents of the water closets and urinals were transported by ten inch and twelve inch barrel drains, along with any surface water, to cesspools in front of the Workhouse. These were judged to be inadequate so in May 1838 a drain was constructed from them, across Mill Hams orchard "to the Back river." It was only in the late 1870s that the Workhouse drains were connected to the main town sewer.

In 1884 Inspector Courtenay proposed that the Guardians review the whole question of Water Closet provision, especially in the Infirmary Wards as one of the closets being out of action in the main building had created serious problems. Once again little seems to have been done. In November 1892 the Guardians accepted a tender of £63 16s 8d from Hill and Son of Bruton to replace all the flushing cisterns and in August 1898 the House Committee recommended additional Water Closets be built in the stone yard and another one by arching over a coal passage. A Plan drawn in 1898 shows twenty-two W.C.s on the ground floor, twenty on the first floor and none on the second floor.

To provide adequate natural light, with the exception of the Workrooms, all the rooms on the ground floor had sash windows which were three feet wide and three feet six inches high. On the other floors they were slightly smaller with the height being the same but were two inches narrower. The majority of rooms had more than one window, with the girls' large dormitory which over-looked their Yard having five. An extension to this was built over the Clerk's Office at the front of the building in 1868 with a further three windows. All the ceilings were white and all the walls in the rooms used by the inmates and all passages were whitewashed with the standard lime white. In addition all woodwork and ironwork was painted in an oil paint but the colour was not specified. Painting was undertaken periodically, for example, in May 1877 Mr Edwards was paid £39 10s 0d to paint the woodwork and ironwork on the outside of the House and Mr Stagg received £28 15s 0d for the same in May 1883 and £45 in 1891. In the same year Charles Mason was employed to paint the inside of the building "under the direction of the Master at 15s per week." Occasionally the Visiting Committee recommended some painting, for example, whitewashing the Infirmary and other rooms and colour washing the Entrance Hall in May 1893 and two months later that the Nurse's sitting room be painted.

At the end of the day for all inmates, both for those who had just suffered the trauma of entering the Workhouse and those who had experienced the boredom of the long hours, there was bedtime. This in itself was not necessarily a pleasant experience for, although heating and candles were available in the bedrooms, by the time the Master and Matron had completed their final visit of the day all fires and candles were extinguished and inmates, including children, left in the dark, locked rooms until the morning bell. Single beds were provided for the men and double ones for the women and children, although infants under two years of age slept with their mothers. The centralization of all pauper inmates in the old Wincanton Poorhouse in 1836 meant that the Master estimated that to furnish eighty beds he required "460 yards of Blanketing 500 yards of Sheeting 75 of Hessens 40 Rugs and Twenty additional mattresses." Some £73 19s 6d was paid to Mr Barrett for bedsteads and he also received £6 12s 0d for towelling, £86 10s 6d to E. Dean and £138 16s 5d to G. Russell for bedding. To make the sheets Kosman was paid £1 5s 0d. So the inmates could expect to have a wrought iron bedstead, sheets and blankets covered with a Rug, on a mattress, initially stuffed with straw or reed but when this proved difficult to obtain in 1860 with cocoa nut fibre instead. An experiment was tried in January 1897 when six hammocks were purchased but it was not followed up. Nothing seems to have been wasted for it was reported in 1895 that when new blankets were purchased the old ones were given to the Matron to put under the carpets. (38)

e) The Visiting Committee

To ensure the smooth operation of the Workhouse and that the conditions of the inmates were satisfactory, all Boards of Guardians were required to appoint a Visiting Committee from out of their number. Their duties were prescribed by the Poor Law Commissioners and included a visit to the House at least once a week, to check the reports of the Chaplain and Medical Officer, to examine the stores and investigate any complaints. They were also required from time to time to record their answers to a list of eighteen questions which covered amongst other areas: the cleanliness of the House and inmates, the work set, the diet, the regular attendance of the Medical Officer and the reading of prayers by the Chaplain. The destruction of all the Wincanton Visitors' Books, except the one covering the period 1893 to 1902, makes any assessment of the effectiveness of their role in the nineteenth century as a whole impossible. Certainly the surviving volume indicates that in the 1890s they covered many topics, heard complaints, made recommendations and expressed opinions. Periodic evidence from the Guardians' Minute Books and their Correspondence with Central Boards indicate that they were active through the decades and that the Guardians usually adopted their recommendations, as might be expected given the committee's composition.

In February 1895, in accordance with a General Order issued by the Local Government Board, an official Ladies Visiting Committee was formed. It is clear, however, that ladies had been visiting the inmates for many years before that. In June 1897 Mrs Barton and Mrs Rogers, the wives of the Chairman and Vice-Chairman of the Guardians, were presented with massive silver salvers and the former with a purse of gold sovereigns as well from eighty-five subscribers in recognition of the fact that "these ladies having long been visitors to the inmates of the Workhouse." No comment was made about their effectiveness although there was implicit criticism in the same year when Inspector Preston-Thomas stressed the importance of lady visitors, "If ladies visited, the rooms would be made to look pleasant with pictures and the lives of inmates would be happier." He informed the Board that he saw no written evidence that the ladies had visited the Wincanton Workhouse for twelve months and when a Guardian claimed that many visits went unrecorded in the Visitors' Book, the Inspector retorted that the book was all he had to go by.

The Visiting Committee obviously did not accept his criticism or change their ways for he noted in the Visitors' Book the following year that he could find that they had made only four visits in the previous fifteen months. Still they did not amend their ways for in 1900 he commented, "The Visiting Committee appear from this book to discharge their duties very imperfectly." The implication of the Inspector's comments was that there was a degree of laxity, not uncommon in the Wincanton Union, which probably meant that visits did occur, possibly not as frequently as they should have and that the questions were not answered as required, but they were not recorded. (39)

Conclusion

When attempting to assess the operation and effectiveness of a rural workhouse, it is helpful to judge it from various perspectives as those who had contact with it had different objectives. For the wealthier classes, the ratepayers, it was a significant part of their strategy for social control. As far as they were concerned for the peace of the countryside and the maintenance of the status quo, which was slanted exclusively for their benefit, it was essential that the poor knew their place and did not seek to rise above their station in life. The threat of the workhouse for a labouring man and his family if he was dismissed from his job and was unable to get another, was sufficient to keep their workforce docile, to ensure that they did not demand higher wages or better conditions. This group would judge the Workhouse to be successful as wages did rise only very slowly in East Somerset and there was little unrest for the remainder of the nineteenth century. In addition it allowed the ratepayers to demonstrate their social superiority as they were in a position to pay the rates which relieved the paupers. For a few of these ratepayers, however, who were small shopkeepers or skilled artisans, they were all too aware that there was a thin line separating them from the poor.

As the ratepayers did not want large increases in their rates an essential function of the Workhouse, as they perceived it, was deterrence. They did not want the poor, and especially the able-bodied poor, to be admitted in large numbers as that would cost too much. They therefore fully supported the imposition of rules, regulations, rigid discipline, a monotonous diet and hard labour, all of which they hoped would discourage admissions. In that sense the Workhouse was for them a great success as their rates did not rise rapidly and large numbers did not seek sanctuary within its walls. On the other hand, the failure to deal with the causes of poverty meant that they were committed to paying their rates year after year without any end in sight.

For those who were charged with the administration of the Workhouse system, from the Guardians to their paid officers, it was an outstanding success, for the simple reason that it worked, and for most of the period under consideration, it worked very, very smoothly. It was in many respects a pioneering system of administration that was to be copied in other areas as the nineteenth century advanced. In 1856 the Wincanton Board of Guardians claimed that not only had they saved their ratepayers £66,220 in twenty years but also,

> "Pauperism here is happily still on the decline, and by a continued firm, faithful, and impartial administration of the law the debasing pauper habits of the past and expiring generation, so dangerous to the public peace and so destructive to the well-being of the labouring population, will be effectually eradicated."

On the other hand, their administration did show the impact of the fear of centralization with its resistance to perceived interference, the lack of any will to undertake large expenditure to improve conditions as this would irritate the ratepayers, and a pronounced element of complacency, conservatism and possibly prejudice against certain groups.

The administrators generally dealt successfully with the change in the nature of the Workhouse from one of deterrence to one which placed greater emphasis upon care for the aged, sick and infirm, along with a permanent core of children. For the Wincanton Board it was a very slow change, usually under pressure from the Central Board and its Inspectors, something which at times they resented strongly. There is no doubt that they could have acted quicker but given the general conservatism of a predominantly rural area, the farmer-guardians were in many cases reflecting the wishes of the ratepayers. With the change in nature of the Workhouse came greater liberalization in some areas, which was well advanced by the mid-1890s, although children had benefited much earlier.

The Wincanton Board was content to undertake its obligations in its own way, preferably without external interference. As a result there may have been some degree of laxity in some areas for while they were committed to maintaining discipline through a multitude of rules and regulations, they were certainly not over-concerned to enforce the work requirement as comprehensively as some of the Inspectors would have wished. The Guardians may not always have monitored the relationships between the various officers as closely as they could and appeared surprised when disputes arose. It may also be that at times they did not supervise the actions of various officers, if some of the complaints from paupers contain an element of truth. The activities of their Visiting Committee were also criticized towards the end of the century, for while they might have undertaken their duties as required, their record keeping was almost non-existent.

While such an approach may not have satisfied the Central Board it may have had a very beneficial effect on life in their Workhouse. By not enforcing every rule and regulation to the letter as a matter of principle, and possibly displaying a degree of humanitarianism, while complaints were quite common general unrest virtually never occurred. The small number of incidents which did manifest themselves were related to a specific grievance and not the operation of the system itself.

The negative aspect of retaining so much local control was that it led to complacency. The Guardians were not innovators in the Wincanton Workhouse which it may be argued was detrimental to the life of the inmates as some areas could have been developed or improved earlier. Two main categories stand out in this respect: medical care, including that for lunatics and their approach to children and their education. What innovation there was came as a result of concerted external pressure and which meant that facilities and policies were often far behind what was available in other workhouses.

After 1834 there continued to be a strong philanthropic tendency in East Somerset as well as a commitment to supporting the concept of self-help. Although some of the Guardians disapproved of able-bodied paupers they were more sympathetic as a result towards other groups. While Charles Barton was Chairman of the Board of

Guardians and a local magistrate, he was also for over thirty years a Visitor of Sexey's Hospital in Bruton. Thomas Oatley Bennett, junior, of Bruton, served as a Guardian between 1877-1879 and 1888-1899 and was deeply involved in many other areas: Steward of the Visitors of Sexey's Hospital; Treasurer of the Shepton Montague Friendly Society; Honorary Secretary of the East Somerset Agricultural Society which gave rewards for long service and good practice amongst labourers; Honorary Secretary of the Managers of the National School; and a member of the Masonic Lodge. While social status and accepting their responsibilities in society played a part in their involvement, it also ensured that they brought a humanitarian approach and an experience of what was happening in other spheres relating to the poor.

From the perspective of the poor the Workhouse was a place to dread, a place to avoid if at all possible. It was to some extent irrelevant whether the stories about the workhouses were true or not, what was important was that many of the poor believed that they were. There were, however, positive aspects for the inmates which some of them may have recognised. The terrible conditions faced by some of the independent labourers throughout the nineteenth century were highlighted in the Introduction. The Wincanton Workhouse at least gave the paupers shelter with a roof over their head as well as some degree of warmth. It gave protection to, and provided some care for, vulnerable groups such as the sick, infirm, lunatics and elderly, all of which would have cost money outside of the Workhouse in the days before the Welfare State and the National Health Service. All paupers in the Workhouse received three meals a day, which may have been extremely limited in scope and monotonous in content, and certainly not the food and drink which many of the inmates would have preferred, but no-one starved to death in the Wincanton Workhouse. Every child in the House was provided with an education, again limited in scope and delivered by teachers with often poor qualifications and few skills but it was compulsory for more than forty years before it became so outside of the Workhouse. Education for the children of labourers involved payment until 1891 and this would have restricted the numbers attending. It may be possible to argue that in terms of education children who were resident in the Workhouse for a long period were actually in a superior position to the children of independent labourers.

The Central Boards and the Guardians tried to emphasize the social disgrace of admission to the Workhouse, but this may have been more a middle class concept as those existing in a precarious economic position in a rural area could not afford to pay too much attention to such disgrace. Casual usage by individuals and families suggest that those facing destitution could not be too worried by the social consequences, especially in periods of economic hardship when many of their neighbours were in a similar position.

On the negative side there were so many aspects of the Workhouse which the poor detested, from the confinement within an institution to segregation to labour to restrictive rules and regulations. Although in the early years of the workhouses horror stories appeared in the press about physical abuses, in reality the number of such instances was very few and virtually non-existent in the Wincanton Workhouse. Some paupers viewed being forced to work as a punishment and that other punishments such as being placed in the Refractory Ward on bread and water, were unacceptable. Judged by the standards of the day when a person could be transported for ten years just for stealing copper wire from the Drying Ground, they were not excessive. Similarly from a modern perspective the corporal punishment inflicted on children under fourteen would not be tolerated but once again contemporary attitudes towards children were different. While many inmates did not like their physical surroundings they were often better than those of independent labourers.

It was not in physical terms therefore that the inmates suffered but rather in psychological ones. For many of the paupers having to go to the Workhouse in the first place was a devastating blow to their self-esteem and pride, especially for some of the elderly who had previously supported themselves and their families for decades. There then followed the depersonalising admission procedure leading to the Workhouse uniform, no possessions of their own and the hated segregation of husband and wife, and parents from children, the anguish caused by the latter being difficult to imagine. As a result of inadequate classification in Wincanton Workhouse, some inmates who had led industrious and blameless lives found themselves forced to associate with those whose outlook on life was substantially different, the local prostitutes and those who had committed a range of offences in previous years.

Even the most resolute of characters must have been worn down psychologically by the monotony of workhouse life. Every minute of every day being regulated and accounted for in some way, from the summons of the first bell in the early morning to the final visit of the Master and Matron at night. Hours of boring work cracking stone, scrubbing, washing or plaiting straw, was interspersed with meals, the contents of which were known in advance and hardly every varied. For the elderly and infirm it could be worse as for them there were long hours with absolutely nothing to do but sit on hard seats in their Day Rooms or Wards. All inmates knew that every aspect of their daily life was governed by rules and regulations and any infringement was likely to lead to internal punishment or a trip to the local magistrates' court to be judged by the very men who were the Guardians, and then on to Shepton Mallet Gaol for a period of time with hard labour. Just occasionally it proved to be too much for an inmate so that in March 1869 John Parsons successfully committed suicide and in February 1897 James Parfitt tried but failed in his attempt when he stabbed himself in the Workhouse garden. Perhaps after all George Crabbe was correct in his observation:

"……..and, far the happiest they! The moping idiot and the madman gay" as they had little concept of what was actually happening.

The final word may be left to George Sweetman, a contemporary local resident, an amateur local historian and who reported on proceedings in the Workhouse in the 1890s for the 'Western Chronicle'. In 1903 he wrote:

> "Only those who knew the building as it was when first erected can realise what a series of improvements has since been made……..It has become more homelike; the

classification is better; the food and clothing are better; the children do not wear the pauper's badge as formerly; they go to the Board School with other children, and their moral tone is altogether raised. In a word instead of resembling a jail, it partakes more of the character of a hospital......It is less a harbour for loafers and women of light character. Each half yearly statement more and more shows that it is the aged of both sexes who go there to rest to the end of their days." (40)

APPENDICES

Appendix 1a

Dietary for the Able-bodied.

		Breakfast			Dinner				Supper		
		Bread	Gruel	Bread	Cheese	Peas or Pots. or other Veg.	Pickled Pork or Bacon with 12 oz Veg. or ¾ lb Peas	Suet Pudding	Bread	Cheese	Peas or Pots.
		oz	pints	oz	oz	oz	oz	oz	oz	oz	oz
Sunday	Men	7	1½	7	1½				6	2	
	Women	6	1½	6	1½				5	1½	
Monday	Men	7	1½	6				10	6	2	
	Women	6	1½	6				8	5	1½	
Tues.	Men	7	1½			12	6		6	2	
	Women	6	1½			12	5		5	1½	
Wed.	Men	7	1½			22			6	2	
	women	6	1½			20			5	1½	
Thurs.	Men	7	1½	7	1½						16
	women	6	1½	6	1½						16
Fri.	Men	7	1½			22			6	2	
	Women	6	1½			20			5	1½	
Sat.	Men	7	1½	6					6	2	
	Women	6	1½	6					5	1½	

The Aged and Infirm, are, at the discretion of the Guardians, to be allowed at Breakfast in lieu of the allowances at these meals, specified in the Table, 1 Pint of tea at each meal together with 8 oz butter weekly, the tea to be sweetened with an allowance of sugar, not exceeding half an ounce to each pint of tea.

Children under 9 years of age to be dieted at discretion, above 9 and under 16 to be allowed the same quantities as Women.

Sick to be dieted as directed by the Medical Officer.

March 1851

(PRO M.H. 12/10567, 11396/51)

Appendix 1b

Dietary for children from 2 to 5 years old.

	Breakfast			Dinner				Supper			
	Bread	Oatmeal Porridge	Bread	Butter	Potatoes or other Vegetables	Meat	Rice or Suet Pudd.	Bread	Butter	Potatoes or Peas	Milk and Water
	oz	pints	oz	oz	oz	oz	oz	oz	oz	oz	pints
Sunday	4	½	5	½				4	½		½
Monday	4	½					8	4	½		½
Tues.	4	½			8	3		4	½		½
Wed.	4	½			10			4	½		½
Thurs.	4	½	5	½						10	½
Frid.	4	½			10			4	½		½
Sat.	4	½					8	4	½		½

10 oz Flour and 3 oz Suet to every Pound of Suet Pudding
6 oz Rice to every Pound of Rice Pudding
Milk and Water. Half Milk
Porridge 12 oz oatmeal to every Gallon of Water.
May 1856.

For children 5 to 9 years of age the dietary was similar except:
    Bread   *1 oz more each time*
    Potatoes etc   *2 oz more except on Tuesday*
    Meat   *½ oz more*
    Rice or Suet Pudding   *2 oz more.*

(PRO M.H. 12/10569, 16427/56)

Appendix 2

Letters from the Workhouse.

a) Letter from Jane Sergeant to the Local Government Board

Union House
Wincanton
November 4*th* 1872

Sir

I have written to inform you that the meat we get hear is not holesome to eat and it is no good to mak enny complaint to the matron are the Master and there is a great deal of difficulty made hear between some of the inmates the mistress and the Master give them the best of everything to live with and some of us sometimes have not our laurince (*allowance*) Sir and I have written to ask you If it is allowed by your wish Sir and I want to know if there is not paid for one inmate as there is for another and the reason that I am in workhouse is for my affliction I am afflicted with the fits but I am not treated as if I am afflicted and some of the women there is hear with children is treated a great deal better then I am

I remain
Your Obedient
Servant Jane Sergeant.
(PRO M.H. 12/10573, 60704/72)

b) Letter from G. Gould to the Local Government Board

Wincanton March 13 1873

Dear Sir

I write these few lines to inform you that the managment of Wincanton Union I have been in here two years whith a bad eye and neck the complaint That I am making as a bout The doctor if I ask him for any Medicine he only make Sport of me if the Master see me in The open air he says that is no place for you why should we poor men be treated in This manner worser then a dog we cannot goes out for a day when we like I remain Yours G. Gould.

(PRO M.H. 12/10574, 17221/73)

c) Letter from Solomon Dewfall to the Local Government Board, March 1884

Dear Sir

I write to you Sir to tell you that the Industrial Trainer of this house when drilling the boys struck me across the head with a stick about One ½ inches round and made a blow in my head and I had a headache the rest part of the day and the day after, and he struck one of the boys whose name was G. Mead 8 years of age and hit him with his fist, took him up with his body and threw him on the floor and made a bruise in his forehead.

Solomon Dewfall

(PRO M.H. 12/10577, 30112/84)

d) Letters from Richard Lewis to the Local Government Board

Richard Lewis wrote many letters to the Central Board, especially in the 1880s and 1890s containing a wide range of complaints and allegations. The following extracts are taken from the year 1891-1892 and are typical of those of that period.

(i) April 15/91

Sir, Since men began to multiply on the face of the earth and forms of Government were established among them there has never arisen more coarsely cruel and wicked set of men than the men that are called the Wincanton Board of Guardians in fact so much have they gained the respect of the poor inmates that as soon as Wednesday comes around the Poor inmates sas this the Forty Teeves day and they have a Chairman whose is Barton whose crime could not be surpassed by any leader of a gang of brigans or robers. Now this man Charles Barton would not alow any poor inmate to make any complaint to any of the merciful Guardians of the Poor but if at any time they should Get an opportunity to speak to any of the Guardians the afore said Barton Would have them locked up……he forses the tramps not only to come to the Men Yard amonst the poor blind & crippled but he also forses the tramps to go up into their bedrooms to throw water about on the floor everyday not for the purpose of keeping it clean but to the intencion of bringing the poor inmates to an untimely end and of making them lowsey and catching all sorts of diseases….

(Alleges that Barton misappropriates their garden produce and other supplies)

Charles Barton has been extremely active in defying the Laws since the present government came into office to prove this I need but say since the present government came to office he has sent me to Shepton Mallet Gaol six times besides having me locked upp several times in what he calls the Union lockup……..

Richard Lewis
A blind pauper of Wincanton Union.

(PRO M.H. 12/10580, 34873/91)

(ii) June 5 91

Sir……..the complaint is There is a poor old woman here nearly 80 years old named Sweet. Now Street the woman that is called the Nurse saa to the poor old woman Sweet I wount have you lying in the beed by day. The poor old woman said I cant get upp Street then said I will see ware you cant at the same time catching hold of the poor old woman draging her off the bed throwing her on the floor and pulling her near to the top of the stairs…..Now I say that Street the Nurse is urged on by Petrie the woman that is called the Matron to do such cruel acts for Petrie herself violently assulted a poor weak minded young woman named Elizabeth Chamberlain on the 26 of May and she relies for support on men who calls them Guardians of the poor……… they are so inchanted by that lovely creature theat they are ready to back her upp in any act of cruelty plunder or murder.

Richard Lewis.

(PRO M.H. 12/10580, 51698/91)

(iii) June 25/91

Sir………Ther is a poor weak minded woman here named Elizabeth Chamberlain now this poor woman was violently assaulted by the old Tory squires. Bartons fancy woman Patery and also by one of his dogs Norris the man who is called the Porter.

(Alleges that she was placed in the lockup on short rations.)

They pulled up her cloths with the object of exposing her nakedness to the following tory scamps, Tory squires Barton, Rogers & Bradney. Tory squire dogs Mackey Hutchings & Boxer….I have also to say that Barton forse woman to take off their clothing and expose their nakedness against their will……..

Richard Lewis

(PRO M.H. 12/ 10580, 57433/91)

(iv) *Undated but received by the Board on 5 April 1892.*

Sir……. 1st the boys have not been allowed to wear hats or caps all this winter when out of doors even though it was snowing or raining second that the children are crying and coughing nearly the whole of the time that they are in what is called the dining Hall and that is sufficient proof to my mind that they are illused before coming in third that the woman are compelled to expose their nakedness against their will 4th that I believe the milk is well skimmed before either the children or the sick people get it…

(He also alleged that the Matron did not allow the potatoes to be washed, that the boys were forced to do the cooking, that the Matron tried to do everyone else's duties and that a carpenter was employed for months making picture frames that no one wanted.)

Richard Lewis
(PRO M.H. 12/10580, 31149/92.)

Appendix 3

Poem attached to a letter sent to the Local Government Board by Richard Lewis in 1884.

Come listen ye men, that labour for nought,
For a man that did so was bitterly taught,
When his labour was ended his employer did say,
Go to the union for there you may stay,

Then away to the guardians to seek relief,
But allas when he gets there they add to his grief,
They tell him that now, his labour is done
To the union workhouse he must surely come

Then cries the old man in wild despair,
Is there no one here who pitys my grey hair,
Will ye not allow me a half a crown each week,
That with that wife myself I may keep.

Then the kindhearted clerk who is too well paid,
Speaking for the board says we can't we are afraid
For if we allow it you'll spend it on beer
So we'll do no such thing but keep you in here.

Then He's locked up in the receiving ward,
Parted from all friends surely his fate is hard,
And there he is kept for 3 nights and 3 days,
That God would take him, he earnestly prays

Then the union doctor at the end of that time,
Goes to visit him and says do you find
Anything the matter with your flesh or your bones,
And Don't you think you could crack a few stones,

So in a close yard he is safely locked,
Whilst cracking the stones on an iron block,
And if he complains, it will sure to be in vain,
For the master will only laugh at his pain,

And if with his food, he ever finds fault
He'll find that the master will not long halt
But catch him hold quick to push him out of door
Saying you idle old scamp you won't get no more

And that's how he ends his miserable life,
When God calls him away from that place of strife
And takes him, to his happy bright home above,
For ever to dwell with the angels of love,

But, listen thou tyrant, though master thou be,
Far away thou shalt be called, thy judge to see,
And he will require of thee thy soul,
That he may send it to eternal Woe

Then howl, ye rich, ye that devour the poor,
And the widow rights, for yourselfs do procoure,
But the widow with children ye send to the gaol
And leave them in sorrow, their fate to bewail.

Now hearken, ye tyrants, ye guardians and squires,
God hath reserved for you a ceaseless fire,
Companions for the devil and his angels to be
Through the countless ages, of eternity.

  From Richard Lewis
  a blind pauper.

(PRO M.H. 12/10577, 47164/84)

Appendix 4

Letter from James Walter to Mr Winter of Wincanton

November 22nd 1847.

My dear Sir,

I write to you from this monastery to employ time, and give a current to thought, which else would become like an Irish bog, stagnant and reeking as a rotten fen. The monkish race in this locale are neither learned nor witty.

"Each ones brains at most,

Would scarcely keep him from a post."

They are the veriest ignorant clowns that ever walked cloisters, the most miserable apologies for humanity that ever ate

"Peas porridge in the pot nine days old."

I have seen much of man and his fantastic tricks, but this specimen of pauper friar's is the *ne plus ultra* of stolidity and low cunning. The most abominably rough hewed sand-stone statues Jove has sent from his probationary quarry. But my dear friend the worst part of the morale, is, they are malignant, envious and slanderous as incarnate fiends, so that one may say "Lord what are such men that thou art mindful of them or the sons of such slaves that thou visiteth them." Now poverty it is said, sharpens our faculties, and is often the hot bed of genius, curiosity and learning; but these underlings have no curiosity, no ideality, they are in the scale of creation behind "The poor Indian whose untutored mind sees God in the clouds, or hears him in the wind." They could never fancy Moses on the mount, nor the transfiguration, which the immortal Raphael did at Rome while painting the glorious picture for the Vatican of the eternal city of pageantry and popedom.

Thanks to Mrs. Winter for soap and huckaback that I may keep this film from my eyes which blinds these barbarians. The plum pudding also deserves praise.

May God keep you and her Sir, from affliction for relieving the woes of

J. Walter.

(Sweetman's Monthly Illustrated Journal, September 1872)

Notes and References

DRO	Dorset Record Office
PP	Parliamentary Papers
PRO	Public Record Office
SRO	Somerset Record Office
WRO	Wiltshire Record Office

1. Speeches of Wakeley and Oastler in the House of Commons cited in D. Roberts, Victorian Origins of the British Welfare State, Yale University Press, 1961, pp. 258, 265; Report of the Poor Law Commissioners, 1834, Appendix B1, Answers to Rural Queries, pt. I, PP 1834, XXX, p. 399; Report of the Royal Commission on the Employment of Children, Young Persons, and Women in Agriculture, 1867, PP 1868-9, XIII, p. 494; SRO DD/SAS/SW/7, Reminiscences of my Life 1901, by George Sweetman, p. 113; 'Western Gazette', 6 December 1872; 'Western Flying Post', 14 December 1852; PRO M.H. 12/10580, Report of Medical Officer of Health, 1891 (Poor Law Papers are catalogued under Ministry of Health, M.H., hereafter PRO is omitted); 'Western Gazette', 24 February 1893; M.H. 12/10577, Report of Medical Officer of Health, 25 February 1884; M.H. 12/10573, Report of Dr. Homes, 1872, p. 3; M.H. 12/10577, Report of Dr. Airy, 1885; M.H. 12/10573, Report of Sub-committee in Bruton, January 1872; SRO D/G WN 8a/16, Minute Book, 5 August 1891 (hereafter Minutes and number of volume).

2. WRO Hoare Papers, 383/961, Scale in the Wincanton Division for regulating the Allowance of parochial Relief; A.J. Carlyle and R.M. Carlyle, ed., The Poetical Works of George Crabbe, OUP 1914, p. 37, lines 215-225; SRO D/P/brut, Overseers' Account Books for Bruton; Abstract of Returns made by the Overseers of the Poor, 1776, p. 43, PP 1731-1800, vol. IV, 1775-1777; Abstract of Answers and Returns relative to the Expense and Maintenance of the Poor, 1813, 1814, 1815, PP 1818, XIX, pp. 110-111; WRO Hoare Papers,

383/125, undated letter from Sir Richard Colt Hoare to Mr Croker; DRO Ilchester Papers, D124, Box 241, Letter from Earl of Ilchester to his Steward, 28 November 1830; 'The Times', 4 December 1830; 'Sherborne Journal', 2 December 1830; DRO 3/B2, Dorchester Jail Register 1827-1834.

3. M.H. 32/85, Correspondence of Robert Weale, 9 September 1837; 'Western Chronicle', 15 January 1897; SRO D/G/WN 32/1, Particulars of Fittings in the New Union Workhouse, Wincanton, January 1838; M.H. 12/10576, Letters from F. Lancaster to Poor Law Board, 17 January and 20 April 1871; Minutes 8a/12, 15 August 1877 and 2 October 1878; Minutes 8a/1, Meetings 27 January, 24 February, 23 March and 27 April 1836.

4. 'Western Flying Post', 9 May 1836; M.H. 34/3, Register of Workhouse Expenditure, Wincanton; Sixth Annual Report of the Poor Law Commissioners, 1840, PP 1840, XVII, p. 57; 'Western Chronicle', 17 March 1899; PRO M.H. 12/10572, Architectural Notes, February 1871; Minutes 8a/18, 7 September 1898.

5. Statistics in Tables 2a and 2b are taken from the Returns made to the Poor Law Commission, the Poor Law Board and the Local Government Board. Minutes 8a/8, 2 June 1858; A copy of the letter which they wrote to the Poor Law Board may be found in P.W. Randell, 'The Wincanton Workhouse in the nineteenth century', in 'Notes and Queries for Somerset & Dorset', vol. XXXI, pt. 321, p. 427.

The statistics in Table 3 are taken from the four surviving Admission and Discharge Books, SRO D/G/WN 50/1-4. These cover the included ten years in full and parts of 1889 and 1893.

External details may be found on a Plan of Road Terrace and internal details in Particulars of Fittings, op.cit., both in D/G/WN 32/1.

Minutes 8a/2, 3 January 1838; Minutes 8a/9, 9 September 1863.

Information on the admission procedure may be found in the General Order of 1842 of the Poor Law Commissioners, published as Appendix 3 of their Eighth Annual Report, PP 1842, XIX, pp. 48-9. See also the Wincanton Board of Guardians own 24 rules issued at their Meeting on 11 May 1842, Minutes 8a/4. Minutes 8a/8, 19

November 1862; 8a/2, 1 August 1838; 8a/9, 6 July 1864, 25 January 1865; 8a/4, 7 April 1841; 8a/6, 7 August 1850; M.H. 12/10567, Letters 21 March and 5 April 1850.
6. Minutes 8a/2, 20 December 1837; M.H. 2/21, Correspondence of Poor Law Commission, 2 February 1846; M.H. 12/10567, 6 November 1850; M.H. 12/10568, 14 November 1855, 30 November 1853.
7. S.G. and E.O.A. Checkland, ed., The Poor Law Report of 1834, London, 1974, p. 430; Minutes 8a/2, 4 July 1838; 8a/1, 1 June 1836, 1 March 1837; 8a/2, 26 September 1838, 13 November 1839; Minutes 8a/5, 19 February 1845, 1 January 1846; 8a/4, 17 January 1842. For events in Andover see, I. Anstruther, The Scandal in the Andover Union, London, 1973. Correspondence relative to Bone Crushing, 1846, PP 1846, XXXIV, pp. 27, 33-4; M.H. 12/10567, Letters 2 and 5 February 1850.
8. ibid. Letter from Robert Clarke, the Clerk, to the Poor Law Board, 2 February 1850; Minutes 8a/8, 27 November 1861; 8a/6 12 January, 9 February, 16 February 1848; Return relating to Industrial Employment of Paupers, 1872, PP 1872, LI, p. 59; SRO D/G/WN 99(a)1, Visitors' Book 1893-1902 (hereafter Visitors' Book); 'Western Gazette', 22 December 1893.
9. Minutes 8a/4, 11 May 1842; M.H. 12/10568, Letter from Robert Clarke to Lord Courtenay, Secretary of the Poor Law Board, 24 August 1853; Minutes 8a/9, 8 June 1864; Visitors' Book, op.cit. 12 April 1893, 5 April 1898; Minutes 8a/1, 24 August 1836; M.H. 12/10567, Letter from Guardians to Poor Law Board, 5 February 1850; M.H. 12/10568, Letter from Clarke to Courtenay, 24 August 1853; Minutes 8a/8, 15 July 1857; 8a/9, 26 August 1863, 29 June 1864; Visitors' Book, op.cit. Entry by Preston-Thomas 4 April 1895; 'Western Gazette', 29 May 1896; M.H. 12/10567, endorsements on letters 5 February 1850, 13 February 1851; ibid. Appointment of Superintendent of Labour, 19 February 1851; M.H. 12/10582, Report of H. Preston-Thomas, 5 April 1898.
10. Report of the Poor Law Commissioners on the continuance of the Poor Law Commission, 1839, PP 1840, XVII, p. 30; M.H. 12/10573, Letter from Jane Sergeant to Local Government Board, 4 November

1872; Reports on Gaols: Shepton Mallet House of Correction, 1838, PP 1839, XXXVIII, p. 136; SRO D/G/WN, 9a/2, General Ledger 1836-1839, 9a/3 General Ledger 1849-1863; 'Western Flying Post', 6 March 1837; Minutes 8a/9, 8 February 1865; 8a/2, 16 May and 13 June 1838; 8a/5, 30 December 1846; 8a/17, 15 July 1896; 8a/15, 11 April 1888; 'Western Gazette', 3 September 1897; Minutes 8a/16, 1 February, 8 February 1893; Visitors' Book, op.cit. 10 May 1893; Minutes 8a/17, 15 July 1896; 'Western Gazette', 6 August 1886; Visitors' Book, op.cit. 14 February 1898; General Ledger 1836-1839, op.cit. pp. 175, 178; General Ledger 1849-1863, op.cit. p. 148; Minutes 8a/5, 14 January 1846.

11. Minutes 8a/7, 15 November 1853, 9 May 1855; M.H. 12/10570, Letter from Clarke to Poor Law Board, 8 June 1864; Minutes 8a/16, 30 March 1892; 8a/3, 17 June 1840; M.H. 32/71, Correspondence of E.C. Tufnell, Letter to Poor Law Board, 5 November 1845; Minutes 8a/5, 20 May 1846; M.H. 12/10568, Letter from Clarke to Poor Law Board, 15 June 1853; Minutes 8a/13, 25 April 1883; 8a/9, 4 March 1863; 8a/15, 18 May 1887; 8a/18, 9 June 1897; 'Western Gazette', 3 October 1890, 1 January 1892, 2 February 1894, 20 November 1896; Minutes 8a/1, 28 December 1836; 'Western Flying Post', 2 January 1860; Minutes 8a/9, 16 December 1863; 'Western Gazette', 1 January 1886; Minutes 8a/16, 20 April 1893, 14 March 1894, 27 July 1892.

12. Report of the Royal Commission on the Administration and Practical Operation of the Poor Laws, 1834, Appendix A, pt. 1, Report of Captain Chapman, PP 1834, XXVIII, p. 466; Minutes 8a/1, 9 November 1836; 8a/4, 20 April 1842; 8a/16, 21 December 1892. For an account of the extent of the Temperance Movement and the spread of Good Templarism, see, for example, Sweetman's Monthly Illustrated Journal published between 1871 and 1879. The statistics in Table 11 are taken from a series of Returns made to the Local Government Board.'Western Gazette', Letter from 'a Special Correspondent', 25 November 1892; Castle Cary Visitor, vol. V, 1904-5, p. 135; 'Western Gazette', 18 June 1909; ibid. 13 June 1883; M.H. 12/10576, Letter from John Gould to Local Government Board, 30 May 1881; 'Western Gazette', 1 January 1897; Minutes 8a/1, 11 May 1836.

13. Minutes 8a/4, 16 February and 9 March 1842; 8a/11, 13 January 1872; 8a/5, 3 December 1845; 8a/6, 9 October 1850; 'Western Flying Post', 20 June 1854; Report from the Select Committee on Aged Deserving Poor, 1899, PP 1899, VIII, p. 194; Return of Paupers over 60 years of Age in Receipt of Relief on 1 September 1903, PP 1904, LXXXII, p. 456; 'Western Flying Post', 13 October 1834; Circular on Workhouse Administration, 29 January 1895, PP 1896, XXXVI, pp. 107-112; Circular on Classification in Workhouses, 31 July 1896, PP 1897, XXXVI, pp. 9-10; M.H. 32/93, Report of Preston-Thomas, 2 November 1898; Fourth Annual Report of the Poor Law Commissioners, 1838, PP 1837-8, XXVIII, Appendix A, p. 50; Second Annual Report of the Poor Law Commissioners, 1836, PP 1836, XXIX, Appendix C, p. 452; Royal Commission on the Poor Laws and Relief of Distress, 1909, Appendix vol. XI, Miscellaneous, PP 1910, LI, p. 174.

14. Minutes 8a/4, 8 September 1841; 8a/6, 19 May, 8, 15, 22 September 1847, 18 April 1849; Twenty-Second Report of Poor Law Board, 1869-1870, PP 1870, XXXV, p. 10; Minutes 8a/8, 19 December 1860, Report of Mr Gulson; Visitors' Book, op.cit. 5 April 1898; Minutes 8a/8, 18 June 1862; 8a/19, 9 August 1899; 8a/9, July 1863; 8a/16, 8 July 1891; Return relating to Workhouse Infirmaries, 1896, PP 1896, LXXII, p. 694; Return showing Paupers on the Workhouse Medical Officers Relief Books, March 1870, PP 1870, LVIII, pp. 847, 872-3, 902-3, 992-3; Return of the Number of Indoor Poor on the Workhouse Medical Relief Book, 1867-8, PP 1867-8, LX, pp. 220-1, 265-7; Return relating to the General Diseases in Union Workhouses, 1877, PP 1877, LXXI, p. 381; Minutes 8a/8, 17 February 1858; 8a/3, 13 January, 13 May, 3 June 1840; M.H. 12/10575, copy of letter of Medical Officer to Board of Guardians, 3 February 1875, reply from Local Government Board, 15 February 1875; Visitors' Book, op.cit. 7 November 1894, 20 November 1895, 21 July 1894; 'Western Flying Post', 21 September 1840.

15. Minutes 8a/1, 24 August 1836; M.H. 12/10571, Letter to Poor Law Board, 7 February 1867; M.H. 12/10569, Letter to Poor Law Board, 28 February 1861; M.H. 12/10574, Letter from G. Gould to Local

Government Board, 13 March 1873; M.H. 12/10570, Letter to Poor Law Board, 21 October 1863; M.H. 32/71, Report of E. Tufnell, 15 July 1842; M.H. 12/10567, 6 August 1851; M.H. 12/10568, 11 May 1853; M.H. 12/10569, 27 March 1861; M.H. 12/10570, 30 March 1864; M.H. 12/10572, 25 May and 25 June 1871; M.H. 12/10577, 17 April 1884; Eighteenth Annual Report of the Poor Law Board, 1865-6, PP 1866, XXXV, Appendix: Nurses in the Sickwards of Workhouses, 5 May 1865, p. 24; Minutes 8a/3, 25 March and 22 April 1842; 'The Lancet', 1866, vol. I, p. 45; M.H. 12/10576, Report of Inspector Courtenay, 25 March 1880; Minutes 8a/18, 31 August 1898, 24 May 1899; M.H. 12/10573, Letter to Local Government Board, 13 June 1872; 'Western Gazette', 2 March and 23 November 1894; M.H. 12/10581, 9 April and 16 May 1895, 24 April and 11 June 1896; Visitors' Book, op.cit. 26 July 1893; Report on Nursing of the Sick Poor in Workhouses, 1902, PP 1902, XXXIX, p. 611.

16. Third Report of the Commissioners in Lunacy, 1848, PP 1849, XXII, p. 7; Thirty-ninth Report of the Commissioners in Lunacy, 1884, PP 1884-5, XXXVI, p. 114; M.H. 12/10572, Report of Visit of Commissioners in Lunacy, 20 August 1862; M.H. 4/1, Extracts from Minute Book of the Poor Law Commission, 1839-1840, 17 December 1839; M.H. 12/10567, Report of Visit by the Commissioners in Lunacy, 11 June, 1850; M.H. 12/10576, Report of Visit, etc. 20 August 1869; M.H. 12/10576, Report of Visit, etc. 30 May 1881; M.H. 12/10570, Report of Visit, etc. 11 April 1865; M.H. 12/10581, Letters to Local Government Board, 1 June, 15 July, 22 August 1893; M.H. 12/10578, Report of Visit, etc. 11 April 1865; M.H. 12/10578, Report of Visit, etc. 1 August 1888; M.H. 12/10569, Report of Visit, etc. 29 June 1861; M.H. 12/10582, Report of Visit, etc. 20 September 1897; M.H. 12/10570, Report of Visit, etc. 4 April 1866; M.H. 12/10573, Report of Visit, etc. 12 November 1872; M.H. 12/10581, Report of Visit, etc. 24 April 1894; Minutes 8a/17, 30 May 1894; M.H. 12/10569, Report of Visit, etc. 20 July 1858; M.H. 12/10570, Report of Visit, etc. 4 April 1866; M.H. 12/10582, Report of Visit, etc. 20 September 1897; Minutes, 8a/18, 16 June 1897; M.H. 12/10569, Report of Visit, etc. 29 June 1861; M.H. 12/10568, Report of Visit,

etc. 27 January 1854; M.H. 12/10572, Report of Visit, etc. 20 August 1869; M.H. 12/10579, Report of Visit, etc. 12 February 1890; M.H. 12/10569, Report of Visit, etc. 11 August 1856 and 19 May 1857; M.H. 12/10579 Report of Visit, etc. 12 July 1886; Minutes 8a/17, 18 February 1895; 'Western Gazette', 23 February 1883.

17. Statistics on the number of children are based upon the Admission and Discharge Books and Annual Returns to the Central Board. Minutes 8a/15, 6 August 1890; 8a/16, 15 April 1891 and 13 April 1892; Return of the Number of Children in Workhouses, 1849, PP 1849, XLVII, pp. 2-3; Minutes 8a/4, 13 and 20 October 1841; M.H. 12/ 10569, Dietary for Children, 1856; Minutes 8a/5, 8 November 1843; 8a/4, 11 May 1842; 8a/6, 23 January 1850; 8a/13, 25 August 1880; Return of Children in Workhouses 25 March 1873, PP 1873, LV, p. 55; Minutes 8a/16, 18 November 1891, 29 November and 20 December 1893; M.H. 12/10576, Letter to Local Government Board, 6 July 1881, Letter of Cornelius Bidgood, 29 November 1880, Letter of Guardians, 17 December 1880; S.R.O. D/PS/winc 1/13, Magistrates' Register 1882-1883; M.H. 12/10576, Report of Local Government Board investigation, 22 March 1881; Minutes 8a/17, 11 July, 15 August 1894, 28 April 1897; Minutes 8a/16, 10 April 1895, 22 and 29 January 1896; M.H. 12/10576, Report of Visit, etc. 22 March 1881; 'Western Chronicle', 18 June 1897.

18. Minutes 8a/4, 9 August 1848; 8a/6, 18 September 1850; 8a/12, 31 January 1877; 8a/7, 23 August 1855; 8a/8, 6 August 1862; 8a/4, 26 December 1849; 8a/17. 15 April 1895 and 14 October 1896; Fifth Annual Report of Poor Law Commissioners, 1839, PP 1839, XX, p. 13; Minutes 8a/1, 25 May 1836; 8a/8, 5 October 1859, 24 July 1861; 8a/9, 23 July 1863; 8a/8, 4 August 1858, 27 April 1859; 8a/16, 25 May 1892; 8a/17, 27 March 1895; S.R.O. D/G/WN 38/1, Register of Young Persons hired from the Workhouse and 38/2, Register of Visits; Return relating to Workhouse and District Schools, 1866, PP 1866, LV, p.467; Tenth Annual Report of Local Government Board, 1880-1, PP 1881, XLVI, p. 326; Minutes 8a/16, 13 January 1892; Minutes of the Committee of Council on Education: Report of J. Ruddock, Esq. in the Southern District for 1850, PP 1852, XXXIX, p. 89.

19. See for example visits Minutes 8a/7, 14 September 1871 and 8a/16, 15 July 1891; 'Western Flying Post', 8 August 1873; Minutes 8a/7, 28 May 1856; 8a/18, 16 June 1897; 8a/16, 11 May and 2 November 1892; 8a/18, 17 November 1897, 25 January 1899; 8a/7, 7 November 1855; 8a/16, 23 December 1891, 1 June 1892, 29 March 1893; 8a/17, 1 April 1896, 27 May 1896; 8a/15, 18 April 1888, 24 July 1889; 8a/18, 6 October 1897, 26 July 1899; Bath and Wells Diocesan Kalendar, 1891, p. 273; Minutes 8a/15, 3 April 1889.
20. Fourth Annual Report of Poor Law Commissioners, 1838, PP 1837-8, XXVIII, p. 290; M.H. 32/85, Correspondence of Robert Weale, 19 September 1837; Fourth Annual Report of the Local Government Board, 1874-5, PP 1875, XXXI, p. 205-6; 'Bristol Mercury', Letter of T.E. Rogers, 22 September 1898; Abstract of the Answers and Returns on Education, 1833, PP 1835, XLII, pp. 218, 229, 790-832; Correspondence of Robert Weale, op.cit. 19 September 1837; General Order: Workhouse Rules, op. cit. p. 56; Minutes 8a/1, 1 June 1836; 8a/2, 25 April 1837; General Ledger, 1849-1863, op.cit.; Eleventh Annual Report of the Local Government Board, 1881-2: Report of Dr. Clutterbuck for 1881, PP 1882, XXX, pt. I, p. 287.
21. SRO WN 32/1 Particular of Fittings, January 1838; M.H. 12/10567, Letter to Poor Law Board, 23 August 1852; General Ledger, 1849-1863, op.cit., p 121; M.H. 12/10572, Letter to Poor Law Board, 2 February 1870; SRO WN 32/3, Fire Insurance Policy, 6 December 1871; M.H. 12/10573, Report of T.B. Browne, 31 January 1872; M.H. 12/10567, Letters to Poor Law Board, 11 August and 2 December 1852; M.H. 12/10567, An Application for the Supply of Books, 6 October 1852; Minutes 8a/12, 1 May 1878; M.H. 32/108, Reports of the School Inspectors: T.B. Browne, 1864; Minutes 8a/1, 17 May and 4 October 1837, 22 May 1839, M.H. 12/10571, Letters to Poor Law Board, 2 November and 17 December 1868; Minutes 8a/3, 12 June 1839; 8a/5, 5 February 1845.
22. Minutes of the Committee of Council on Education: Report of J. Ruddock for 1849, PP 1850, XLIII, p.103; Report of J. Ruddock for 1851, PP 1852, XL, p. 143; Minutes 8a/6, 5 December 1849; M.H. 12/10568, Report on the Schoolmaster by J. Ruddock, 16 June 1853;

M.H. 12/10569, Report on Wincanton Union, 11 June 1861; M.H. 12/10571, Report of T.B. Browne, 19 February 1867, p. 4, 30 January 1868, p. 4; M.H. 12/10572, Report of T.B. Browne, 28 January 1869, p. 4, 16 March 1870, p. 4; M.H. 12/10574, Report of Dr Clutterbuck, 15 May 1874; M.H. 12/10570, Report of T.B. Browne, 15 March 1866; M.H. 12/10573, Report of T.B. Browne, 31 January 1872; Royal Commission on the Poor Law and Relief of Distress, 1909, Appendix, vol. XI, PP 1910, LI, p. 174; Minutes 8a/13, 4 July 1883; 8a/16, 13 May, 20 May, 17 June, 24 June 1891; 8a/17, 13 March 1895.

23. M.H. 12/10569, Letter to Poor Law Board, 15 August 1857, Minutes 8a/8, 18 November 1857 and 26 May 1858; 'Western Gazette', 2 August 1872; M.H. 12/10580, Report on Industrial Instructor, 25 November 1890; M.H. 12/10575, Report of Dr Cluttercuck, 14 August 1876; Return of the Names of Adult Paupers, 1861, PP 1861, LV, p. 350; Report of T.B. Browne for 1872, PP 1873, XXIX, p. 105; Report of Dr Clutterbuck for 1886, PP 1887, XXXVI, p. 277.

24. Report of the Royal Commission on the Administration of the Poor Law, 1834, Appendix B, Answer to Rural Queries, PP 1834, XXX, p. 407, Q. 49; Minutes 8a/2, 12 September 1838; Return of the Total Number of Children in the Workhouses, 1841, PP 1841, XXXI, pp. 31, 35; M.H. 12/10568, Letter to Poor Law Board, 24 January 1853; Return showing the Number of Bastard Children born in the several Workhouses, 1864, PP 1864, LII, p. 88; Minutes, 8a/2, 13 December 1837; M.H. 12/10568, Letters to Poor Law Board, 1 June and 1 March 1853; Return relating to the Classification of Workhouse Inmates, 1854, PP 1854, LV, p. 660; Royal Commission 1909, op.cit. Appendix vol. XI, p. 174; Minutes 8a/7, 5 October and 12 October 1853; SRO WN 50/1, Admission and Discharge Book.

25. Circular to Boards of Guardians, 15 February 1841, PP 1841, XXI, p. 175; First Report of the Poor Law Board, 1848: Vagrancy, PP 1849, XXV, pp. 24-5; First Report of Local Government Board, 1871-2, Appendix, PP 1872, XXVIII, pp. 58-60; Minutes 8a/10, 24 April 1870; M.H. 12/10577, Letter to Local Government Board, 1 March 1883; M.H. 12/10573, Report of E. Wodehouse, 24 January 1872; M.H. 12/10572, Report of Colonel Ward, 12 May 1869; Minutes

8a/4, 11 May 1842; 8a/5, 10 January 1844; ibid. Letters 12 August and 18 November 1846; Visitors' Book, op.cit. 4 April 1895; Reports on Vagrancy by Poor Law Inspectors, 1865, PP 1866, XXXV, p. 636; Visitors' Book, op.cit. 15 November 1893; 'Western Gazette', 17 January 1896; Minutes 8a/17, 15 April 1896; 'Western Chronicle', 17 March 1898; Report and Communications on Vagrancy, 1848, PP 1847-8, LIII, p.321; M.H. 12/10570, Letter from Clarke to Poor Law Board, 6 May 1863; 'Western Gazette', 13 March 1896; 'Western Chronicle', 10 March 1898; ibid. 17 March 1898; Castle Cary Visitor, vol. I, 1898-7, p. 38; 'Western Flying Post', 4 November 1862; SRO D/PS/winc 1/7, Magistrates' Entry Book, 1868-1871; 'Western Gazette', 6 April 1886, 6 May 1881; 'Shepton Mallet Journal and East Somerset Herald', 2 October 1863; 'Western Flying Post', 2 March 1846.

26. Minutes 8a/4, 14 June, 6 July 1842; M.H. 12/10567, Letter to Poor Law Board, 21 March 1851; Minutes 8a/6, 15 January and 5 February 1851; SRO Q/AGs 14/1, Shepton Mallet General Register 1855-1862; Minutes 8a/3, 19 August 1840; 'Western Flying Post', 4 March 1870; 'Sherborne, Dorchester and Taunton Journal', 1 November 1881; Minutes 8a/4, 13 January 1841; 'Western Gazette', 28 June 1872; Minutes 8a/16, 20 May 1891; M.H. 12/10576, Letter to Local Government Board, 30 May 1881; 'Western Gazette', 5 September 1879; Minutes 8a/2, 30 May 1838; 8a/4, 8 June 1842; 'Western Flying Post', 13 January 1844 and 25 March 1843; Minutes 8a/3, 13 March 1839; 8a/4, 10 March 1841, 14 September 1842; 8a/5, 2 November 1842; 8a/6, 31 March 1847; 'Western Gazette', 9 April 1886; 'Western Chronicle', 17 September 1897; Minutes 8a/16, 27 January 1892; 8a/18, 25 March 1898; 'Western Flying Post', 30 October 1868; Minutes 8a/17, 11 March 1896, 15 May 1895; 8a/16, 10 May 1893; 8a/4, 24 February 1841; 'Western Gazette', 28 June 1872, 25 December 1874; Minutes 8a/6, 27 January, 2 March, 23 August 1893; 8a/17, 6 February 1895; Visitors' Book, op.cit. 10 May 1893; Minutes 8a/17, 11 March 1896; 8a/5, 14 August 1844; SRO D/PS/winc 1/1, Magistrates' Entry Book 1854-1857; D/PS/winc 1/7, op.cit. 1868-1871; 'Western Flying Post', 4 November 1862; Minutes

8a/16, 19 July 1893; 'Western Gazette', 30 July 1886, 1 November 1889; Minutes 8a/1, 21 September 1836; 8a/4, 20 April 1842; ibid. 10 February 1841; M.H. 12/10576, Letter to Local Government Board, 11 July 1877.

27. Minutes 8a/1, 1 June 1836; 8a/4, 4 July 1838; WN 32/1, Particulars of Fittings and Plan of 1898 by A.J. Picton; Minutes 8a/5, 3 January 1843; 8a/4, 11 May 1842; 8a/9, 30 May 1866; Return relating to Industrial Employment, 1872, PP. 1872, LI, p. 465; Minutes 8a/5, 4 October 1843; 'Western Gazette', 28 June 1872; 'Western Chronicle', 12 March 1897; Return of the Number committed to any Prison for any offence in a Union Workhouse, March 1835 to March 1842, PP 1843, XLV, pp. 344, 351, 367; Return from Workhouses, 1 January 1853, PP 1852-3, LXXXIV, p. 466.

28. M.H. 12/10567. Letter from Poor Law Board, 6 February 1850; M.H. 32/93, Letter from Lord Courtenay to Local Government Board, 28 October 1895; Royal Commission on Poor Law 1909, op.cit. p. 174; M.H. 12/10567, Letter to Poor Law Board, 23 January 1850 and from P.L.B. 6 February 1850; Minutes 8a/7, 16 December 1840; 8a/10, 14 February 1872; M.H. 12/10568, Letter to Poor Law Board, 25 April 1855; M.H. 12/10573, Letter to Local Government Board, 27 December 1871; Minutes 8a/12, 22 November 1876, 21 February 1877; M.H. 12/10575, Letter to Local Government Board, 24 November 1876, 2 August 1877, Letters from Jones to L.G.B. 11 July, 18 August 1877; Minutes 8a/16, 19 August 1891; M.H. 12/10581, Letter to Local Government Board, 21 March 1895; Minutes 8a/2, 26 July, 20 December, 27 December 1837, 16 March and 28 September 1838; 8a/3, 6 November 1839; 8a/16, 18 November, 22 July and 29 July 1891; 'Western Gazette', 24 July 1894; M.H. 12/10576, Letter from David Jones to Local Government Board, 11 July and 18 August 1877; Minutes 8a/17, 7 August 1895; 8a/6, 23 January 1853; Minutes 8a/16, 17 May 1893.

29. Census of Great Britain: Religious Worship, PP 1852-3, LXXXIX, p. 367; Minutes 8a/1, 1 June 1836; 8a/2, 4 July 1838; 8a/4, 11 May 1842; SRO WN 78/1, 78/2, Creed Registers 1869-1900; Minutes 8a/2, 15 August 1838; Report of Poor Law Inspectors: E. Gulson, 1866, PP

1867-8, LXI, p. 224; Fifth Annual Report of Poor Law Commissioners, 1839, PP 1839, XX, p. 44; Return relating to Workhouse Chaplains, 1880, PP 1882, LVIII, pp. 766-7; Minutes 8a/13, 25 August 1880; 8a/15, 27 July and 3 August 1887.

30. SRO D/G WN 69, Register of Deaths 1866-1906; Minutes 8a/16, 18 November 1891; 8a/8. 9 March 1858; Visitors' Book, op.cit. 14 February 1898; Minutes 8a/15, 19 December 1888; 8a/17, 16 and 23 September 1896; M.H. 12/10567, Letter to Poor Law Board 16 April and Reply 3 May 1851; Minutes 8a/9, 7 November 1866; 'Western Gazette', 29 May 1896; Minutes 8a/19, 8 November 1899; 'Western Gazette', 26 June 1896; Minutes 8a/6, 17 April 1850; 'Western Flying Post', 24 July 1868; 'Western Gazette', 11 April 1873; M.H. 12/10572, Letter to Poor Law Board, 18 March 1869; 'Western Gazette', 6 February 1885; Minutes 8a/1, 23 November 1836 and 'Western Flying Post', 28 November 1836; M.H. 12/10568, Letters to Poor Law Board, 13 and 20 December 1853.

31. Minutes 8a/1, 1 June 1836; 8a/2, 4 July 1838; 8a/4, 11 May 1842; 8a/3, 16 October 1839; 8a/5, 2 October 1844; 'Western Flying Post', 11 January 1841; 2 January 1860, 1 January 1861; 'Western Gazette', 31 December 1880; 'Western Chronicle', 15 January 1897, 3 February 1899; 'Western Flying Post', 2 January 1860; 'Western Gazette', 31 December 1880; 'Western Chronicle', 3 February 1899; 'Western Gazette', 4 January 1878; 'Western Chronicle', 31 December 1897; Visitors' Book, op.cit 6 July 1893; 'Western Chronicle', 2 July 1897, 16 September 1898; Minutes 8a/4, 11 May 1842; 8a/5, 20 December 1843, 2 October 1844; 8a/16, 12 November 1890; 8a/18, 16 June 1897, 9 March 1898; 'Western Chronicle', 16 June 1899; 'Western Flying Post', 16 September 1870; Minutes 8a/17, 17 January 1894; Visitors' Book, op.cit. 31 January 1894, 3 February 1895.

32. Visitors' Book, op.cit. 19 December 1894; M.H. 12/10576, Letter from John Gould, 30 May 1881; Minutes 8a/16, 16 December 1891, 25 October 1893; 8a/17, 9 January 1895; 8a/4, 13 January 1841; 8a/5, 23 August 1843; M.H. 12/10576, Report of Inspector Courtenay, 18 May 1882; Minutes 8a/16, 17 May 1893; 8a/5, 12 April 1843; 8a/4, 24 February 1841; M.H. 12/10576, Letter to Local Government

Board, 6 July 1881; M.H. 12/10567, Letter to Poor Law Board, 16 July, 25 July 1851 and from Poor Law Board to Cox, 31 July 1851; M.H. 12/10577, Letter of Complaint, 18 March 1884, Letters, 2 April, 10 April, 24 April, Report of Clutterbuck, 23 July 1884, Report of Courtenay, 21 August 1884, Letter of Reprimand, 20 September 1884; Minutes 8a/12, 4 July 1977, 17 March 1880; M.H. 12/10576, Report of Inspector Courtenay, 18 May 1882; Minutes 8a/17, 7 August 1895; M.H. 12/10580, Letter from Richard Lewis, 14 April 1892; 'Western Gazette', 1 November 1889; M.H. 12/10582, Report of Inspector Preston-Thomas, 26 April 1897; 'Western Gazette', 30 July 1886; Sweetman's Illustrated Journal, September 1872

33. Eighth Annual Report of Poor Law Commissioners: General Order, Workhouse Rules, PP 1842, XIX, pp. 60-62; 'Western Flying Post', 26 May 1871; Visitors' Book, op.cit. 13 March 1895; Minutes 8a/3, 24 July 1839; M.H. 12/10567, Endorsement to Letter, 2 February 1850 and Letter to Sealey, 6 February 1850; Minutes 8a/6, 12 February 1851; 8a/9. 8 February, 29 March and 23 March 1865; M.H. 12/10568, Letter to Poor Law Board, 15 February 1854; M.H. 12/10569, Letter from Matron, 26 February 1861, Letter to Poor Law Board, 13 November 1861, Letter to Poor Law Board, 15 June 1859; Minutes 8a/9, 22 July, 29 July, 5 August, 9 September 1863; M.H. 12/10570, Letter to Poor Law Board, 13 January 1864, Letter endorsed by Gulson, 27 August 1866; Minutes 8a/15, 19 February, 12 March, 2 April, 23 April 1890; 8a/16, 21 January, 8 July 1891; 8a/17, 3 September 1896; M.H. 12/10581, Letter 20 October, 21 October, 7 November 1896; M.H. 12/10582, Letter 17 October 1898; Minutes 8a/4, 10 November 1841; 8a/3, 12 June 1839; 8a/5, 18 October 1843, 23 September 1844, 19 February 1845.

34. PRO Ed 7/104, No. 52, Preliminary State of Income and Expenditure: Bruton Mixed School; 'Western Flying Post', 10 March 1871; General Order: Workhouse Rules, 1842, op.cit. p. 64; Minutes 8a/7, 21 November 1855; 8a/12, 27 March 1878; M.H. 12/10578, Letter to Local Government Board, 24 July 1886; Report of Dr. Clutterbuck for 1881, PP 1882, XXX, pt. I, p. 288; Report on the Training of Pauper Children, 1841, London, 1841, p. viii; M.H. 12/10567, Letter to Poor

Law Board, 8 September 1852; M.H. 12/10570, Letter to Poor Law Board, 27 August 1866; M.H. 12/10574, Report of Dr Clutterbuck, 15 May 1874.

35. Minutes, 8a/2, 28 November 1838; General Order: Workhouse Rules, op.cit. p. 63; Minutes 8a/2, 4 July 1838; M.H. 12/10568, Letter to Poor Law Board, 22 June 1852; M.H. 12/10569, Letter to Poor Law Board, 25 March 1857; Minutes 8a/11, 18 March and 25 March 1874; M.H. 12/10576, Letter to Local Government Board, 13 February 1879; Minutes 8a/6, 1 October 1851; 8a/12, 27 March 1878; M.H. 12/10580, Appointment of Porter. 1 October 1891; Minutes 8a/17, 2 October 1895; M.H. 12/10572, Letter to Poor Law Board, 25 May 1871; M.H. 12/10569, Appointment of Porter, 12 March 1856; M.H. 12/10568, Appointment of Porter 7, 12, 14, 21 September, 1853; Minutes 8a/17, 22 July 1896; M.H. 12/10567, Letters to Poor Law Board, 26 November 1854; M.H. 12/10570, Letter to Poor Law Board, 21 October 1863. "The Abode of Love." This group was established in 1846 in Spaxton near Taunton by Henry Prince. He was the vicar of Charlinch until his license to preach was revoked by the Bishop of Bath and Wells for alleged 'carnal insinuations' with lady converts. After a period in Suffolk he moved to Weymouth where he undertook a revivalist campaign which achieved many converts and raised a considerable amount of money which allowed him to buy an estate in Spaxton. This consisted of a house with eighteen bedrooms, spacious grounds with outbuildings, stables and several cottages. It also had its own chapel which was furnished with easy chairs and a billiard table. Prince was viewed by his devout followers as the embodiment of the Holy Ghost. In this community love was meant to be spiritual but over the years there were a number of sex scandals often centred on Prince himself. The group was widely attacked in the popular press and it horrified respectable society, especially as there were the moral implications and accusations of brainwashing. Despite all this it survived the death of Prince in 1899 – itself a devastating blow as many believed he was immortal – and finally closed in 1956. For more details see, C. Mander, The Reverend Prince and his Abode of Love, EP Publishing, 1976.

36. S.G. and E.O.A. Checkland, ed., The Poor Law Report of 1834, London, 1974, p. 375; M.H. 12/10572, Report of Colonel Ward, 12 May 1869; M.H. 12/10578, Report of Mr Courtenay, October 1887; M.H. 12/10581, Report of Lord Courtenay, 4 April 1895; Minutes 8a/5, 23 December 1846; M.H. 12/10572, Letter to Poor Law Board, 2 February 1870; Minutes 8a/9, 30 May 1866; M.H. 12/10581, Letter to Poor Law Board, 24 July 1893; M.H. 32/93, Classification of Workhouse Inmates: Letter from Lord Courtenay, 28 October 1895, Reports of Preston-Thomas, 27 October and 2 November 1898; 'Western Chronicle', 18 June 1897; Visitors' Book, op.cit. 30 May 1902; Royal Commission on the Poor Laws, op.cit. p.174.

37. General Order: Workhouse Rules, op.cit. pp. 55-57; M.H. 32/85, Correspondence of Assistant Poor Law Commissioners, Letter from Robert Clarke, 6 September 1837; Minutes 8a/18, 20 April 1898; 8a/4, 3 March 1841; 8a/3, 16 October 1839; 8a/8, 24 August 1850; General Order: Workhouse Rules, op.cit. p.62; SRO D/G/WN 9a/2, General Ledger, 27 December 1837, 27 June 1838; 9a/3, General Ledger, op.cit. 28 July 1852; Castle Cary Visitor, vol. V, 1904-5, p. 82.

38. D/G/WN 32/1, Particulars of Fittings, op.cit.; WN 32/3, Fire Insurance Policy, op.cit. 25 April 1838, endorsed 28 February 1844, 6 December 1871; Minutes 8a/6, 9 October 1850, Visitors' Book, op.cit. 24 September 1894; Minutes 8a/2, 1 August 1838; 8a/7, 11 August 1852; M.H. 12/10580, Reports of Mr Courtenay, 27 December 1890, 28 November 1891; Minutes 8a/17, 7 March 1895; M.H. 12/10581, Report of Lord Courtenay, 28 September 1896; Report of Edward Gulson, 31 December 1866, PP 1867-8, LXI, p. 224; D/G/WN 32/1, Contract, 13 September 1836, Agreement, 16 May 1838; M.H. 12/10577, Report of Mr Courtenay, 16 December 1884; Minutes 8a/12, 20 May 1877; 8a/13, 30 May 1883; 8a/16, 27 May and 10 June 1891; Visitors' Book, op.cit. 24 May and 26 July 1893; Minutes 8a/1, 27 April 1836; 9a/1, General Ledger 1836, op.cit, entries for 4 May, 22 June and 28 September 1836; Minutes 8a/18, 27 January 1897; 8a/17, 20 February 1895.

39. General Order: Workhouse Rules, op.cit. pp. 58-9; Minutes 8a/16, 15

February 1893; G. Sweetman, The History of Wincanton, Wincanton, 1903, p.113; 'Western Chronicle', 18 June 1897, Visitors' Book, op.cit. 5 April 1898, 14 August 1900.
40. M.H. 12/10569, Financial and Statistical Statement during the year ended Lady Day 1856, p. 2; 'Western Chronicle', 19 February 1897; Sweetman, op.cit. p. 111.